Helen Gurley Brown's

Outrageous Opinions

 PUBLISHED BY BERNARD GEIS ASSOCIATES
IN COOPERATION WITH AVON BOOKS

AVON BOOKS
A division of
The Hearst Corporation
959 Eighth Avenue
New York, New York 10019

First Avon Printing, June, 1966

Cover design by Avon Books

FOR REX BARLEY
AND
ED GRADE

TABLE
OF
CONTENTS

Let's You Be a Real Good Guest • Dear John
or Dear Just Anybody • Gifts and Loans for
Men • They're All Married but You • You
Have a Guy—She Doesn't • Tell Them How to
Mix and Match You • Hot- and Cold-Running
Friends •

The Terrible Twenties • Sex and the Older
Woman • But You Look Ten Years Younger! •
Delectable After Forty • The Friendly Forties •
Never Mind the Dialogue, Where Are the Men?
• Happy Fiftieth Birthday! • In Love with a
Younger Man! • When Your Traveling Com-
panion Is a Man •

Who Cares If You're a Mess? Everybody! •
The Flattest Tummy in Town • Be a Lazy
Summer Beauty • More of You Shows in a
Swimsuit . . . Including Your Insecurity • Who
Wants to Be a Health Nut? • Look Ma, I'm a
Yogi! • Beautiful on the Inside • The Sexy Plain
Girl • Young Lady Slobs • How to Be Very,
Very Popular with Men • What Are You Doing
to His Eardrums? • Are You Using Your Voice
to Get What You Want! • How to Be Cool and
Daring • Legs Are In, Bosoms Are Out . . . Well,
Sort of • Let's Stir Things Up a Bit • Bless Your
Heart! • No Nose for Compliments • Do You
Dress for Him or You? • To Be a High Liver,
It's Liver, Darling! • Scared Stiff? That's Good!
• The Big Yes • The Villain Could Be You •

To Shrink or Not to Shrink • If You're Shy,
But Oh My . . . • A Special Kind of Problem •
Flight from Depression City • What to Do
About Your "Craziness" • "Eat Beautiful" and
Feel the Difference • The Gourmet in You •
The Mole on the End of Your Nose • Are You a
Scaredy-Cat? •

How to Lose a Man on the First Date • How to
Say Goodbye and Make It Stick • Should She
or Shouldn't She? • Well, Should She or Shouldn't
She? • Let's Face Facts—We Outnumber Them
• Happy New Year All Alone • The Rich, Full
Social Life—What's That?• Surrounded by Loved
Ones, but Oh So Lonely • Getting a Lonely
Young Mother Out of the Gloom • The Week-
end That Was • How Do You Keep from Get-
ting Murdered? • Last-Minute Christmas Gifts
of Love • And Bring Your Young Man . . . Oh
Sure ! • How to Argue and Be a Lady • Joseph,
the Fiend, Took Her Flying Machine • They're
Needing You More But You're Needing Them
Less •

INTRODUCTION

ATTENTION, GIRLS WHO'VE NEVER MARRIED, WIDOWS AND DIVORCEES

or,

How to Get

With It (and Him)

After *Sex and the Single Girl* was published, I began to get a lot of mail, mostly from single girls—spinsters, widows, divorcees—who wanted to know *more*. I thought I'd said everything I knew to say on the subject of unwed blessedness in the *book* but these girls felt, I guess, that I might have something special to offer toward solving Their Particular Problem. (Since "Sex" was published in twenty-eight countries and sixteen languages, a lot of letters came scribbled in something I couldn't quite understand, and we had to spend a little time getting them into *my* mother tongue.) Well, more "to answer the mail" than anything else, I began writing a syndicated newspaper column called "Woman Alone" in the spring of 1963. I tried to cover subjects I hadn't covered in the book and also wrote more fully on some subject I *had* covered before—careers, apartments, diet, entertaining, clothes, beauty, etc. Naturally every second column dealt with *men* because that's what every second *letter* dealt with. (Really it was more like *every* letter.)

Anyway, here are some of the more successful of these columns collected in this book.

What makes me think the opinions in them are outrageous?

Well, after the column got going (and about seventy-five newspapers signed up for it) every two weeks or so one of the subscribing newspapers would get the Los Angeles Times Syndicate manager on the phone and start screaming something like, "Rex, this time this dame has really done it. You expect us to run this stuff in a *family newspaper?*" Suffering Rex would assure them that Phoenix or San Jose or Portland was running the column they objected to, but the caller usually wound up replacing it with a "safe" one that he or his staff wrote on crabgrass-killing tricks or favorite banana bread recipes of all time. It would have been a fairly simple matter for me to write a few "safe" (i.e., nonoutrageous) columns for the syndicate to have on hand to replace the ones that were considered too hot to handle, but the newspapers never agreed on which ones these were and I would have had to write *two* sets of columns each week—a "safe" set for them and a hot set for me.

Because you're a reasonable girl, I don't think you're going to find any of the columns truly outrageous . . . only full of what I hope is honest, girlish, straight-from-the-soul frank advice from one female to another. (Of *course* you should tell your mother you're having an affair if you're thirty-eight and she's sixty-five. She's got to get to know you *sometime* if you're to remain friends. Of *course* it's better not to marry the miserable creep you're having an affair with just because guilt and age-consciousness are closing in on you and you figure this may be the last man on earth you'll ever have a hold on.)

Before I had to stop writing the column to become editor of *Cosmopolitan* (a girl has just so many hours and so many brain cells. Besides, the Hearst Corporation, which owns *Cosmopolitan*, had its own syndicate and they didn't fancy my continuing to write for a competitor), it ran two years —from April 1963 to April 1965.

People have asked from time to time what gives me the idea I'm *qualified* to offer advice to women alone. Well, I *was* a woman alone for thirty-seven years and I think people who went through something themselves often know more about it than the "experts." Anyway I've never felt any hesitation about telling the things that have happened to *me*—or to friends—and saying what we did under the circumstances (or under the pressure or under the hairdryer or wherever). I think many another "civilian" woman could write her own column just as I did if she feels strongly about something and can write.

What I've written comes from my own struggle to build a better life as a woman alone. I hope it inspires you to do much much more.

Calling All Widows, Divorcees, Bachelor Girls

Are you a single woman? Do you know how many other women in America over the age of eighteen have no husbands, except possibly an ex? The total count is in excess of 24 million!

So you see, you have lots of company, and in many cases the company you're in is the best! Many single women are among the most interesting, admirable and even enviable citizens of our time.

Of course, you do have certain problems getting along in a world in which the majority of people are married, and in recent years, no single voice has been representing this large and growing larger segment of American women—the single ones. That's why this book, some of it based on my newspaper column "Woman Alone," has come into being. It will be devoted especially to you . . . your joys and problems.

In it we'll discuss jobs—how to up-grade one if that's your desire and how to find one if you aren't already working. We'll deal with the managing of money as well as managing the people who are trying to marry you off, but have no constructive help to offer (*i.e.*—introducing you to some eligible men!). We'll delve into wardrobes, beauty tips, entertaining and decorating advice to help you live your single-woman life in superlative style.

Naturally we'll discuss that very important subject, the men in your life—how to deal with the ones who are already there, how to attract new ones.

We'll also have a few words for happily married women whose husbands must necessarily be away much of the time. Some, but not all, of the same advice on getting along alone will apply to you.

How Do You Rate as a Prospect?

An attractive but "jilted" switchboard operator recently told me this story:

"I went out with this wealthy and attractive man six times," she said, "and I thought we were getting along fine. Then I read in the paper last night that he's engaged to marry a Chicago debutante. It doesn't seem fair! She's no prettier than I am. Her family probably has money, but I'm sure I'd make him a better wife."

Would she make him a better wife? Is there any reason to believe that a debutante is a poorer marriage risk than a hard-working switchboard operator? Sorry, the answer is no!

I'm always for hard-working girls, because *I'm* one! Furthermore, I don't think girls who dream of marrying well-to-do husbands are necessarily the creeps of the earth.

There are *worse* people to marry than those who can carry you off to Europe and pay painlessly for houses, cars and minks. If these fringe benefits are bestowed by a man you could love just as dearly without them, nothing could be finer!

How can you begin to fit into such a picture? Well, if you're going to dream of a wealthy "catch," you first have to be realistic! I once heard a shrewd trial lawyer I worked for say this to a gold-digging client who'd asked his help in her pursuit of a hotel owner:

"Look, Miss J., you gotta figure out what's in it for *him*. Sure, you're pretty, but I've seen prettier. A lot of other dames are as young as you are. These wealthy guys maybe aren't so hot-looking or don't have such hot dispositions, but they can choose from thirty, forty dames they already know and a couple of thousand they haven't met yet! What have you got that's so special he should pick *you*?" Miss J. was crushed!

Some important men do marry nice, "simple" girls, but not all that often! Movie stars usually marry other movie stars. Wealthy men marry heiresses. Politicians marry girls whose fathers can help them get votes. When Prince

Rainier decided to take a wife, he didn't pick a dairy-maid. He chose a Philadelphia society girl *and* an Academy Award-winning actress.

Even wealthy men who leave their wives rarely take up with Miss Subways. This is not intended as criticism of the men. If you were an internationally famous bachelor, you might play it the same way!

But if you would marry a man who is eligible in character with professional standing, charm, tenderness and brains (never mind whether he's rich), it doesn't hurt a bit to be something more than just a nice, sweet girl!

If you aren't a great beauty, a flowering seventeen, a famous sportswoman or an heiress, I suggest one way you can interest a "good" man is by becoming a very special person yourself. Usually you do it through your job. Having a great career is a proven way to get to the men. More about that later.

Sometimes the Losers Don't Lose

Do you think I don't *know* that while I sit here telling you to be smart, quick, well-informed, lovely and to live up to the best that's in you, some seemingly helpless, dumb, disorganized, just plain dreary girls are making off with the men? And the reason isn't that they have such beautiful souls. Some of them have terrible souls. Nor is it that they're so sexy. The North American porcupine has more sex in his make-up than some of these women.

What do they have then? I'll tell you what I *think* they have. Oatmeal-bland exteriors and interiors. Some men want a girl who isn't going to give them any trouble. I mean *none*. She isn't going to want to eat pheasant breasts when he's in the mood for pork and beans and vice versa. His whim is her absolute command. She will be home by the hearth and he can *depend* on her being there regardless of when he calls during the day and despite the fact he gave her thirty-five cents all her very own to spend when she *does* go out.

Although some men like having a wife that every other man in town would be proud to introduce as his dearly beloved, some men *don't* want that kind of wife at all. She

19

would make that kind of man feel uneasy and insecure if she were great. He wants a girl nobody else is going to be after.

I think many men secretly enjoy loving a woman only they and possibly the girl's mother could consider lovely or lovable. Perhaps that famous male ego takes over just a little when a man marries an almost-less-than-average girl and pretty soon he is seeing her as Galatea and himself as Pygmalion—he having made her into something wonderful and beautiful although her new wonder and beauty isn't apparent to anybody else in the world.

Some men marry girls who will be *sure* to give them trouble and they too secretly want it that way. I watched a brilliant young physicist court a medium-good-looking, *known* to be alcoholic. Long before they married she was missing days of work at a time and passing out at parties. Two years later, she is now his wife—and he is still tender and passionately devoted to this girl, although the blackouts come more often and her job and housework have been discarded altogether.

Come to think of it, why should men be any exception in preferring trouble-free mates? Some women don't want Sean Connery or any other winner. For all the reasons a man doesn't want a highly "successful" girl, a woman prefers not to marry anybody who will challenge her, upgrade her, give her high standards to live up to or an uneasy moment with other women.

Why then do I keep telling you to try to be the smart, pretty, witty and wise girl who definitely frightens some men away? Ah, because you don't scare *all* men away when you live up to the best that's in you. You don't scare off the secure and self-assured men.

There's also a little matter of there not being enough husbands to go around for single girls at any one time—I mean husbands you can marry. If you are without one, I think it is far and away better to be the finest, most hip, energetic, "successful" person you can possibly be—it being understood different people have different raw material to work with—than to be a loser. If you never get married, it's the *only* way to fly—high, wide and admirably.

Why Isn't a Nice Girl Like You Married?

A single woman who has never married sometimes wishes she could carry a document around which would verify the fact that at least somebody asked her . . . or maybe several somebodies! It might be an old love letter containing the important question or the sworn statement of a beau that he proposed, or she might even tote around the old beau himself!

The trouble is that proof of proposal probably wouldn't quiet her tormentors. They would want to know why she didn't accept one of the offers and avoid this miserable, pitiable state she's now in.

The divorcee faces a different kind of criticism, though often tacit. At least half of her friends privately wonder why she gave up a husband who, with all his shortcomings, surely was better than no husband at all. (That's *their* opinion!)

The widow's cross turns out to be the pals who simply assume after a "decent interval" she can or should settle down into a comfortable, compatible, safe but exciting *new* marriage when, in fact, she does not have the ghost of a prospect on the string. Or, let's face it, perhaps she is delighted to be free! There *are* widows whose period of mourning *ends* with their husband's death.

Spinster, divorcee, widow—how do you deal with the people who are trying to marry you off?

If you really don't want to be married or remarried, you can simply say with conviction that you've *had* it or don't want it at this time. As for girls who really are perishing to get married, a close-to-honest answer is still best. Yes, you'd like to be wed, but you're going to take your time and marry someone you would honestly be thrilled and happy to marry.

Aren't you being too particular, even neurotic? No! It's all right to know what you want in the way of a husband—what could be a more important "investment"—and to stick by your guns. Turning off your friends' anxiety (and near insults) should be done in good humor even if they're being boors.

21

The way to convince them you really aren't a hardship case is to go around living the most exciting, enviable, useful single-girl life you possibly can.

And starting with Part I, we will deal with specific ways to help you achieve this kind of single-girl life.

ONE | LOVING EVERY SINGLE MINUTE

or,

*Live Alone
and Orgy!*

The trouble with a lot of people who live alone is that they never realize how delicious it is until they've up and moved in with somebody or the other way around. *Then* they could kick themselves for being so dumb but it's too *late*. These next pages tell you some of the ways to have fun . . . *alone* . . . and about some girls who are doing just that.

Live Alone and Orgy!

It's roundup time. Time for you to think of all the selfish, impractical, indulgent, lovely things you can do when you aren't married and live by yourself. You can do most of these things with somebody around, of course, but you're apt to get funny looks, if not downright howls of complaint. Have you forgotten how nice it is that—

1. You can get into bed the minute you're home from work, have a peanut butter sandwich and lemon No-Cal for dinner, read a novel straight through from beginning to end if you want to.

2. When you're wide awake for no reason at four in the morning, you can turn on your bedside lamp and read, do your nails, put up a hem or do any other whimsical thing that appeals to you.

3. You can bake a batch of gingerbread, sop it with gobs of sweet butter, eat right straight through the whole thing.

4. You can collapse in bed all weekend—go without make-up or even without clothes. (Be sure the shades are down.)

5. When getting ready for the party of the year, you can

whip the dress, the shoes, the wrap, the face, the figure, the hair into shape four nights in a row and no one will know how narcissistic you are. Only the results will show.

6. You can postpone all housework until something *must* be done—not bore yourself with it daily.

7. You can play your new Andy Williams record eighty-two times in a row without driving someone to the nut house.

8. You can burrow-in uninterrupted with work from the office—the kind that's going to make you high-powered and rich someday.

9. You can talk on the telephone for hours.

10. You can hide the phone under blankets and never answer.

11. If a beau calls at 10 P.M. and says, "Come on, let's go to a discotheque," you can jump up and go go. Nobody around to say, "Be sensible."

12. You can sink up to your elbows in plants, paints, beads, clay, tile, sequins, yarn or any other hobby that pleases you.

13. You can call up people and have a sudden party because you're in the mood—nobody to consult who may *not* be in the mood.

14. You can leave the radio or television set turned off for eight weeks at a time, or you can play them nonstop.

15. You can have private conversations with your cat, dog, parrot, parakeet without somebody implying you're a nutburger.

16. You can eat loads of little green onions and garlic toast without driving anybody away.

17. You can sleep with the windows closed, or wide open.

18. You can do absolutely *nothing* for hours.

Raw, Naked Ambition— Naughty, Naughty, Naughty?

Ambition is a quality often attributed to the harpy-eagle wife who tries to push her doltish husband up the business ladder or a mother intent on getting her daughter into the movies. The word is also used in connection with girls who have a hankering to become rich and/or famous. Any girl who has a hankering to become rich and/or famous usually figures out in no time at all that she'd better keep the hankering to herself if she wants to avoid long, putting-down lectures from her friends and family ("You're a very talented girl, Shirley, but I'm afraid you'll just break your heart reaching for the moon.") and having men back away from her altogether. She discovers that ambition is a very dirty word.

I'd be the first to go along with the idea that ambition is something to hug to yourself. When you go around yapping about it, you dissipate it. Ambition, however—naked, raw ambition—I not only don't think is a dirty word, I think it's a lovely, honorable, admirable, scintillating, beautiful quality for any girl to have and people with ambition are more fun to be around than people without it. Women alone should and *can* have it in spades.

I will never forget the time I saw the Arthur Miller play, *After the Fall,* and a heretofore unknown actress named Barbara Loden nearly took my breath away. There were several good actresses in the play but Miss Loden was electrifying. She shimmered. She shone. When she left the stage, I missed her dreadfully. When she came back again, I sighed and waited for her to open her mouth again. (She played the difficult role of a sexpot, possibly the late Marilyn Monroe, who must make you understand the torture in her soul while every man in the world worshiped and desired her.) I may be wrong but I *think* every female in the audience admired Miss Loden's fantastic performance and wished, however unconscious the wish, that she could have *been* Miss Loden giving that performance. Yet most of the audience would say, I imagine, that ambition in a woman is unwomanly, a naughty, dirty thing. Right? Apparently it only gets to be acceptable when you already *are* a star.

We can't all be Broadway meteors but we can be *something.* Talent isn't usually what's lacking. All of us have some of that. We really *do.* Some of the most scintillating successes of our time have less natural talent than less-famous contemporaries but they have honed it and used every erg of it and that suffices. (Maria Callas doesn't have the greatest operatic voice nor Peggy Lee the best pop one, but look what they've managed with those voices.)

Most of us aren't fortunate enough to know the one thing we'd like to do as young women. So you just begin by putting one foot in front of the other and doing what's *there* the best that you can do it—being the best waitress, best piano teacher, best secretary. If you keep doing that one thing with extraordinary verve and skill, I firmly believe something better turns up—and better and better. That's about all ambition is and how it works.

Ambition-ridden women are rarely old maids, you know. They love, they marry, they have children, they give of themselves to their community and their country and they give *more* because they've developed more to give. I hope *you're* not trying to stamp out naughty old ambition when it lifts its proud head.

Are Men More Susceptible to Nurses?

Let's visit an attractive registered nurse at one of Los Angeles' major hospitals and see if it's true that a man in a weakened condition is an absolute pushover for the nurse who cares for him during his illness. (We certainly want to know any and all ways of getting to a man, don't we?) I won't use this young lady's real name because she might be drummed out of the nursing corps, but she's a real person.

"Yes, of course men are susceptible to us when they're sick," says twenty-four-year-old blue-eyed and brown-haired Stephanie. "They are subject to fantasy. They figure we're all starchy and efficient on the outside and soft and girlish on the inside. They also think we're some kind of angel as we flutter about. The only trouble is that you can't keep a man bedded down handing him potions and taking his pulse forever. After they get well, they sober up and you have to take your chances among the other girls they know."

"Don't you have a good head start, however?" I asked. "I mean you've had the man all to yourself maybe for several weeks or months."

"Yes, I'd say you have a distinct advantage," Stephanie

said. "Certainly many nurses *do* date patients and marry them because they've had a real chance to sink into a man. I've found though that patients often want to skip all courtship procedures when they get out of the hospital and *do* take you out, however. They've been fantasizing about you for weeks and just want to get right down to business. They may take you to a bar for a drink, then rush you home and try to get romantic, muttering something like, 'I've wanted to kiss you for weeks, Stephanie, and now I finally have you all to myself.' They don't realize *you* may not have been thinking the same thing about them at *all,* so of course your responses aren't co-ordinated."

"Do the doctors you work with make good date prospects?" I asked.

"Very," said Stephanie, "and many smart nurses grab off the doctors while they're still interns. It may mean the girl has to help support her husband until he's through with his training, but she figures it's an excellent investment because doctors always make a good living."

"How much does a registered nurse make?" I asked.

"One hundred and eighteen dollars a week gross," said Stephanie. "This is after three years of nursing school and possibly four years of college. Of course you save money on food and clothes because uniforms aren't as expensive as tweed suits you'd wear to an office and the hospital feeds you."

"Have you ever fainted in the line of duty?" I asked.

"Yes, on my very first day of training when they took me through the morgue. I just felt so sorry for everybody. I also fainted three other times during baby deliveries. I kept imagining it was me having the pain. I'm much stronger now. I don't even mind the sight of blood although I do still get shaken up by smells."

"What would you say is the biggest satisfaction in nursing?" I asked.

"Helping people. This really does mean something to most of the girls in the profession, I believe. You also get to meet challenges and this brings out the best in you."

"And the men?" I asked.

"Yes, the men are nice, too," Stephanie said.

How the Hostess Gets Her Man

By now you must know I have your best interests at heart and am always trying to find coveys of nice men for you to flush out.

Having heard that airline hostesses meet more men than anybody, I decided to check out this rumor with a genuine one. I asked Shelly Brownlee, a brown-eyed, peach-skinned stewardess with Trans-Canada Air Lines if this was true.

"We do meet a lot of men," Shelly said. "Probably ninety percent of our passengers are men."

"Do you ever go out with any of them?" I asked.

"Oh, yes," she said. "Also with the crew members. They're absolute darlings."

"How do men you meet in flight go about asking to see you again?"

"Well, first you may flirt with them a bit," Shelly said. (I *suspected* as much. Stewardesses *flirt*.) "When passengers first get on board, you get a kind of picture of who's nice.

"Then, after you've been up and down the aisles a few times, you narrow the field down and pick out two or three men to concentrate on during the flight. You stare at them as you go by, and usually they stare back. After this eye-to-eye contact they generally feel free to talk to you when you serve lunch, or they may come back to the galley when you're working."

"I assume that men you *haven't* been flirting with take a fancy to you occasionally, too," I said.

"Yes," she said. "One chap last week passed love letters to me while I was getting lunch. He said he did that because he didn't want the other hostess to know he'd fallen in love with me and have her feelings hurt. It was sort of the thoughtful approach."

"What if the man who asks you out is married?" I asked.

"Well, then you don't go, of course," she said, "but you've done all that good flirting and made someone happy."

"Does anyone ever get terribly fresh?"

"Occasionally. One day a well-known boxer and his wife got on board. She was really glorious—so was he, for that matter. She sat by the window, he sat in the aisle seat, and every time I went by he just sort of reached out and patted me—well, it was awfully weird."

"Is anyone ever so persistent you have to call the captain?"

"Heavens, no," Shelly said. "Nearly everyone treats you like a princess, especially the older people. They're awfully sweet. One day a nice little old lady told me that although it was her first flight she wasn't going to be afraid because her folks had said I would give her an anti-fright tablet.

"I was about to tell her they were kidding, but instead I got her a 222 (a strong aspirin). She took her 'fright tablet' and was happy as a clam the whole trip."

I wanted to know if she had ever spilled coffee on anybody.

"Just last week I dumped a cup of coffee on a man," she said. "He had a business appointment the minute he got off the plane and no change of clothes. We sponged him off, and he stood up with me in the galley the entire flight so he wouldn't ruin what was left of the crease in his pants. He really was a darling."

"Did he ask you out?"

"Oh, I imagine so," Shelly said.

Do you suppose she did or did not pour coffee on that man on purpose? We'll never know. I just know that although I'm too old or something to be an airline stewardess, I for one am going to watch what stewardesses do the next time I'm on board, because it seems they not only meet the men, but they are making *off* with a lot of them.

Girl Races Motor and Makes Men Happy

Every so often a girl doesn't play it the way other girls play it and absolutely beautiful things happen to her. Take Virginia "Pooky" Baker. Pooky was her family's name for "fat baby." Twenty-year-old Pooky is blonde, five feet six with a pouty mouth like Brigitte Bardot. She sells Hondas, the lightweight Japanese motorbikes, to men and sometimes women customers in a jazzy, glassfront showroom on New York's Madison Avenue.

"Put a pretty girl in the window and you really see action," says the company's manager. Pooky happens to be his top "salesman," her record being three Hondas and one Lotus (small English sportscar) in one day. She gets a twenty-percent commission on these sales. About eight men a day ask her to go out with them but she doesn't go.

"It wouldn't be good for business," she says. "If you're dating, he won't buy."

She does get rather close to her customers, however. In demonstrating the motorbike, Pooky hops on with the customer and tells him to put his arms around her waist. "Some of them seem to take a bit more coaching than others," she says. "Mostly they hang on tight and get the hang of it very quickly. Men like to be mothered, I guess. When a woman shows them how to ride, they lose their fear. I guess they think if a woman can ride this thing, so can they."

Can men possibly take her seriously when she talks about the mesh transmission and dual cam-type brakes?

"I don't dwell on those things," Pooky says. "I just say, 'This motor doesn't give you any trouble, so why know about it? It's built for American abuse.' They seem to trust me implicitly."

"Why don't more girls have unusual 'men's jobs like yours," I asked her, "when they're able to be so good at them? Is it because they meet management resistance when they apply?"

"The only thing that holds women back is they won't go in and try," Pooky said. "I think most companies would be glad to give a girl a break selling if she wanted it. Females are certainly needed in marketing. After all, women control most of the money in this country. I think women don't have these jobs because they're afraid of losing their femininity. They're always worrying about whether their hair is in place. Actually, you can be just as frilly and feminine in this kind of job as you can nursing or teaching, and you certainly meet men. Of course, I think you should remember at all times to let the men you meet light your cigarette and open car doors —or help you on the bike."

Pooky, who rides to work every day in skinny skirts

and high heels on one of the two motorbikes she owns, lives with a family which has three children (a very good thing to do when you first move to a big city), but is in the process of getting her own apartment. She is also hoping to get some girls interested in road-racing which, so far, is not open to women on the East Coast. A serious art student, Pooky paints on her day off and will eventually use her commissions to study art in Europe for a year. "I'll go back to selling motorbikes when I come home, however," she says. "I expect I'll do that even after I'm married. I just love dealing with customers and helping them be happy."

The Loneliness of the 3 O'Clock Ironer

"There I was at three o'clock in the morning ironing this stupid blouse," said a chestnut-haired young computer operator. "Then I ironed two cotton shirts, some denim slacks and sat down and cried!"

The tears were not from lost sleep or exhaustion or even because she scorched the second shirt. And you're wrong if you think she was weeping because of a traitorous boyfriend, a crisis at work or family troubles. She was crying over the seeming idiocy of being *able* to iron at three o'clock in the morning—or any other time she pleased!

I'm sure her depression went even deeper. Perhaps she was thinking, "Where am I headed?" "What's going to become of me?" "How much longer can I stand this stupid life?" All perfectly good, normal, run-of-the-mill, three-o'clock-in-the-morning thoughts for a single girl!

Even if thoughts like these haven't plagued you recently, have you noticed how they sometimes arrive with sudden fury after you've been to the wedding reception of a friend? The more handsome the groom, the heavier the gloom!

It may interest you to know that on the same night you are crying your heart out, your married girl friends could also be weeping up a small storm! A husband may have been overbearing and impossible for weeks, or all

33

the money so carefully saved for a trip has had to go for a new roof. Crying isn't your exclusive prerogative!

Have the blues if you like, but if you're depressed because there's nobody to object to the kooky hours you're able to keep, forget it.

The rhythm of a single girl's life is *different* from a married woman's, and it's nothing to cry about! Scheduling your chores at the exact same time those "normal" married people do would be impossible. Chances are you work all day, and the last person caught ironing a collar at work was under observation at a local clinic.

I say iron at three o'clock in the morning if you like, then pop in your car, lock the doors and go watch a dawn come up someplace. *You* can be as noncomformist as you like.

Do the dusting just before guests arrive for your party. Get into bed with a jar of yogurt the minute you're home from work and read from supper to dawn! I promise you this—unchaperoned freedom will be one of the things you'll miss when you marry.

Three's a Crowd and Even Two's Too Many

To be or not to be alone, that is the question. Whether 'tis better to bring a warm body, just anybody's body, to the party, the movies, the restaurant, the theater or strike out by yourself is not much of a question as far as I'm concerned!

If there's nobody to bring or nobody you care a poof about bringing, you should go by yourself. Some very dull girls I know are afraid to venture out to the grocery store without a beloved friend in tow. It's got to be twosies or threesies at all times. Consequently all members of the party get to looking and sounding exactly like each other.

Some far more scintillating single women start out alone at least and find more interesting things and people happening to them. Ava Gardner is one. I keep reading that she's been to this restaurant or that night club quite by herself, and there's a girl who could have as many escorts as she pleases, I'm sure.

If there's ever a time in your life when you're so surrounded by people your only moments alone are in a locked bathroom, you'll look back and treasure this time when you could have prowled, explored, meandered and adventured without several people trailing along.

Have you considered these unescorted and unaccompanied possibilities?

A woodsy walk. I took these many times when I was single and alone and sometimes the "aloneness" fell on a national holiday, too! I brought along a tangerine or some "prize" to reward myself with when I was halfway through the allotted three miles.

The movies. I have a friend who won't even *go* to the movies except alone. She likes to sit in the last row of the theater, rest her knees against the seat in front of her, eat two or three bags of unbuttered popcorn and simply luxuriate in the story being unfolded on the screen.

Theater (drama, musical, ballet, concert). You dress to the teeth, build a little fantasy about yourself as being a glamorous, visiting countess about whom people are saying, "Who is that woman?" You also congratulate yourself for being an art lover and able to afford the ticket.

Train ride. Give me one good reason *not* to get on a train some Saturday morning and ride to a nearby town. Club cars are fabulous places to meet and talk to strangers. It's hard *not* to talk even if all you had in mind was riding and thinking.

Lecture. Prepare a cogent question to ask the speaker when he's finished.

Brokerage office. I guarantee if you drop by every day to sit and watch the big board ten or fifteen minutes, you'll start talking to *other* regulars, mostly men. It might be nice to have a share of stock to watch go up or down.

Library. One of the truly fascinating places of a big city. Take your pile of books over and sit down next to an interesting-looking man.

Brunch. A single-girl friend buys the Sunday papers and takes herself to the poshest hotel dining room in town every Sabbath. It could just as well be a neighborhood coffee shop. An extravagant breakfast is something that should be prepared *for* you occasionally.

Flower, produce, fish market. Get there early in the morning when they're unloading. Ask questions.

A Single Girl's Letter to Santa

DEAR SANTA:

Although there are a lot more impressive things I could ask for for Christmas (and I *have* been a very good girl this year), I am going to confine my list to these seemingly trivial items. They aren't trivial to *me*, you see, Santa. I've been needing some of these things desperately for quite a long while:

1. The ability to have a nice fat argument without losing my temper. As you know, Santa, I get so emotional when I argue about religion, sex, politics and civil rights, I start talking too loudly and interrupting whoever is talking and pretty soon I'm talking more and people are listening less and I never get the feeling I've convinced anybody of anything.

2. Some black magic that will make men have a strange, craven urge to kiss me even though we don't know each other very well and they don't do anything about it.

3. Some new jokes to cheer up my mother when she gets depressed because I'm not married.

4. Some tactful phrases to explain to my boss that it is better to do all the dictating at one time, preferably early in the morning, instead of piecemeal throughout the day up to and including when it's time for me to go home.

5. Some patience with the fellows who keep telling me how beautiful my beautiful girl friend Mary Ellen is and asking how they can get a date with her. She really is a doll and I like to look at her, too, Santa, but I don't seem to be as thrilled as I should be when fellows keep raving to me about her.

6. The hypnotic power to make that new attorney at the office say, "Will you have lunch with me, Catherine," before January 1.

7. A system of staying with my self-improvement programs through the eleventh day. I get along just fine, Santa, for about ten days and then—pow!

8. Some telephone conversation that makes a man see *me* all over the page of the book he's reading long after he's hung up.

9. Some new disgust words that are not as unladylike as swear words but not as tired as all the ones I've been using such as phooey, nonsense, rats and that's what you think.

10. Stardust to dust all over me before parties so I'll shimmer like a blonde starlet in a sequined gown although I'm a small brunette.

11. Some nice understanding smiles for my father who thinks every boy I go out with should ask me to marry him. He asked Mother on their first date, Santa, and it's very hard for him to get it into his head that nowadays it may take a girl a little longer (even if she's interested).

12. Somebody to be *that* interested in. You know, Santa, really cuckoo.

13. The energy to tuck my hips under and *keep* them tucked under at a cocktail party when I'm stuck with one person too long.

14. The guts to wear one of those new low-plunge necklines although the plunge isn't going to be *that* spectacular.

15. A small mechanical failure of the elevator in our building so it will give me a chance to start a conversation with that dreamboat who gets on when I do in the morning.

16. A year without any dreadful surprises, but if they happen, lots of courage to spit in their eye.

Yours truly,
CATHERINE

Dreams of Glory

Imagine, if you will, that this is the year of our Lord nineteen hundred and sixty-six, but some drastic changes in population figures have taken place. *The bachelors outnumber the single girls.*

You might overhear a conversation something like this:

"You see, I'd walked her down Elm Street on purpose so we could pass Fogelson's. They had some beautiful French Provincial stuff in the windows, and do you know what *she* said?"

"What?"

"She said, 'John Whitehouse, if you walk me past this furniture store one more Saturday afternoon, I'm going to

37

refuse to go for walks with you any more. Don't you know by now I'm just not interested in furniture?' "

"I guess you should have been more subtle."

"That's right. Phyllis is a pretty perceptive girl and I shouldn't have tried to ram this household stuff down her throat so fast. Well, we went over to Gallagher's to have a soda and I was determined to be casual and nonchalant the rest of the day the way she likes me but this couple came over."

"What happened?"

"The girl showed Phyllis her engagement ring. She was a drab little creature naturally and old Phyl carried on like she was really impressed. After they left she said, 'Imagine, getting married!'

" 'What's the matter with getting married?' I asked. I could feel my blood pressure beginning to rise.

" 'Well, nothing, I guess,' she said, 'but when two people are having a perfectly dreamy romance, I can't see their wanting to spoil everything by getting married.' "

"Typical female attitude."

"Well, frankly, Joe, tears were beginning to well up in my throat and I couldn't say anything for a minute. Then Phyllis looked at me and said, 'What's the matter, darling? You look funny.' 'Oh, nothing.' I said. I'm just depressed.'

"Well, she kept asking me what was the matter and finally I blurted out, 'Here I am going on thirty-two and you don't want to get married and I just don't know what's going to become of me. My folks say if I don't get married in a year or two at the latest, I'll be past the age when any girl could possibly want me.' "

"Ye gods, man, you didn't say *that*? To a girl like *Phyllis?*"

"I knew it was a terrible mistake so there was nothing to do but try to gain back some of the ground I'd lost. I broke our date for Saturday night."

"Was she impressed?"

"Seemed to be, and of course that tickled me, but then she said, 'Well, I'll just have to go to the party alone!' Joe, I could shoot myself. She's going to be at that party with God knows how many single men and I haven't a thing to do Saturday night but maybe do my toenails or clean out my golf bag. Listen, you wouldn't like to go to a movie?"

38

"Sure, why not? I gave my phone number to a couple of cute girls this week, but you know how it is. They never *really* call."

"Great, I'll pick you up, but we'll have to go someplace out of the neighborhood. I wouldn't want to run into old Phyl and have her see me with a guy when I'm supposed to have a red-hot date."

"Sure thing, John. And listen, don't answer the phone this week. It could be Phyllis, and you want to give her a good scare while you're at it."

The Loved Ones

A gentleman asked me the other day if I was aware that some girls give their cars names. "A girl I know," he said, "kept talking about Carl this and Carl that and how sick he'd been. I thought *he* was her brother, but *he* turned out to be her Austin-Healy."

"You're asking *me* this question?" I replied. "Who has been closer to Gloria Hibiscus, Appletrees, Catherine Howard and Bismark (a 1935 Pontiac, Buick station wagon, '49 Chevy and Benz 190-SL respectively) than I have been to some of my friends?"

"But how can you be maudlin about something that gets flat tires and dead batteries?" he asked.

"Do you cut people out of your life because they have scarlet fever or migraines?" I asked.

I *could* have told the gentleman that some girls even name plants. My sister has a philodendron named Florence and a rubber plant called Rupert. A friend and her mother refer to a small pine tree that resides in their foyer as Philip. "Have you fed Philip today?" one will ask the other. Another friend has dubbed her two wigs Rapunzel and Griselda.

I like to think girls endow inanimate objects with human qualities because we are hopelessly imaginative and quiveringly sensitive. (It has nothing to do whatever with being nuts!)

One girl has carried it further than anybody I know by feeling guilty about showing favoritism toward a particular paring knife. "I've been making a concerted effort," she

39

says, "to use some of the other knives which are just as deserving." Another girl I know has been consoling a brand new mohair sweater with, "Now, now, no hurt feelings. I haven't worn you because I'm saving you for a very special occasion." (No need to say these things out loud, of course, because objects can read thought waves.)

I'm certain girls would give more, not fewer, things a name if they just knew enough good names. They're easy to find, however. *Webster's New Collegiate Dictionary* (which you probably see at work) has seven tightly packed pages of wonderful given names—Daphne, Deirdre, Demetrius, Derek, Drusilla, Duncan and on and on and on.

Cars are easy to christen (although you mustn't break a champagne bottle over their hoods), inasmuch as they have origins and personal characteristics just like people. A Mercedes Benz would be Wolfgang, Kaiser Wilhelm II, Tristan, Wilhelmina or Liebchen. A French Renault would be perfectly happy getting named Pierre, Gustave, Maurice or Cherie. A peppy Mustang would like to be called Frantic or Playmate or Benzedrine. I'm sure a Buick Riviera with its gorgeous lines would respond nicely to Aphrodite, Dagmar or Elizabeth Taylor.

How do you know if a car is a boy or a girl? There's no official way to tell, but most people get emanations. You look at a Cadillac Coupe de Ville and just automatically say, "Maude!" (or Winifred or Abigail). Somebody meeting a Chrysler 300 for the first time will say "Hello there, Gregory, Dominic or Humphrey." If you aren't sure of its sex you can always play it safe but nongender with Buttercup, Lambiepie or Dreamboat.

I hope you're looking around for something to name this minute. I don't think a woman alone can be too tender.

27 Ways to Spend Saturday Night

It occurs to me that a lot of women alone would like to know how to spend Saturday night either by themselves or with only another girl as a date.

First off, I'd say to avoid that spinsterish, no-men-in-our-lives feeling, don't go where dating couples are. Skip taking yourselves to dinner in that *intime* little French restaurant, and don't go see a first-run movie where the lovers are queuing up. These are possibilities:

1. Think of somebody or several somebodies over sixty-five and ask them to dinner. If that's too ambitious, call up and ask if they'd like you to come over and visit them.

2. Write ten letters—five to people you've owed, four to people you never wrote to before (newspapers, magazines, politicians). Then write one letter to your mother or father or both saying, "I never told you this before, but I think it's wonderful you had me, and I appreciate how you brought me up." Don't be shy. They'll love it.

3. Exercise one full hour (or as long as you last). Then take a nice long bubble bath. Dry off and give yourself the pedicure and manicure of all time.

4. Develop a sense. Play this by phone with two other friends. Each of you go rummaging and see how many smells you can "collect" from your apartment—leather, spices, paints, newspaper print, closets, desk equipment. Whoever has the best list gets treated by the others to a butterscotch sundae.

5. Make out your will. Write some gratitude notes to be opened after you're gone. Don't play this too long. One thing might lead to another, and if you're really lonely. . . .

6. Pick a subject. Check out five books from the library during the day and bone up that night. When you get through with "Thirteenth-Century Torture," you may feel you never had it so good. (Or you could pick a pleasant subject.)

7. Give your apartment a scrub-down as though it were harboring yellow fever germs.

8. Put on some records—jazz, classical, cha cha cha —pull down the shades and dance naked a couple of hours.

9. Buy a cheap old piece of furniture and refinish it. (This may take three Saturday nights.)

10. Buy a few yards of loose-weave fabric and "fringe" place mats for Christmas presents.

11. Start making your Christmas cards. (Sounds gruesome, but you could be plenty happy in November.)

12. Try on everything you own. Throw out about a

third of it. Decide how to bring the rest up to date. Start sewing right then or pack it off to the dressmaker Monday.

13. Volunteer to sit with a young couple's children free—no strings attached.
14. Bake something immoral (brownies, date-nut loaf). Leave plates of it at the neighbors with a note "From the fairies."
15. Fast. Drink just a few liquids all day. By eight o'clock you won't feel like doing a thing but piling into bed.
16. Make a list of all the men you've kissed, another of the men you'd like to. See how they compare.
17. Repair, restring, reorganize your junk jewelry, and throw out a lot of it.
18. Ride a bus or streetcar to the end of the line.
19. Explore a neighborhood you've never been in before.
20. Turn the garage light on and wax the car.
21. Call up a man you're absolutely certain doesn't know your voice, and tell him you're in love with him.
22. Paint the bathroom.
23. Make a list of people you hate, and hate them for an hour. Think of every last crumby thing they've done. Then one by one forgive them all.
24. Have a jacks game.
25. Sleep out of doors.
26. Collaborate on a foreign dinner. If it's Armenian, one girl brings the shish-kebab, one the stuffed vine leaves, one the goat's milk, etc.
27. Buy several yards of brown paper, small cans of enamel or flat paint, cheap brushes. Spread everything out on newspapers and paint murals.

How to Be a 'Loner' in Style

"Dear Mrs. Brown: As one of your staunch supporters, I find I must take issue with your Twenty-Seven Ways to Spend Saturday Night. Granted, some of your suggestions have merit (having some old ladies in to dinner), but aren't there plenty of other nights in the week for that? You mention avoiding public places like the plague. I can think of no quicker way to become a hermit."

You are absolutely right. There's no reason in the world for women alone to avoid public places. Did I really say that? I don't think so. I suggested that Saturday night per se was not the time to take yourself to the romantic little French restaurant frequented by couples in love or the first-run movie where dating couples stand in line.

I think a girl is in trouble who feels that Saturday night is a terribly big deal and she must do the closest thing possible to what she would do on a date. Her big night may just as easily be a Monday or Thursday if that's when a date turns up. In my opinion, all days of the week are equally lovely, work the next day notwithstanding.

Halloween night or Thanksgiving Day can also find a girl quite alone. No reason to commit hari-kari. I feel a girl's best bet is to take Saturday nights and holidays quite casually if she isn't booked and do the most constructive and off-beat things that present themselves. What better night to have elderly friends in for dinner?

Of course you must go into the world of people by yourself, and go on Saturday night if it pleases you. To be among the "twos" when you are the only "one" at least gives you an idea of the condition you hope to achieve. The twos are your inspiration.

If you decide to go to a concert or ballet by yourself, I have these suggestions:

1. Dress yourself very beautifully. Don't try for one instant to blend with the woodwork.

2. Congratulate yourself on the following: You can afford the ticket. You like yourself enough to put on a pretty face and a pretty dress. You have taste. You are curious. You don't take yourself too seriously. If the performance is great, this may be a very memorable evening.

3. Keep the anxious look off your face. Keep your mouth relaxed and serene, your eyes smiling. Look around and case the joint. You are an art lover.

4. Amuse yourself with Walter Mitty fantasies. Decide that you are a woman of mystery. People are curious about you (it may or may not be true). They are not thinking "poor little thing." They are wondering, Who is she? Does she live here or is she from out of town? You can also consider that probably your exact counterpart is

43

somewhere in the theater—a man alone, also attractive. You don't have to track him down or speak if you see him, but you can keep your eyes open.

That's another advantage of being alone. You can people-watch to your heart's content.

So Why Aren't You?

I think the time has come to decide once and for all on a sensible answer for you the next time somebody asks, "Why isn't a nice girl like you married?"

I've found, based on a small recent survey among unmarried women, that the two most popular answers are, "I've never been asked" and "I haven't found the right man yet."

Both answers, in my opinion, are terrible. As for not having been asked, most girls who get married were never out and out asked either. They usually did the asking themselves. As for not having found the right man yet, that has nothing to do with getting married either. Legions of girls marry the wrong man every year (there's a catch to even the best of men).

Not having suitable material would never keep a real marryer from marrying. I think your answer should be more honest. I suggest one of the following (you could try out each one until you find the answer that works best for you). Questioner: So how come a nice girl like you isn't married?

1. Oh, but I am. My husband is being detained out of town for just a little while. It was really I who signed Jean Paul Getty's name to that check, but darling Frank wouldn't hear of my going to jail.

2. My first five marriages were so ghastly, I simply haven't been able to face a sixth.

3. I could never bring myself to make one man happy at the expense of making so many men miserable.

4. I *was* married once. I was nine years old, and my father had it annulled. My poor husband killed himself.

5. I've been in love with Cary Grant for ten years and have just never been able to catch him between wives.

6. I've never really wanted anybody but Howard

44

Hughes, and he's been very hard to pin down to a date. As a matter of fact, I haven't been able to find him for six years.

7. (To a man) It's very simple. I just never met anyone as charming as you are. (Go wash your mouth out with soap after this one.)

8. I guess it's because I'm such a flighty thing. Someday I suppose I'll come to my senses and settle down to real happiness like all you married people have. (This is hitting below the belt, but who said anything about being fair?)

9. I don't really think a girl is ready for marriage until her children are in college.

10. It's kind of a difficult question to answer. Suppose you were single and somebody asked you why you weren't married. What would you say to them? (You'll have your inquisitor sweating out answers for ten minutes while you go off for a lemonade.)

After He's Gone

A grief-stricken girl friend called me yesterday to say she had just been dropped by her beau. Brushed. Bounced. Kissed off. She is in pretty bad shape.

There are worse pains than man trouble in a girl's life, but not *much* worse in my opinion. Is there anything whatever you can do to ease the pain?

First, you can talk about it. You can talk to some kind and understanding girl friend who's been through it herself. You can talk until you are blue in the face. Then you can start all over and talk some more. Explaining, exploring, remembering virtually every hour of your relationship and probing what must have led up to the trouble seem to provide a certain solace. At least you ascertain there's probably nothing you could have done to make it turn out any differently. (Some girls prefer a professional listener—psychiatrist or psychologist—as well as a girl friend.)

You're not in the mood to reason, of course, but here are two thoughts you might consider.

The fact that somebody breaks clean and says goodby is really better for you than being kept around like a plaything. You know where you stand. It may be

45

at the bottom, but now you can pick yourself up and get on with living. It's even more honorable on the part of the man than dangling you like a yo-yo.

Secondly, keep in the back of your mind the great new burst of "love" and "nobody else will do" feelings you have for him are partly predicated on the brush-off. Because he's gone, gone, gone, all of a sudden he's bigger than life-size and more appealing than Charlton Heston. He'll get back into proportion when a little time has gone by.

As for trying to drum him out of your heart five minutes after you've parted, impossible. Give him a decent mourning period. Hurt all you want to inside, and don't even try to be a big brave girl. Don't worry that you'll carry on like this forever because you won't. Time and nature will get you on your feet again.

As for active therapy, when you're over the worst grief-torn period, you must start your chores. Night school is one of the best I know. Two night classes a week in French, modern dance or principles of cost accounting on top of your job will keep you pretty engrossed. Giving a party is also therapy. So is a frontal attack on skiing or tennis or cooking.

Then when your insides are further healed, I think you must have a stab at making every man you can fall in love with you. I can hear the squeaks and squawks and howls of rage. It is immoral to try to make men fall in love with you when they belong to somebody else. Well, I don't mean really fall in love. Not more than two per-cent of them would succumb anyway, so nobody is in great danger. But you can make men feel a little bit more like men and happy to be alive. The idea is not to pine and mope for a new Mr. Right to replace old Mr. Right who turned into Mr. Wrong.

Be a living doll to every man you know—your most charming, beguiling, interested, vivacious attractive self. Mr. Right will come along sooner.

I Couldn't Be Bothered!

"Iron all those ruffles? Why should I bother, with this marvelous little hand laundry down the street that does up the dress for $3.50?"

46

"I used to knock myself out making hors d'oeuvres, but then I found this marvelous woman. She does all the shopping, brings four different things to your house—two spreads, one dip and a vegetable bowl. So why should I kill myself?"

"Put up a hem? Let somebody who's a professional do it."

"Do my own nails? It takes too long. Besides I always manage to smear them."

"Life is too short. My time is worth more than that."

This kind of talk, which I hear all the time, is fine for heiresses, but in my opinion, it's practically immoral among girls who support themselves.

All girls deserve luxuries. I can't pick yours for you, but the ones that flip me are those you can see, touch, feel, look at, wear, drive, bask in, show off to friends and remember (such as a trip to Bermuda) the rest of your life.

Luxury in the form of hiring somebody to do what you can do perfectly well yourself gives you so little to show for it the next day. And the girls who indulge in those "I'm too much of a lady to do that grubby stuff" luxuries so rarely can afford the other kind—the ones you can see, touch, feel and look at.

A few hedonists demand both kinds, of course. For example, one woman I know would never wear anything but Mainbocher suits to the office. A *blouse* cost $250! She made over $30,000 a year for a while and figured she could afford *anything*. She had a full-time maid and the most expensive attorney in town to handle minor legal affairs. Last year at age fifty-seven she had a serious illness. Her minuscule bank account was gone in three weeks, and she is now a tired, poor lady who must start over with a mountain of debts and no luxuries of any kind for a while.

I don't often say there aren't at least two ways to handle your life, but I'm rather pig-headed about this money thing. My credo is that you live carefully on a day-to-day basis and don't treat yourself like a maharani so that you can pop for really lovely things in your life when you want to. That would include helping a friend in need on occasion.

I hear so many girls say, "But my time is worth more than that." Sure it is, honey, but is anybody coming to you between the hours of 5 P.M. and midnight to *pay* you what your time is worth? Mightn't you just as well be washing the car, ironing a blouse or doing any of the stuff you're *able* to do yourself?

I don't believe in trying to make your own furniture or candles or even your own clothes if you don't know how. Heavy housework I'm always for turning over to somebody else *when* you can afford to. But I *do* think it's pretty nutty to start delegating every last chore to somebody before *you* have your first mink coat and some rainy-day money in the bank.

Test Your Rating as a Woman Alone

There are test-yourself questionnaires to find out how smart you are, how happy you are, how quickly you react to danger and practically anything you've ever wondered about. I don't see why we shouldn't have a test to find out how successful a woman alone you are. Get out your pencil and check the correct answer to each question.

1. A boy friend has brought you home at three in the morning from a very swinging cocktail party. You should:

   a. Drive him home in his car, return to your own home in his car and figure out a way to get his car back to him in the morning.

   b. Feed him six cups of black coffee and make him walk around the block with you six or eight times. Then send him home.

   c. Let him sleep on your couch.

2. You have been going with a man one year and he hasn't proposed. You should:

   a. Propose to him and see what happens.

   b. Continue to date him until the whole situation is too big a drag and tell him good-by.

   c. Stop seeing him like *now*.

3. Your mother is badgering you because you haven't married some nice boy. You should:

   a. Move away from home.

   b. Find somebody to marry.

   c. Turn your mother's voice off in your brain so that

48

you really don't hear when she begins to nag.

4. An attractive fellow at work has been pestering you to go out with him. You like him but there's a company ruling that employees may not date. Your best bet is to:

   a. Take a job someplace else so that you can date this man freely.

   b. Date him now but be careful.

   c. Tell him one or the other of you will be leaving the company someday (nobody keeps the same job forever) and you should both be patient until that happens.

5. You've been dating a very nice chap but he doesn't know how to kiss. You should:

   a. Attempt to tell him or show him how to kiss better.

   b. Continue to go out with him but stop kissing him.

   c. Don't see him at all.

6. You are going to a fabulous party and would like a smashing dress to wear which isn't in the budget. You should:

   a. Buy the dress anyway (put it on your charge account).

   b. Borrow a dress from a friend.

   c. Be creative and make something out of inexpensive yardage or draperies like Scarlett O'Hara did.

7. You've been yearning to go out with a man who doesn't seem to know that you exist. You should:

   a. Call him up and ask him to come over.

   b. Call him up and say you're coming over *there*.

   c. Give a party and invite him to it.

(*All* the answers for questions one through six are correct. None of the answers to question seven will do. A man who's deaf, dumb and blind to your charms doesn't deserve you.)

Do You Know Anyone Who Makes These Common Errors?

It's only too true that a lot of nonsense is still being circulated about single women. The women themselves know how silly these old wives' tales are, but they can't get anybody to listen—especially men.

As a former single woman, I'm going to take it upon

myself to put down some myths held by men about "our group," together with the facts.

Myth: A single girl is single because she couldn't find anybody to marry her.

Fact: A single girl is single because she's too choosy, too neurotic, too wedded to her parents, too frightened, too insecure or too happy being single, but rarely because she couldn't come up with somebody—or several somebodies—to marry during her single span.

Myth: Girls become very excited when a man tells them his secret fantasies about them. The more blushing and outrageous they are, the more aphrodisiac.

Fact: Girls are usually only moved to tears or laughter by secret fantasies. What actually moves them is the physical touch, being held warm and close and tenderly.

Myth: A girl who holds a very high-powered job doesn't like men.

Fact: A girl who holds a very high-powered job often got the job by being tremendously interested in men—knowing how to talk to them, get through to them and charm them. She often has a lover. Oftener she has a husband.

Myth: Girls who act aloof with men are often a flaming cauldron inside.

Fact: The aloof girl usually doesn't like men very well or is scared to death of them. Her insides are not very flaming.

Myth: A girl who would rather go to an expensive restaurant than a pizza parlor is showing her gold-digging tendencies.

Fact: A girl who would rather go to an expensive restaurant than a pizza parlor is showing some consideration for her stomach lining, plus showing that she's humanly attracted to luxury. Most women prefer posh to hash on dates if given a choice.

Myth: A girl who lets a man know she is seriously interested in getting married ruins her chances.

Fact: A girl only ruins her chances if she nags about marriage. If a man gets hopelessly scared off merely because she states her desires, she never really had any chance of marrying him in the first place.

Myth: When a girl wears a low-cut gown, she is mighty keen about her date and probably is trying to seduce him.

Fact: When a girl wears a low-cut gown, she may be

only keen about her own body and showing it off. Or she may be keen about some unknown person she hopes to meet at the party her date is taking her to.

Myth: Girls prefer tall men.

Fact: Girls who aren't very tall themselves may be downright uncomfortable with a tall man. A short man is able to make a small girl feel like a glorious hunk of woman for a change, while a big man only makes her feel skimpy.

Myth: A girl who doesn't like other women and prefers to be with men is sexy.

Fact: A girl who doesn't like other women and prefers to be with men *all* the time (I think) is sick.

Myth: In spite of what you say, most girls secretly want to get married.

Fact: That's no myth. That's a fact!

Lonely, Lonely, Lonely, Lonely, Lonely— Oh, So?

A major newspaper recently ran the following words in display type on the front page of its women's section: "THE LONELY ONES . . . in our town there are literally thousands. The majority are women . . . for the most part they go their way unknown, unheard and certainly unsung. Their existence is an unhappy one. They are the lonely ones. They are the women who walk by themselves and cry by themselves, who dine alone and remember alone and whose companionship with hope has not taught them that there is a longing without bitterness. They are the lonely ones, etc., etc., etc." At the top of the page there is a picture of a very handsome woman with her hands in her pockets, photographed on a city street, presumably just standing there being lonely.

I just wonder who in the world all these lonely creatures *are*. I live in the city the writer is talking about and, frankly, I never see these hordes of lonelies out prowling the streets. I don't even know any who are sitting home in their apartments. Every unmarried (single, divorced, widowed) woman I know always has somebody she could haul in for company if she *wanted* to.

Many unmarried women do indeed dine alone. I wish to heaven I *could* sometimes as does many another married woman. Then you could eat the noncaloric, no-preparation-at-all cottage cheese you'd really like instead of digging into the 9,000-calorie beef stroganoff you've prepared for the family.

As for crying alone, I find it's the *only* way to cry. Cry with somebody else in the room and they're always trying to pat you and pet you and get you to stop when the only thing in the world you want to do is have a good cry. (You have to get rid of the mob to get the job done.)

As for remembering alone, that's how most of us remember, married or single. Once in a great while you say to your husband, "Darling, do you remember that gondola ride we had up the Grand Canal in Venice in 1948?" More often you are remembering a boat ride you had up Lake Minnetonka with some boy who was on the scene long before your husband came along and doing this reminiscing out loud certainly won't cheer up your beloved.

There is loneliness and loneliness, and I wish people would stop pretending it all belongs to women who don't have official mates. *Men* are lonely. One recently said to me, "Stella and I live in the same house, but she pretty much goes her own way. I supply money, of course. My kids haven't consulted me about anything in years. At fifty-four, I happen to be the oldest employee in my company and haven't a lot in common with the younger men."

A thirty-year-old wife laments, "What if you had a husband who was never particularly hot-blooded to begin with and whose ardor through the years has cooled until you might as well be living with a kindly uncle. A new perfume, new attitude, pleas and threats don't get through to him. Children help ease the loneliness, but they are no longer babies and are beginning to live their own lives. Sometimes I feel absolutely cut off from life."

I'd hazard a guess that the thoughts going through the head of that "lonely" woman with her hands in her pockets in the picture might be: "I probably shouldn't have left the apartment at the exact time I said I'd be home. Oh well, he'll call back. He *always* calls back. If he only wouldn't call back just *once*, I might find him a little more amusing." Or, "I suppose I should be over there

52

baby-sitting for Clara so she and George could go to that movie. I do love my grandchildren, but this would be the fourth time this week. Clara must learn that having children involves giving up things, and Grandma can't always be around." Or, "Maybe if I go for a ten-minute walk alone, I can think of those nine ideas I'm supposed to have for the meeting tomorrow." What she *isn't* thinking is, "Oh, if I just had someone to walk *with* me."

The Poor Gertrude Vacation

"In the company I work for, you have to take your vacation by September," Gertrude said. "And all summer I've been in a mild panic and depression about it. This has been the year of the new inlays, the year of helping my brother with my nephew's college tuition, the year of paying off the hi-fi and stereophonic equipment I thought I couldn't live without. I didn't have enough money to take myself to a country *inn* for the weekend, much less to a different country entirely for a really glamorous vacation."

"And what did you do?" I asked.

"July thirty-first I found one of my friends was in the same boat. So we said, 'Okay, it would be plain stupid to miss this vacation entirely. Let's take it together and map out a poor Gertrude and poor Eloise (that's my friend) itinerary that will at least give us *something*.' Actually it turned out to be one of the best vacations I ever had because I didn't *expect* anything.

"We played tennis every morning. We were so terrible people sometimes stopped and watched just to get a good laugh, but we felt very virtuous and healthy and kind of young, you know. We went through a rock mine just out of town. We visited a lion farm, a bakery and an advanced judo class. The last two weren't open to visitors, but Eloise told them she was writing a magazine article and they let us in. One day we had a movie orgy—four in one day—a silent, a foreign and two Hollywood ones. I cooked crepes suzette one night for the first time in my life."

If you're hard-up for vacation plans and vacation money, here are a few suggestions:

53

1. Ask your company if they would let you work straight through your vacation this year and pay you an additional two weeks' salary. If they have to hire summer replacements for the girls on vacation, they might be only too happy to have you stay. Use the money all in one heap for some gorgeous possession or bank it for a big vacation next year.

2. See if you can cat- or dog-sit for people who are out of the city and get paid for this before your vacation starts. Even though pets are well-treated in kennels, many pet-owners feel guilty about leaving them there. You can take the pets to your house or move into the pet owners' house. Your rates should be kennel rates so that you can stockpile vacation funds.

3. Make a bargain with friends who have a car to let you keep it while they are away and give it its exercise. (Most cars get cross and cranky when they are unused for two weeks.) Take your vacation at the same time they do and you will have a car at your disposal.

4. Scrupulously make a list of the museums, galleries and historic landmarks in your city that you have never visited and go see them. *Do* it! You've always *said* you would.

5. Have a delicious, inexpensive little dinner party for four friends—all girls, if you've run out of men. Part of what makes a dinner party memorable is having time to add the special touches and take pains. You have the time! Mexican or Chinese dishes can be very inexpensive and people will gobble them up.

6. Read and eat in bed for one whole day. I'm *always* plotting and scheming for ways to do *that*.

Imagine having a whole week for this madness!

Smartening Up the Pad

In giving "how to" advice on improving your face, your figure, your wardrobe and your outlook, a writer has to watch herself every minute to keep from telling people to spend a lot of money. (Naturally, anybody's outlook is going to improve with a round-the-world cruise, but whose budget does *that* fit into?)

Unfortunately, improving a house or apartment can take

more money than a cruise. Crazy old buffets that used to be stolen from junk shops for $7.92 don't even blush at wearing price tags of $100 these days. Nevertheless, it's possible to give your home some lovely touches of glamour without spending a fortune. New York decorator Thelma Gill has these inspired ideas:

No matter how modest your home, it can have the aura of great beauty if you have personal taste. This you aren't born with. It's acquired by immersing yourself in beautiful things. You should haunt museums, antique stores, study the beautiful homes you visit, also the decorated rooms of new apartment buildings and department stores. Gradually the taste and the need and desire for beauty will be transferred to your own surroundings.

When you start to work on your house, stand in each room and ruthlessly see what you can throw out. Better to be sparsely but nicely furnished than saddled with monsters. Regroup and rearrange what's left. Let some new thoughts in.

"Re-think" your dining area to make it more of a living room. Push the table up against a wall. Put a lamp, a plant, some bric-a-brac on it, pull up an arm chair and treat it as a desk. Two or three people can still use it as a dinner table without moving a thing. Shoo a couple of dining room chairs out to the living room or some other area.

Use inexpensive fabric, but plenty of it to cover architectural faults—jagged corners, wrongly placed windows or no windows. Drape the fabric from the ceiling to the floor instead of just from the top to the bottom of a window.

"Paper" a whole wall or room in fabric—nothing could be more feminine. Try for 25-cents-a-yard material. (You can dye cheesecloth or unbleached muslin gorgeous shades in the bathtub or washing machine.) Sew strips together and thumbtack to the wall in pleats or straight across.

Take up that filthy, scruffy carpet and give it to the Salvation Army. Rent equipment and sand your floor, or perhaps it needs only wax and polish. Throw on a throw rug or two. You can spatter-paint an unattractive floor with several shades of brightly colored enamel. Dribble shocking pink from a sponge all around the floor. Let it dry. With a clean sponge, use turquoise next, then, lime green and moss green, drying between coats. Use any color combination you wish, and take your time. You're an artist.

Drape the cheapest kind of round-top table (24- to 36-inch diameter) with fabric. A round plywood top can be made for any table you own. The fabric should hang to the floor all the way around and be hemmed or finished with fringe or braid. Put a photograph and flowers on top. Very feminine.

Use extravagant bunches of fresh leaves in vases—huckleberry, lemon or whatever your florist has. Mix leaves. They are inexpensive and should last weeks if you clip the stems.

Hang a splashy curtain from ceiling to floor in the bathroom to screen off the tub. Install a rod in the plaster and make your own curtain of a fabulous floral or abstract. It can be tied back on each side like draperies or left closed.

Change china occasionally as you do dresses. Buy two new plates in one design, two new cups and saucers in another, desserts in a third. It will cheer your dining alone. Many chic hostesses wouldn't dream of having huge matched sets of anything.

How to Give a Dinner Party With No Man and No Maid

One of the best dinner parties I've been to in ten years was given by a single working girl last week in a one-room apartment with a kitchen the size of a pea-pod. She had nobody to help her play hostess, no host and no money to throw around. These are Miss Kelly's party rules:

1. Forgive the expression, but you *must* create an image —one of a smooth, pretty, gracious, at-ease, charming, relaxed hostess. Do that and you can stop worrying about the food—and the man, and luxurious surroundings you can't produce. How to bring this off? Plan every last detail of the party ahead of time and work like a rat. There is nothing dimple-simple or easy-does-it about a good party.

2. Keep the menu simple. Don't be afraid of underfeeding the guests. A rich casserole and salad will do it, plus hors d'oeuvres, wine, coffee and dessert. (Charlotte's

menu was shrimp with red sauce and marinated artichoke hearts served with cocktails, chicken breasts in wine with seedless grapes and slivered almonds, green salad, coffee and two kinds of dessert—fresh fruit and lemon chiffon pie.)

3. Make a list of every last party detail, then check off each thing as it's done. This will include purchases for house and hostess, primary grocery list, last minute grocery list (ice, flowers), apartment chores (table setting), kitchen brigade.

Whatever you buy, put the money where it shows—glasses, dishes, napkins and on your back. Ancient, unglamorous utensils cook just as well.

4. To bring off the image, these are musts: candlelight (plus soft electric lights), music, fresh flowers, wine, cocktail napkins (but no coasters), place cards and a long skirt and blouse for you. No slacks, capris. Place cards are not just for show. During "rush hour" a harassed hostess can literally forget where she wanted people to sit.

5. Clean your apartment several days ahead and get it out of the way. All it will need before the party is a touch-up.

6. Do the major cooking the night before the party. Set the table, get your own clothes ready, decide on a place for guests' coats. Have a "dress rehearsal." Wherever you seat yourself, be sure there is furniture nearby that you can stack dishes on—hi-fi set, card table or whatever.

7. Night of party: start with empty wastebaskets. During last-minute cooking, clean up as you go along until first guests arrive. After that, forget "keeping up with the dishes." Only empty ash trays. Your place is with guests, not out in the kitchen being a compulsive housekeeper.

8. In serving, bring everything to table on an enormous tray. This should require two trips at most. Don't let another girl help you in the kitchen. Shows "poor little me" tendency. After putting food on table, set tray on hi-fi or table behind you. When main course is over, let guests pass dishes to you at head of table. Stack dishes on tray. Take everything to kitchen and return with dessert and coffee. Forget about dishes.

9. Sleep late next day. One of the bonuses of being a "woman alone" is that you can clean up after the party two days later, if you like.

TWO | STALKING THE WILD MALE

or,

When a Lady

Goes Hunting

It's been suggested that the advice I give girls about men is a little on the "grabby" side—i.e., how do you grab one before somebody beats you to him, what are the grabbiest of all little dinners to serve him, is having a hi-fi set or owning a motorcycle a better way to his heart? Well, for goodness' sake, if I didn't think—*know*—men are important, I wouldn't care whether you grabbed one or not. I just figure you have to have (grab) one before you can love him up close and forever. What good does it do you to be lovable if he's off having a grabby dinner with some other girl . . . or his mother or his *boyfriend*?

Very well, what with the larger ratio of single girls to single men in most cities, sometimes a girl needs help to bring a man into *her* orbit. After he's there I figure you'll *know* what to do with him.

Where the Men Are

It's time for a rundown of cities in terms of their being good places or bad places for single girls to find men to date. This information comes from correspondents whom I've questioned and I have three "goods" and one "bad" to report on.

Washington, D.C.: Terrific. "You've heard of all the girls working for the government here? There are just about as many corresponding men—all the staff members of the various cabinet officers, senators and representatives, young attorneys, labor executives, foreign legations, the hundreds of people who come here to lobby. You have to be hep and bright. They don't like marshmallowy girls who have nothing but marriage on their minds, but if you can talk well and look sharp and don't bear down on marriage, you'll have a ball."

Miami: Not too encouraging. "You can have a great job, belong to a swinging club like the Racquet Club, support the musical and social events, but there are still a lot of widows and divorcees just like you doing the same thing and some of them are wealthy, which helps. It's a beautiful, luxurious city but bachelors or newly divorced men don't last any longer than a dab of butter in hot oatmeal. Somebody grabs them off quick."

Toronto and Montreal: The greatest. "Men abound in both cities, not just single men under twenty-five but bachelors into their forties. Immigrants pour in here by the thousands—English, Scots, South African, Australian and European men who normally don't marry until they're at least 26. I'd say single men outnumber women about eight to one both places.

"Montreal is more difficult for a single girl to find a job in because of the language barrier, but if you can speak French and don't mind the cold, it's a fascinating city. In Toronto jobs are crying and you are surrounded by the University of Toronto, outdoor cafés and entertainment places of all nationalities.

"There are social clubs on every corner (dues are minimal), art galleries, parks, skating rinks, tennis courts, swimming pools, squash courts, indoor badminton, symphonies, great stores, amateur and professional live theater, folk dancing, free courses in languages and the arts. Anybody who's tired of the American bachelor and his 'eternal games' really ought to try these places."

Rome (and other European cities): Excellent. "There are just nests of lone men in Rome and Berlin, many not married—U.S. businessmen transferred here, military personnel, diplomats (senior and junior). The only reason U.S. men marry foreign women is because there aren't enough of their own nationality to go around when they're stationed abroad. I've watched it happen for fifteen years. There's a big turnover of men, too, on the overseas scene so you have a chance at new ones all the time."

Where the Men Are—
Under Your Nose Division

Even though I've just told you cities where men are in great numbers I still believe that it doesn't do a scrap of good for a lonely, man-hungry girl to move there. If she isn't meeting the men where she is *now* (there are always some men around, you know) she isn't going to do a great deal better where they're denser. A girl who likes men will meet them wherever she is.

Let me tell you about Joyce, one of my dearest friends and that's her real name. She's an executive secretary, divorced and forty years old, I believe. Joyce has been visiting me from California these past few days, but I'm so busy just now I haven't been able to go out and sightsee with her one single day. That hasn't bugged Joyce. Every morning I take her out to the elevator, send her down to the street and she's off to do her own sightseeing.

In the two days she's been here, she's covered five museums—the Museum of Modern Art, the Frick, Guggenheim, Whitney and Metropolitan. At the Metropolitan this afternoon she tells me she picked up a man. "We were in front of a Jackson Pollock and he said, 'There *is* an order to what he does.' And I said, 'Of course there is. He's planned!' And now we have a date to go and see the Museum of Natural History tomorrow." (One hopes when they run out of museums, they'll have the sense to branch out into theater or concerts and not just let the friendship peter out.)

I think you could put a girl like Joyce down a mine shaft and she'd find a man or he'd find her. And she's not a huntress or predator. She's interesting—and interested in *life,* not in nesting. She also adores men.

"I have very few lunches with girls," says Joyce. "If there's no man to have lunch with, I read or work. I never stalk men, however. Tracking them down like a bloodhound doesn't work. But they're always there, you know.

"I was having a hamburger at a counter a few months ago, minding my own business, reading. Naturally I had my glasses on. The chap sitting next to me asked if I thought the bug in that story (Kafka's "Metamorphosis") is the size of a man or just an ordinary bug-size bug. I thought for a minute and said I felt it was better not to close in on his size. That would spoil the story. We chatted and he turned out to be the president of the student body at a nearby university (I won't tell you which one).

"This boy has been to my office twice just to talk, and last week we went to a movie. I had a ball. Corrupting young manhood? My eye! Girls his age are so vapid he probably can't talk to them, but I wouldn't be caught dead having a romance with him. We're *friends*."

Could you find it in your heart, do you suppose, to like some men you aren't going to marry? Could you keep your pores open and your valves adjusted to accept people merely because they're interesting and have something to say? Could you get yourself interested in the world and what's going on out there so that *you'd* have something to say instead of fretting yourself nearly to death about lifetime companionship? I think you'd meet a lot more men if you did that. I assure you they're out there—if not to marry at least to have as friends.

Haunting and Hunting Men, 1966

It's well into the new year and time for an entirely new list of places where a girl without a steady beau can meet some new men. The two most reliable methods of meeting men are still, in my opinion, through a job and through friends. If there aren't any men where you work, you may have to change jobs, of course, or switch fields. Also, married friends sometimes have to be hustled a bit to do a bit of hustling. They may know a perfectly good, eligible man and not realize that the two of you would be interested in each other. In that case, speak up. "Look, Jack and Eloise," tell them, "this is the year I plan to meet a really good man and get married. I think the time has come. I just feel it in my bones. If you know anybody I might like or who might like me, then I want you to be sure to get us together." You have to be firm and not embarrassed. There's nothing to be embarrassed about.

Now, if you've already exhausted the meager man-supply of friends or your job and have also given up on political clubs, church socials and such, here are some new 1966 sources to check out.

1. Walk a dog. All dogs who live in apartments and have no yard to play in have to be walked daily. So nobody can accuse you of having ulterior motives as you sally forth looking gay as a Gauguin. People who have no dog may stop and pet your dog. (A friendly poodle or spaniel is preferable to a man-eating German shepherd for widening your social horizons.) If you should meet a man walking his dog, friendship can develop between your dogs even if the two of you are too shy to speak at first. If enmity develops, so much the better. The owners can hardly remain uninvolved with each other when one dog is trying to bite the other.

2. Take your laundry to a laundromat. Some very chic and polished bachelors take theirs there, too. You'd be surprised. If, after a few tries, the laundromat nearest you doesn't provide anybody interesting, sample a new location. If anybody ever questions the fact that you are eighteen miles away from home with two bedspreads and one pink blouse, say it isn't necessarily true that all laundromats are alike. The action out here in Cliffwood is gentler. Bring a good book to read while you're waiting and casing. If you see a likely man, ask if he'd watch your things while you go next door for cigarettes—not that anybody has ever stolen anything much from a moving washing machine, but this is only a get-acquainted gambit.

3. Join a flying club. It costs money to learn to fly but the ratio of boys to girls in these groups is exceedingly high. The instructors are practically all men so there's your first prospect. If you crack up, there's no end to the crowd you attract.

4. Join a motorcycle club. More boys than girls here, too. Ditto on the accident.

5. Study photography. There will be more men than women in your class and photography offers many postgraduate benefits. Go to the park with your camera and make like Cartier-Bresson. You don't even have to have film in the camera, if you're broke from paying for it. The fellows are tossing a football to each other? Click, click, snap, snap. A man is alone on a park bench reading? Snap, snap, click, click. Take down names and ad-

dresses and offer to send prints. If you haven't actually
been using film, there can always have been an accident
in the dark room which calls for another shooting session.

6. You could join a nudist camp. They're always screaming for new girl members. Don't apply if you're just
going to scoff. They are very dedicated people and take
themselves seriously.

Spending Up a Storm to Impress a Man

If by chance you're thinking I'm against spending a lot
of money to impress a man, you're wrong. I think it's a
great idea, if you can afford it.

The idea is not to spend the money on *him* necessarily
but to spend it on *you* and, well, just things that add to
the impression of you as a glamorous woman—dinner
parties, clothes, trips, good furniture. Men are human (I
have *never* said anything to the contrary) and like you,
my dear, are impressionable.

Let me get personal.

I don't think there's any doubt the man I married was
impressed that a week before we met I had paid all cash
for a sports car. My husband-to-be had barely known a
girl who paid all cash for a can of hairspray, much less a
car. (Let it be said the car's purchaser had worked whirl-
ing-dervish fashion for eighteen years to be able to afford
such a bauble, moving up from streetcar to a disinte-
grating thirteen-year-old Buick to a slightly younger
Chevrolet to plunge finally, at age thirty-six, for a brand-
new car.)

Here's another "girl buys man's interest" story. A girl
accountant I know had the astonishing foresight to buy
fifty shares of I.B.M. at eighty dollars a share. The fifty
shares are now worth roughly $25,000. Last year my
friend fell in love with a man who was not keen to get
married. He liked her well enough but marriage he'd had.
The first thing she did was put up half the money for a
sailboat he fancied.

As joint owners (she got it in writing), she figured she
could always buy him out or the other way around if
love cooled. They next bought a Texas oil-well together—

not producing at the moment but they have high hopes. A few months ago they started looking around for a four-unit apartment house. Just last week Natalie told me her friend had started to figure things the way she's been figuring them for ages—they're in so many deals together, maybe they should get married. (No, it isn't romantic but most proposals aren't.)

One more example of Girl Impresses Man. Elizabeth grew up on a beautiful farm in Ohio. She now works in an ad agency on the West Coast but every Christmas or Thanksgiving she takes one of her young men back to the farm for a real slice of farm living. The man buys his ticket. The hospitality—sumptuous—is on Elizabeth and her folks, who can afford it. They give parties, hayrides, go visit the neighbors, ride the horses and sample the vintage wine. Elizabeth has not met the man she wants to marry, but this back-to-the-farm American holiday trek goes over tremendously well with her beaux.

Yes, dear, I know there's a little thing you can offer a man called love, which is the most priceless thing you *can* offer him. It doesn't hurt, however, to bedazzle him a bit with your accomplishments and possessions if you have them. You *don't* have them usually when you're twenty. Making something of yourself and acquiring some money is something to work toward if you think there is the remotest possibility you might be forty years old some-day and looking for a man.

Get Out of Town on a Plane

Airplanes are a good place to meet men. I know you don't travel by plane every day of the week, but I do think your next air trip is something you can look forward to with pleasure.

Airliners have built-in advantages for getting acquainted. You sit so close—especially tourist class. And unlike trains, once you're seated next to a man, he's yours for the length of the trip. This contrasts sharply with the measly amount of time allotted you standing beside an attractive stranger waiting for the elevator, for example. Ten seconds to make good just isn't enough. I won't say the men you meet on planes are always "take-home" men (and I'm not allowed to take any home any more anyway because I'm married), but they can make you feel rather princessy and glamorous while the trip lasts. There's something about talking to a charming man—quietly, intimately, in flight—that leaves you with the impression you yourself are smart, sophisticated and charming (whether a dinner date develops or not).

You don't always have anything to say about whom you sit next to on a plane, of course. On long flights, most seats are reserved in advance. There's always the possibility somebody nice will be assigned next to you, however. On flights where you are able to pick and choose, it's simple to pop down next to a man. There isn't anything to feel brazen about. Men love to be popped down next to. It makes them assume, "I must be a very attractive citizen. She picked *me*."

Here's another tip. If you are shy, which I am though it probably doesn't sound so sometimes, I've found the best ploy for getting acquainted if he doesn't open the conversation first is to comment about what he's reading. You just look over his shoulder and read along with Mitch or Bill or whoever he is until he finally looks up to see what in the world you're doing.

Nine times out of ten he will be reading a trade publication of which you really can't make head or tail, and when he looks up and finds you reading, you say, "What are cathode rays anyhow?" First thing you know he's explaining and you're off to the races.

There's also a more direct get-acquainted approach if the silence except for the motors has become deafening. Just look him right in the eye and say, "What *are* you going to Pittsburgh for?" He's usually delighted to tell.

With a little sacking of your shyness, I'm convinced you can have great fun on a plane.

Mama, How Can I Meet That Man?

Every so often you hear about a dreamy man you'd like to meet. He's a bachelor, what else! And a very good bachelor (right age, right job, right looks). Perhaps he's a man you've met once and would like to see again, but so far as you know the desire is all on *your* part.

Here are some legitimate and illegitimate ways of getting *to* him. I know this advice will bring a spate of "Oh, for goodness' sake, do you think all women think about is chasing *men*?" comments. It will also elicit some cluck-clucking over the suggestion that a girl use these "unnatural" means to meet a man. Never mind if they are "unnatural." They work. I met my husband by using one of these eleven proven methods. I won't tell you which one.

1. Enlist the aid of someone who knows your heart's desire and ask that friend to arrange a date or to invite both of you to the same party. Married women are sometimes awfully good about helping you with your little schemes. Men can be cooperative, too, provided they don't have a hankering for you themselves.

2. Give a party. If you've met the man once, a simple telephone call may get him there. If you don't know him, find out who does and ask them to bring him to your party.

3. Figure out how the business he's in ties in with yours so that you can make a legitimate business call. He leases office space. Your company is looking for a new location. He doesn't have to know you aren't the company's official scout.

4. Ask him to be a guest speaker for your club or sorority.

5. Get him put on your list to solicit for a charity drive.

6. Whatever he's selling, make up your mind to buy it —insurance, cars, stationery, rugs.

7. Ask if you can interview him for an article you're writing. Tell him what publication you have in mind. You can say you haven't been commissioned but you're pretty sure the article will sell.

8. Track him at his favorite sport. If he skis, you ski. He plays tennis. You play tennis. Follow him around the golf course. (To find out where he does these things you will again need the help of friends or possibly he has a secretary who can be made a buddy.)

9. Let his hobby play into your hands. He loves sports car racing. He's an amateur photographer. He paints on Sunday. He's a rock hound. He's a baseball fan. Turn up to root for his team. Join the organization he belongs

to or take lessons from the same teacher (golf, art, music).

10. Get active in a political organization (it should be *his* party, of course) and ask him to do a special assignment for you—write a pamphlet or whatever.

11. Call the man up and ask him to have coffee or cocktails with you. Don't say why, only that you want to see him. When you meet, with candor and charm tell him there was no burning issue except that you simply wanted to see him. So what is he going to do, *hit* you?

GOOD LUCK!

How to Propose to a Man

Even though it's not leap year, I have compiled a handy-dandy list of thirteen ways to propose to your man.

Bear in mind that even proposals from man to girl are not always straightforward, will-you or won't-you propositions. Sometimes the hint at marriage is so oblique that a girl is hard-put to decide did he or did he not suggest they get together for keeps. Several of these "proposals" from you to him are not of a direct nature either. They will definitely give him the idea that you have marriage on your mind, however, and if he shows up for your next date, I think you can be reasonably optimistic.

(At his apartment) "Darling, you really do have the greatest Miles Davis collection in the world. Won't it be wonderful when I can add my Dave Brubecks to it and we can have a *house* full of music?"

(Consulting calendar at *your* apartment) "Harry, what are you doing June nineteenth? If we happened to get married that weekend and took a two-week vacation, it would bring us into the Fourth of July holiday and we'd get three extra days."

"Isn't it just too good to be true we *both* like sailing. I was thinking we might buy that sloop you had your eye on. I'd put up half the money. I'm sure we're going to be involved in each others' lives (throw in a long slow look here) a very long while."

"I think it's wonderful that *your* dog and *my* cat get along so well together, don't you? Do you think they can ever both sleep in the same room or should we give Benjie the back porch and Raffles the kitchen?"

"I'd love to go to Las Vegas with you, Harry, but of course I wouldn't dream of traveling with a man I wasn't married to."

"I don't think men should ever help with the dishes or housework, do you? Oh, I know a lot of men do it, but I wouldn't want *you* and *me* to have that kind of arrangement, would you?" You must not murmur these birdbrained words unless you are positively willing to live by them. Just gaining a current advantage doesn't justify their use.

"My mother and father don't really approve of you, darling, but I've told them I'm too old for them to have anything to say about the man I . . . well, the man I . . . I mean, the man I . . ." (He finishes the sentence.)

"Dearest, since Fred and Doris give you such a pain in the neck, I've decided we won't see them any more. I'd rather we made some new permanent friends together."

"Do you think we should have a baby . . . what I mean is, should *any* girl have a baby . . . the first year she's married?"

"I have to name a beneficiary for my life-insurance policy at work pretty soon. I have no immediate family and it occurred to me that you . . . well, we're such good friends and seem to be seeing so much of each other . . ." (Stay off the end of the pier after this action unless you trust him completely.)

MORE DESPERATE MEASURES—

"Johnny, I have to decide whether to renew the lease on my apartment for another year, or do you think I probably will be living somewhere else?"

"Dearest, there's a fantastic sale of Swedish chairs at the Furniture Fair this week. Should we drop by just to browse?"

"All right, Paul Applegate, I'll give you two more weeks to make up your mind!"

So He Won't Marry You

Some girls are born marriers. You turn one loose with a man for fifteen minutes and the man has not only asked for the next date but has also asked her to spend the next fifty or sixty years of her life as his beloved wife. I had one girl friend who never just *went* with anybody. She was always engaged. She was gentle, virtuous, soft, blonde, beautiful and a wow with the boys' mothers. The boys never took a chance on losing her. They signed her up as a fiancée even if she hadn't said Yes for sure. About the fourth one she married.

This kind of girl friend and these stories of proposals are very depressing to girls who are going with men they would give anything to marry, but the men won't.

The con game is depressing, too. Most girls are not cut out for it. We were taught that boys chase girls so how come things got switched around so completely that here you are laying down the law like Matt Dillon—"I will give you until February to make up your mind, and if you can't, then it's good-by."

The very fact that a man has to *think* about wanting you is humiliating. After all, you aren't a painting, an apartment to sublet or even a secondhand Thunderbird. You're you, not an object for appraisal.

I believe there is a reluctance on the part of most men to commit themselves totally, and for goodness' sake, why not? Only a salmon or a nincompoop splashes into matrimony blithely. Most men, genuinely in love with a girl, will hesitate and hedge just so long, however, and, rather than risk losing her, will marry. The marriage usually works out fine.

When a man won't marry after this normal, gentle prodding process, what do you do? Well, you can prod some more. I invested a year in the waiting game myself (kicking and poking all the time), and I think a year is not too unreasonable a time to wait. Many men are convinced more quickly, of course.

If a man objects obdurately and violently for any longer period, I think you must ask yourself why and face

72

the answer woman-fully. He may have a very valid reason.

A dear friend of mine handed down her ultimatum four months ago to a pretty terrific guy, and it was not accepted. She took a long trip but is now returning to him to try again. "I believe I can convince him this time," she says, "and I must." Then she explained quite honestly that her friend has an extremely delicate emotional problem that could affect their whole marital relationship. "He doesn't want to marry me until he's absolutely certain this thing is solved, but I know I can help him."

What an ungrateful girl! This man is trying to save her a nightmarish existence but she refuses to be saved.

I'm not the person to delve into why she has to have this man above all others. I don't even know why I wanted the man who wouldn't marry me those many years ago. I do know there is no one man for every woman. That is idiocy. And I do firmly believe with all my heart that you should never force someone to marry against his will. It doesn't work and you deserve better. You'll have it, too, if you take "no" for an answer and figure it's the best thing that ever happened to you.

The Dating Game—Rules for Him

A friend of mine who is just about the datingest girl I know has given me her impressions about what can reasonably be expected of a man in the dating game in this year of 1966. Here is Ann Pearson's (a Southern belle with a sense of the way things are *now*) list:

Compliments: The finest thing a man can do for a girl he's dating is lavish her with well-placed compliments, and she can never receive too many. These should be spontaneous, inspired by something she's wearing or saying or doing at the moment. Compliments are just his way of letting her know he really *sees* her and *notices* her and that he likes what he sees and notices.

Clothes: A man's clothes don't particularly matter. Naturally, it's more pleasing to a girl if he dresses nicely. But if a girl is going around with a guy who dresses like a slob, she knows that's the way he is and she accepts that as part of his "package."

73

Money: He doesn't have to spread a lot around on a date just to be impressive. Most girls are willing to let a man fit his plans to his budget unless he's really a pathological cheapskate, and then he has to be jarred out of it. Going to a great restaurant *once* in a while is usually appreciated by a girl if a man can afford it, but if she knows he can't she doesn't hold it against him for one minute.

Date plans: The most flattering thing a man can do is take a woman some place she couldn't go without him —to dinner at a friend's or boss's house, to his club if he's that wealthy, to a charity benefit. It's also heady if a man finds out what a girl really likes and is interested in and makes arrangements for that kind of evening. "A man I dated knew I loved sketching," says Ann. "He enrolled us in a sketch class for thirteen Wednesdays in a row. That was a compliment because he was willing to commit himself for thirteen weeks. Of course, it was a compliment to him that *I* was, too."

Advance notice: A man doesn't need to call up a week or even three days in advance to ask you out. That's an old-fashioned notion. Maybe he doesn't know in advance whether he can make it. Maybe you don't know, *either*. A call on Saturday morning for a date Saturday night is quite acceptable. (I've said this myself!)

Presents: What girl doesn't love them? Hopefully he should buy the kind he can afford so they don't get repossessed. She can't help but be moved by flowers. Maybe, however, he'd be a little wiser sometimes to spend the same money for something she can keep around to be reminded of him by, such as matched glasses, cigarette case and coin purse. Lingerie is too personal, but I don't see anything wrong with some kind of wearing apparel that's different and fun—an offbeat sweater or beach hat. When he says, "I saw it and knew you'd look marvelous in it," she has to be pleased.

Etiquette: Yes, he still fetches you from the car. "I'll sit all night and wait for him to come around," says Ann. Helping you off the curb he shouldn't do, because that deprives you of the privilege of taking his arm and batting your eyes at him as you cross the street—something no girl should be denied and *is* if he's got you by the elbow. Yes, men should still walk on the outside of the street, because that gives you a whack at the store windows.

Telephone: Certainly he should keep in touch with you through the week even if he isn't asking you out for a date. Presumably, if he likes you well enough to date you he must have some things to say to you from time to time. No, there's still a double standard about girls calling men, and we should only do it to ask them to a party or for some really good cause.

Obligations: A man should never let you down when you really *need* him to take you to a wedding or company banquet or family gathering. If it's an evening during which you know he's really going to be bored to tears, however, you should keep him involved in it for the least possible time. Start a little late. Leave a little early.

Children: If a dating woman has children, a man should suggest taking them along *some* of the time on dates, but not nearly *all* the time. A woman should never ask a man to pay for the baby sitter (some women alone don't agree with Ann). That's her personal responsibility, and she should no more ask a man to assume it than she'd ask him to pay for someone to come in and clean up the apartment after she cooked his dinner.

Transportation: It's all right to meet a man in your own car if there isn't time for him to come and get you or he's already where the evening is to begin and it's miles from your house. Still, I don't think a man should let a woman drive around by herself after midnight. I still like to be considered fragile and in need of protection.

How to Be a Great Date

It occurs to me that I haven't said anything to you about how to be a great date. I've just taken for granted that the only challenge was to get the man to go out with, and after that everything was straight downhill. How shortsighted! A couple of wrong moves during your initial engagement, and it could be good-by, Miss Chips. Very well, here are the ground rules. Some are as old as Tutankhamen's mummy, but there haven't been any better ones invented so far as I know.

75

1. On a first date a man needn't ask you too far in advance. I think he can even call you that afternoon for the evening. It's all a big adventure anyway, and you don't start playing games (*i.e.* laying down the law about advance notice) until some time later.

2. It cannot possibly hurt to be on time. You may be dodging around posts later in the evening to escape with your virtue, but you really ought to show up when you said you would. (If he has to wait and wait, it gives him too much time to wonder how your rug happens to have nine cigarette holes in it and if he's going out with a pyromaniac.)

3. Regardless of the difficult parking situation around there, he picks you up *inside* your apartment. If you start getting whisked up off the curb in the beginning, the one time you're late and he has to drive around the block seventeen times the evening will be spoiled. Sometimes it's cold and rainy out there, too.

4. Look sensational. There's no other way to play it.

5. If you have roommates or parents, let everybody meet on this initial date. If they're an asset, you need them. If they're a liability, you want them brought into focus immediately so you can start rising above them.

6. Some men are talkers. Others are listeners (very rare). A listener can be even more pernicious in his listening than a talker, however, and you must be well stocked with gossip tidbits as well as juicy filet-mignon conversational entrees. Obviously every girl should be able to switch from talking to listening as easily as she changes from T shirts to cocktail sheaths.

7. Speaking of cocktails, you may serve him one if that's your habit with other men. If it isn't, don't lay in any supplies. If he should continue to drink your booze for over an hour with no sign of dinner, you must be firm. "Harry, there are the eaters in this world and the drinkers, and I'm afraid I fall in the former category."

8. Once goaded, he should have in mind a place to take you. Go there and shut up. A second date is time enough to refuse to be poisoned at the same chili parlor twice. If he asks you which of three restaurants you'd prefer, the correct answer is, "I love every single one of those places, but I think I'd like————." Name the least terrible. If he doesn't have a restaurant in mind, he's asking for trouble, but you must nevertheless suggest

two or three in the *medium* price category. If they don't seem flossy enough to him, he can move you up to a better category.

9. Certainly you kiss goodnight, *if* you like the man. No grabbing his ears and dragging him inside your door if he hasn't thought of the advance himself. A man should still make the first move.

See Europe and Live

Have you been to Europe yet?

Well, we've got to get you there before somebody gobbles you up and marries you and you miss one of the most enchanting of all female experiences, being a woman alone in Europe.

It's an investment all right but doesn't cost that *much*. Your plane or boat transportation is the big item. Then you can actually see Europe, if you want to play it frugally, for a ridiculously small outlay. I had so little money saved for the trip, I borrowed from a friend, thinking I'd probably get stranded, but I was able to bring all the borrowed money right back home again.

If you book lower-class accommodations, which I did, your hotel rooms may have crepe-paper curtains and the bathtub may be on a different floor, but how much will you be in your room anyway, and how many baths do you take every day?

For lunch I often bought fruit, cheese and pastry at the local stands, which saved enough francs or lira for dinner at the poshest place every few days. By careful managing you fit in luxuries, too. I'm saying don't wait to see Europe until you can travel like a maharani. Go now!

I'm all for your making the trip alone rather than toting along even one girl friend. People will often invite one girl to join them for dinner or cocktails. They will ask you to their homes. Two girls together don't look as though they need rescuing.

By all means badger your friends at home for names, addresses and phone numbers of their friends in Europe. Get them to write these people about you in advance if you can. Once in the city, ruthlessly call everybody up. Some of them will be sweet and take you in.

What about men? If you're looking for a husband, you and I are finished! Hunters never track anything anyway. As Hildegarde Dolson said in a charming article in a recent women's magazine, "How to Travel Alone and Like It," she never saw a man chasing a bloodhound in her life. Asking a pleasant girl to dinner is something else again. Go to Europe to enrich your life, not to get married. You may or may not have a romantic fling. Chances are for it if you travel alone, have your figure and clothes in shape and are friendly and not frantic.

It's good to let a travel agent map out a tour for your first visit. This doesn't necessarily mean that you'll be "conducted" but only that you'll know in advance which countries you're going to, and how long you'll stay. They'll also make your hotel, bus, train, boat and plane reservations.

I think it's great to see as many cities as you can the first time rather than specializing in one or two. You can see an amazing lot in two days and at least get the feeling of whether you want to return to the place.

There are all kinds of special tours for those interested in photography, gourmet food and art treasures, and your travel agent can fix you up with those, too. There are even conducted tours for unmarried girls and bachelors, if you want to throw all my advice to the winds. Some people have been known to enjoy them.

Fever-Ridden, But That Didn't Stop Him

What would you do if you were really sick while living by yourself? I polled several girls on this question, and here are some of the answers:

"My mother (father, sister, aunt) would either come and stay with me, or I'd move to her house until I got well."

"I'd go to the hospital right away. I almost died once not having anybody to look after me and decided after that I would always go to the hospital *sooner* rather than later."

78

"I'd throw myself at the mercy of my landlady. She lives downstairs and is pretty nice."

"I'd call up my boyfriend (girl friend) and let him (her) take charge."

"I'm too healthy ever to be *that* sick. I'll always muddle through alone."

"I'd keep in touch with the doctor and if I got worse let him decide what to do."

"People from my office would take turns looking after me. We've done that for each other many times."

As fraught with terror as the prospect of being sick alone is, apparently something or someone nearly always comes to your rescue. Here's the poignant story of one girl whom I polled about illness.

"I've lived alone for years," she said, "and had head colds and chest colds and every kind of cold you could have, plus a few other things, but I was never seriously ill until this winter. Then I came down with old-fashioned flu that made me so sick I didn't even want to answer the phone though it was right by my bedside.

"A couple of days went by and I was really delirious when I heard my door opening and there was the landlord and a fellow who lives in my building. I thought it was the landlord who'd decided to make the call, but it was the other fellow. He said he'd seen my car in the carport for several days and the mail piling up in my mailbox and wondered if anything was wrong.

"Something was wrong all right, and he just took over. After taking my temperature and calling the doctor, he fixed me some hot soup, straightened my bedclothes, brought me fresh pajamas and tidied up my apartment.

"For one whole week that man baby-sat with me when he wasn't working—fed my cat, fed me and saw that I had all my prescriptions filled. He made me feel like a child—helpless, dependent and terribly grateful for the cold cloths, the hot soup and flu tablets.

"It's funny how being sick can make a man feel needed, and all men need to be needed. It didn't matter that my hair was scraggly or that I didn't have on make-up and that I was terribly unglamorous. This man was all tenderness and love. Now that I'm well we've become close friends, and he really believes that if he hadn't been with me I might have died and that his love saved my life.

"He says he was aware of me around the building, but it took my illness to get me in focus. I don't advocate becoming sick to catch a man, but in my case it seems to have worked out like that."

Another girl polled says, "Never mind about *your* being sick. Watch out for any bachelors of your acquaintance—especially in your apartment building—who are felled with illness and use this chance to become indispensable to *them*."

It's a naughty old flu bug that blows nobody good.

What If You Want to Marry a Millionaire

Someone recently complained to me that all people who advise girls about finding a man usually suggest that she should settle for a nice, readily available man and not set her sights too high.

"But what," she asks, "if you want a completely beautiful and seemingly unattainable man such as Frank Sinatra or the young Aga Khan?"

She goes on to describe herself as a "slim, lithe, quite beautiful, intelligent, charming girl of twenty-three." Here is the rest of her letter.

"I have been in love several times and many men have pursued me, but something inside me always says, 'No! You can do better. You know you can.' But how? That question I am never able to answer.

"My father is moderately wealthy and I shall graduate from a good college this year, then travel in Europe and study in Paris next year. I feel this might be my perfect chance to meet a French Cary Grant. But what would I do if I did meet him, aside from saying how much I admire him? Can you think of anything probable that I could possibly do to get someone like this to marry me? How could I even *meet* these famous men?"

This letter perhaps has you clucking and wanting to straighten the young lady out. It also has me clucking a bit but not too loudly.

It is not immoral to want to make a good marriage. In all the surveys compiled to determine why so many people get divorces, money problems are high on the list.

I think it is possible to fall in love with many different people in a lifetime (hopefully at a time when you are free to fall in love) and one of them may as well be rich. Many a wife of a famous man set her cap for just such a man and got him. Having got what she wants, she plays fair and makes the man a good wife. What's wrong with that?

I would tell this young lady and others with similar aspirations that a *job* is usually your entree to an important man. This is perhaps the sixtieth time I have said it. You may be getting bored. No matter *how* beautiful and young you are, just standing there like a cupcake hoping somebody will want to gobble you up is quite stupid. A few terribly rich girls are able to be nothing but cupcakes. However, they are so eligible themselves that people are trying to meet *them*.

Perhaps it would not be tasteless to mention some girls who met their famous husbands through their work. Veronique Passani was a reporter for Paris-*Match* when she met Gregory Peck. Jacqueline Lee Bouvier was an inquiring photographer for a Washington newspaper when she met John F. Kennedy. Kathy Grant was an actress when she met Bing Crosby. Swedish beauty Ingrid Goude was a model when she met department store magnate Jerry Ohrbach. Happy Murphy worked on Governor Rockefeller's political campaign. Mr. Rockefeller's son, Steven, married a young lady who had worked in their home. Frances Miriam Cranshaw was an airline stewardess when she met multimillionaire Peter Widener III. I could really go on and on.

Even if you aren't mad about your job, it puts you in touch with the men and gives you something to talk about. You also stand for something besides cup-caking, and that makes you more attractive to worthy men. I do hope, of course, that you *love* the man you marry or I shall feel that I've done you both a grave injustice in getting you together.

The Girl with a Past ... Any Future?

"I'm thirty-four," Adeline told me. "I've had more men in my life than most girls have birthdays.

"Some of them were seriously in love with me. I never cared a thing about getting married before, and I know this was neurotic, but now I think I'd like to be. I'd like a good husband I could be true to and children and a house. The trouble is, I've probably loused up my life, and no man is ever going to want to marry me."

"The only thing that might keep you from having the husband and children and home you want is your attitude," I said. "The man himself isn't going to be the problem.

"A man who falls in love with a woman is so vulnerable and trusting and so *hooked* he will often help a girl whitewash her past with a bigger bucket of paint than Tom Sawyer used to paint the back fence."

"How could that be?" Adeline said. "Maybe a man marries a girl because she's convinced him she's an innocent flower, but then I'm sure eventually all these men in her past come out."

"It doesn't work that way," I said. "Except for real country bumpkins, most men are pretty shrewd. They know what kind of girl they've got. But, like women, a man in love will often blank out anything unpleasant about a girl's life because he doesn't want to think or hear about it. He will also marry the girl and never question."

"Isn't this a shaky basis for a marriage?" Adeline asked.

"Not necessarily. Some been-around girls make marvelous wives. When the girl does settle down, she is faithful as a saint. She's had all the playing-around she could ever want and is ready to devote herself to one man. She can also be a wonderful mother. No one would recommend she live her life as she has, but now that it's done, the situation isn't hopeless."

"You make it sound very simple," she said. "Why did you say my attitude has something to do with finding the man?"

"Because, Adeline, you're so used to thinking of yourself as a scarlet woman that whenever you meet a man you assume he is thinking the same thing. Certain girls are talked about and speculated about, to be sure. But a man never knows for *certain* about your past.

"If you're ready to get married and plan to be a *good* wife, you must assume that a man would be lucky to get you, so act that way.

"Another thing. It may be necessary for you to meet a different kind of man than you have known before. Because you never cared about marriage, you may automatically have sought out men with whom it wouldn't be possible. Now you must gravitate to the possibles."

"Have you known girls like me to make good wives?" Adeline asked.

"Dozens of them," I said. "Some are quite famous. Their husbands are madly in love with them and think they are the most wonderful women in the world. It's up to you, dear."

How the Girls Got the Men

Now we're going to hear from two former bachelors about how they got landed by their wives. They both claim it was the girls' seeming indifference to marriage that landed them. The girls were very casual throughout the courtship. This is something advisers are always advising: "Don't let the gentleman know you care." And I'm always coming right along behind the advisers and saying just the opposite. "Why should you pretend not to care when you care? Why does a girl have to be an actress and a phony?" I did promise to tell you the men's side of this not more than a minute ago, so here it is.

Ex-bachelor #1 is a newspaper columnist and a television personality. (These are real people, of course, with names changed.) He is quite dazzling though not young. When Mack was a bachelor, having been divorced, he was a bachelor of the first magnitude and considered wildly eligible. Girls pursued him as girls do anybody who is semi-famous and in a position to get married (or not in a position to get married).

In Mack's own words, "I went out with some lovely women, divorcees, starlets, actresses, a few career girls and a rich widow or two. The pattern was always the same. Getting the girls to be amorous was no problem—if not on the first date, then on the second. I don't mean to shock you or to sound conceited. That's just the way it was.

"After the fifth date at the latest, they took me home

to have dinner with their families. Then they moved in for the kill. When were we going to announce our engagement? I would feel like a drowning man.

"Meanwhile, back at the television studio, there was a girl who'd been working with me for five years—pretty, smart, but kind of aloof. If there's one thing she wasn't, it was after me, but she ran my television show with class and skill. I began to fall in love with her, but she couldn't have cared less.

"Finally I got disgusted, went to Las Vegas, met a really stunning showgirl, brought her back with me and intended to marry her. At that point old Claudia came to, I guess, and decided she'd better not let me get away after all. She managed to break up the romance with the chorus girl and send her packing. We waited another year and got married. The thing is, six years later, Claudia still has me convinced I married the prize of North American womanhood. She was the only one who didn't chase me."

Ex-bachelor #2 is a university professor. "I met Phyllis three weeks before she was leaving for Yucatan to set up shop as an artist. This impressed the daylights out of me. It takes a lot of guts for anybody, man or woman, to give up a good public relations job, which she had, and go off and paint somewhere. It didn't impress me enough to stop her from going, of course.

"I vaguely suggested she ought to stick around. She didn't stick but went right ahead with her plans. We corresponded the whole year she was down there. She wrote fantastic letters. Finally I couldn't stand it anymore and went down there and got her. We were married three weeks later. I know if she'd been here under my nose it wouldn't have worked out that way. Other girls had tried."

On closer examination I don't think either of these girls was "acting" or being a phony. The first one really didn't care for the man until later. The second didn't have enough encouragement from the guy to fall in love. It started very cool, so off she went to Mexico. It occurs to me that what both girls did that was admirable was go about their lives as though finding a husband were *not* life's only goal. And they got one. (Mother Brown is not above using sneaky testimonials from ex-bachelors to drive home a point.)

THREE | # THE BIRDS
IN YOUR
HAND

or,

The Availables

and Others

It isn't always baby-oil smooth with the particular man you've chosen to grab—i.e., marry or date or just plain be in love with—and I don't think there's a pain invented that's comparable to the kind you get when things are going wrong with *him*. Here are stories of what some of my girl friends and I went through in blackest, lovesick hours and how the problems got solved. Maybe you'll find something helpful here.

How Choosy Should You Be?

Many a girl has wondered if she should settle for a man she doesn't really love (and is *barely* proud to take to a party) in order to be married to *somebody!*

I've been talking to a young divorcee who is pondering this question right now. Her used-car salesman is solvent and attentive and sweet enough to include her mother and her two children on many of their outings.

Still, when they're alone, she can't for the life of her keep from getting exasperated at his grammar and the small range of subjects that interest him (she is a Radcliffe graduate). He also doesn't stimulate her libido!

My advice is to date the man as long as he is a nice escort, never, never to mistreat him, but not to *marry* him, either! And if the best thing to be said about *your* marriage prospect is that he isn't too bad and you think you can *get* him, maybe you ought to wait for somebody a little bit *more* could be said about!

As I've written previously, there's a catch to everybody. If love has blinded a bride and groom to any shortcomings in each other, a few years of marriage will miraculously restore their vision. He discovers she is a spender right out of the court of Louis XIV. She finds he has a temper like a hungry cougar, especially at *her* family reunions.

That doesn't mean they haven't a good marriage or that any girl should wait for the "perfect mate." (Who's going to *live* that long?) It simply means you should be reasonably certain you aren't going to be more bored and discontented *in* marriage than you ever were single.

During my single years, I turned down a clump of proposals (and this isn't meant to be bragging)! One was from a chap who held hands with his mother when the three of us went to a movie. I declined two other gentlemen (separately, of course!) because it looked as though I might be supporting *them*.

Two others I just couldn't see myself fetching slippers or baking waffles for with much enthusiasm. It wouldn't have been any better if *they'd* offered to bake the waffles. They all married somebody else, and I finally landed a dreamboat who is the world's most miserable driver and couldn't change a washer on a faucet if the kitchen (or the whole bloody house!) were under water.

I beg you not to "settle." You deserve somebody whose "catch" is at least no worse than *your* catch (or could co-exist *happily* with yours). Five, ten, even fifteen years later, you can assuredly find somebody as good as the "loser" your relatives claim may be "your very last chance." And if you shouldn't, you're still better off waking up by yourself!

It Meant More to You Than to Him

Every so often in the life of every single girl there's an evening of pure magic. (The "single girl" can be a widow or divorcee, too.) He came to the office to see your boss and asked you out to dinner. He was introduced to you by friends and turned out to be a dreamboat. He's somebody you've known for ages who never seemed attracted to you, then out of the blue he asked you to a party.

88

There are dates and there are dates but for some reason this particular date had shimmer and stardust to it from the beginning. When you danced with him, you clung. When he talked to you, you were mesmerized. When he kissed you goodnight—or perhaps several goodnight kisses later—you did the closest thing to swooning a modern girl can do. Later alone, hugging your pillow, you remembered and remembered and remembered.

It's not that you never saw him again. It's just that when he called there was no indication that anything special had happened to *him*. You wanted to say, "I'm different. You turned on my dreams and desires last night and now I can't get them turned off again. Please fall in love with me because I think I've fallen in love with you." He just says, "It was a lovely evening. I'm off to Buffalo —or wherever he's shuffling off to—and I'll call you when I get back." Clearly he was not as moved as you are moved. In certain dire cases the man doesn't even call to say it was a lovely evening, hello, good-by or *anything*.

Why, why, why, when you are so rarely affected by someone like this is he not affected back? Ah, my dear, because two people are not always starving at the same time. There's been a void in your life and this man seemed to be the one to fill it. Perhaps there's no void in his life at all. I think that is more often the case than that you were not charming or pleasing to him. Your need is simply greater than his.

Sometimes a man—or woman—is not able to love *anybody,* of course, and that is always rough on the people who happen to love them. More often, however, I think the timing is what's off. Usually, when you're very much attracted to someone they're attracted back. Probably your date of the evening was attracted, too, but he may already have a girl friend or a wife or a full social schedule or be much older than you and a little blasé about romance or indeed it may be somebody who doesn't know how to love anyone very truly or very well.

While we're into this little philosophical discussion, I think it's safe to say that women who sustain the fewest hurt feelings or shattered emotions in life are the ones who "tune in" to the other person's wave length.

It's really quite pathetic to see a girl knocking herself out chasing the person who doesn't want to be chased. (If there's a possibility the person *does* want to be chased, then you know I'm all for chasing, but you should be able to *tell* after a few chasings who's responding and who isn't and let up.) It doesn't have to be a man that the girl chases ridiculously and without much chance of success. The girl may be in pursuit of friendship with another woman who is really not all that interested or of appreciation from a boss who simply is never going to give it. You just have to keep your antenna brushed off and working all the time or you can wind up depressed and disappointed for no good reason other than that you were unable to read the other person's wishes.

The Razzle-Dazzle Man

My friend Paula called to tell me she was having lunch with her guy again. Apparently, they are fabulous luncheons. They start with champagne, continue through flaming crêpes, and then I think perhaps through a flaming kiss or two as he drives her back to her office.

Her man, I gather, is a *somebody*. The whole restaurant hops to when he's there. He takes phone calls at their booth, the results of which cause stocks to go up or down. He also has a car and driver. He's in a different league than most of the men Paula dates.

She has never told me for sure, but I imagine he is married. Paula never sees him any other time than at lunch. If he weren't married, there would be no reason for them not to meet in the evening because he seems fond of her.

Criticize Paula for having lunch dates with her friend? Not me. I know exactly how she feels. These are glamorous little oases in her life. The conversation is stimulating. She's thrilled to death that a man of this caliber wants to see her. But I also know how she feels when lunch is over. She wonders, "Is this really the way it's supposed to be between a man and woman? Aren't you supposed to go to parties with a man, to play tennis with him, to be able to show him off to your friends?" Of course you are.

You know that I am not one to tell you that impressive people—tycoons, movie stars, entertainers—even if they're married—are not impressive. Everybody is impressed by *them,* for heaven's sake. I'm not one to tell you it's more fun to go to the movies with the boy next door than it is to have lunch with Mr. Somebody either. But I will tell you this. Romantic lunches are definitely not enough if that's the only time the romance occurs. You deserve better, and with somebody who isn't married.

Not everybody wants to settle for the nice boy next door. I didn't. I wanted a *somebody* when I married, and that's what I got. I'm not saying this is normal or right. I'm just saying this is the kind of man some girls, including me, insist on having—and for keeps.

If you want marriage or at least an out-in-the-open dating friendship to be with this kind of man, a somebody, I think you get it by getting to be more on his level yourself. A few princes of industry pick peasant girls, but very few. Inch by inch, day by day, year by year, you must get to be a somebody, too.

I don't advocate thinking about marriage to this man every hour, in your every prayer and striving toward it. That seems rather crass, and also it doesn't get you anywhere. But I think if you forget the kind of man you want to marry, all the while working to be the best *somebody* you know how, a *somebody* is the kind of man you eventually attract—not just for flaming kisses at lunch but forever.

The *somebody* doesn't have to be rich either. He just has to be *somebody*. That could be the minister, the poet laureate, the owner of the hardware store or the lad you think can *become* somebody.

On Your Mark, Get Set, Fire!

Injustice collectors, which many single women happen to be, are a bore.

If they're crossing the street against the light and a bus almost hits them, the way they tell it, the bus had it in for them. If their mail isn't delivered in a snowstorm, the postal department is trying to cause a rift between them and their loved ones. Collecting injustices is a somber, debilitating, frustrating, joyless, self-defeating personality-destroying way of life.

On the other hand, not speaking up when you have a

legitimate grievance is almost as bad. How do you know when the grievance is legitimate and you should speak up and when you're just "injustice collecting?" When you have held your tongue for a long, long time but finally the outrage, unfairness and one-sidedness of a situation comes sweeping over you like a blast from a bake oven, I don't think there's any longer a need to pipe down. You should rant and rave in good health.

Here are some situations which I think call for a woman alone to speak up:

The Man Who Came Back. You and he went together for years but he married someone else. His marriage has not worked out too well and he's back . . . with all his problems. Although you're over him, you figure it never hurts to have an admirer. You occasionally see him just to hear all the flattery—you're so sexy, so marvelous, he's missed you so. As a matter of fact he's missed you so he'd like to resume your old relationship. You're tempted. There's nobody very exciting around right now. Hold on! If you're so wonderful, how come he married the other girl? Is he divorcing the other girl to marry you now? Apparently not. Who needs a devoted admirer who is still married? Tell him!

The Noble Soul. Every sou he makes he gives to his mother, his needy friends or his brother with five children. The other day you watched him buy a $35 fire engine for his ex-wife's child by her new husband. "They haven't much money," he explains. Hold the phone! On your birthday you went to a movie and came back to your place for scrambled eggs. The last four Saturday nights in a row he's had dinner at your house. Nobody wants to be a gold digger but maybe you'd rather back the real Community Chest instead of this character who's acting like one with everybody but you. Speak up!

The Deaf Cassandra. She's a little older than you, more glamorous, richer. She's always impressed the daylights out of you, and you listen by the hour as she tells you of trips, dinner parties, purchases and of course her vexing little problems. Does she know that one whole lunch hour she talked to you while your mouth was full of novocaine and you never even had a chance to tell her you'd been to the dentist? Not that she'd ever be the world's best listener even if she did shut up and let you on, but tell her you'd like equal time.

Arrested Development Friend. This couple knew you when you were making eighteen dollars a week as a clerk behind a candy counter. Now you own the candy store. Your friends see you only as you were then—helpless, frightened, two-foot-tall little waif with them as a strong influence in your life. Let's talk about who you are now. Make them stop putting you down.

When to Date or Not to Date the Boss

There's nothing morally wrong with dating the boss if he is single. You may feel that's so unlikely there's no use even discussing it! Not necessarily! With one marriage in every three ending in divorce, a lot of bosses are going to be "free" at some time in their lives. One of them may be yours.

I'd say this. If he's an attractive, interesting man you'd be foolish to turn down a date just because he's your boss and because the situation might get sticky later on. Let it! Probably one of the reasons you work is to meet men. If you have to leave your job eventually it may be worth it to have had a lovely romance that *could* have ended in marriage.

If your boss is already married, well, I don't know a top-flight secretary or businesswoman who doesn't have lunch and occasionally dinner with her boss if a business situation warrants it. Lunch is okay, in my opinion, even if it has nothing to do with business. If the two of you can't be trusted to eat lunch together away from your desks, you can't be trusted out of your cages *anywhere!*

If the dinner invitation is strictly social, however—and your perfectly good single-girl judgment will tell you— that's a different story. Infatuation may set in for one or both of you. You're almost sure to be hurt and then you'll be too angry and humiliated to be able to keep your job. You'll have to give it up, not for a lovely out-in-the-open romance with the possibility of marriage but for a clandestine never-had-a-chance relationship.

I believe it's all right in certain instances to have dinner with a married man who is in your city on business. If he doesn't stay too long or come back too often I don't think either of you or anyone close to him can get too hurt. But when you are under a boss's nose all day long and he's married, it's trouble, my friends, in *any* city.

'No' to the Boss

A young lady told me recently that she had changed jobs six times last year because every place she went the boss always asked her to go out with him and he was usually married. A chap listening to us suggested she wear thick glasses, dresses with high necks and long sleeves and eat garlic and cucumber sandwiches for lunch.

"Oh, I couldn't do that," she said, and I'll have to admit those are rather desperate measures for a pretty girl who hates covering up all her assets. Taking her problems to heart, I have prepared a list of replies she, or you, might give to the next married boss who asks either of you out.

1. Mr. Bates, I fall in love with every boss I ever go out with. I don't mind for myself, but it's usually a little hard on his wife. She doesn't object to sharing him with me at the office but she hates my monopolizing his time on weekends and of course I never could do anything just halfway.

2. I'd love to have dinner with you, Mr. Bates, but I'm having a series of X rays in the morning and am not allowed to eat anything all evening. (The thought that you may have some ghastly physiological hang-up will give him pause. Most men don't want to get involved with a girl who's just about to have an operation either.) If he tries again later on: Isn't it hysterical, Mr. Bates, they took the wrong X rays last time. They were supposed to be barium and they took chest ones instead. Now I have to do the whole thing over tomorrow morning.

3. I'm so glad you thought of dinner, Mr. Bates. Two of my mother's sisters are here from Keokuk and I'm sure the four of us could have a lovely time together.

4. Oh, I was hoping you'd ask me out! My ex-husband beat up the fellow I usually go out with and he's in the hospital. It's been mighty lonely these past few nights.

5. Isn't that funny? I was going to ask you to have dinner with me. You see I'm very interested in your job and I thought if anything ever happened to you, well, maybe I could sort of take over. Perhaps I could start learning the ropes this evening.

6. Dinner? What a wonderful idea. But do you think we might have lunch together first? We could pop by the bank and take care of my loan first. I've been looking for somebody to co-sign. Then we could go someplace for lunch and celebrate.

7. I knew you were friendlier than everybody said you were, Mr. Bates. Just wait until I tell the girls in the steno pool that you've asked me out and then tell them all about our evening.

8. I love the idea of your wanting to see me after work, Mr. Bates. Ever since I started to work for you you've reminded me so much of my father. He was a wonderful man, Mr. Bates. I wish you two could have known each other. He was just your age.

All right, so you aren't a comedienne and you want a straight answer. I always found something like this worked if you're sure you *don't* want to go to dinner with the man: I'm flattered more than I can tell you that you want to have dinner with me. You're an extremely attractive man. I'm afraid I could develop quite a crush on you. It's just that I've had disastrous experiences dating anybody I ever worked for and I don't want to jeopardize this job. I hope we'll be wonderful friends. I want to work for you a long, long time. Perhaps I'll change my mind later on. Let's just wait and see.

The "Keptive"

Three years ago, a friend of mine decided to be a "kept woman" . . . in the classical sense of the word. Her rent, food, clothes, investments and vacations would be paid for by a benefactor. She in turn would be at his beck and call exclusively.

She had the offer—from the wealthy man she worked for as a bookkeeper. She planned to continue with her job, but, instead of earning $62.50 a week, her income and fringe benefits would soar to approximately six times that.

It sounded like such a sensible step! She was a poor girl without spectacular looks, education or any particular talent by which she might acquire a healthy bank balance. She presently had a number of debts and obligations.

While not madly in love with the man of the offer, she was not repelled by the thought of a physical relationship. Miss X frankly stated—though not to him—she planned to stay with the arrangement a year. By then she should have achieved enough financial security to make the rest of her life easier. At twenty-six, she felt she could spare the year.

Would you like to know how Miss X made out? The liaison lasted exactly six and a half weeks, but did not end for the reasons you might imagine! Towering guilt never overcame her! What depressed her was that (1) she was not able to amass any nest-egg money to speak of, and (2) she was bored almost to distraction.

Being "kept" necessitated moving to a lavish apartment, stocking gourmet foods and wines and making a staggering investment in negligees. It was very hard to put anything aside! Her friend was maddeningly slow about buying into General Motors for her. Perhaps he sensed that as soon as she had a portfolio she might take off with it. Glamorous trips didn't materialize because he couldn't get away and didn't trust her to whoosh around alone.

Miss X wasn't free to date, and her friend rarely took her out. She found she could stand just so many concerts, art exhibits and ballets with girl friends without feeling like a convent girl. She even ran a little short of G.F.s, because everyone who guessed her situation was so snidely critical that it wasn't pleasant to be with them.

Then, horrors, she found herself getting wildly jealous of the man's wife—not because she'd fallen in love with him, but because "the other woman" got to go to all the good outings!

My friend said *adieu* to her friend, moved to a small apartment, joined a different company. She reports she is making less money, but enjoying it more. (She has even revamped some of the negligees into blouses.)

There is no moral to this story. It's just a recounting of what happened to one girl who thought possibly she had it made, but didn't!

Why Doesn't He Get Off the Dime?

"We had our little talk," Evelyn said, "and I was astonished at how well it went. He didn't turn beet red or bolt out of the room or anything. Of course, I didn't out-and-out say, Will you or won't you. I just explained we'd been going together almost a year, and I wanted to know about the future."

"And where do you stand now?" her older and glamorous friend inquired.

"Well, that's the funny thing," Evelyn said. "We had our talk on Friday. I didn't expect to settle anything then, of course. I just wanted him to know how I felt and think about it. Sunday we went to the movies and he was adorable. Tuesday we had dinner together, but do you know, not a single word about the subject I brought up, and it's been a week since our talk. I'm really beginning to wonder if he *heard* me."

"He heard you," her friend said. "What he is doing now is engaging in a little war maneuver called 'total evasion.' By evading the subject in conversation, he hopes it may possibly go away."

"Of *course* it isn't going to go away," Evelyn cried. "And I may have been tactful and subtle, but there wasn't much doubt he was supposed to let me *know* one way or another."

"Don't get agitated," her friend said, reaching for a carrot stick. "This is traditionally the way males act who don't want to get married but don't want to lose the girl either—nothing to be alarmed about."

"How do you know he doesn't want to get married?" Evelyn said, sounding *thoroughly* alarmed.

"Because he hasn't asked you, has he? And he still isn't asking."

Evelyn's big blue eyes began to mist over. "Does that mean it's . . . hopeless?" she asked.

"Not at all," her friend said. "But it may take more than polite conversation to make him see it your way. As a matter of fact, and listen to me, you may have to clear out completely before he'll come around. Then

97

when you vamoose, you must be sure in your own heart you'd rather give him up than stick around on his terms, too. If you merely bandy threats around but are actually prepared to keep him on any terms, he senses it and there'll be no real incentive for him to give in."

"It's awful," Evelyn moaned. *"Men* are supposed to chase. It's all so unromantic. I feel so unfeminine."

"Unromantic, perhaps," her friend said, "but not unfeminine. Girls have been handing down ultimatums, or their fathers have for them, since antiquity. It's just something many girls must go through—like trying to get the landlord to paint your apartment."

"When will I know it's time to take a stand?" Evelyn asked, determined now to be sensible.

"When you have heard him say for the twelfth time that he adores you, he dotes on you, you are the most beautiful girl at the party, why don't you take your vacation together this summer, you will make a wonderful wife someday, you are a gentle, loving girl—everything but the words you want to hear which are, 'Which weekend shall we get married, Evelyn?' "

"I wasn't going to have dessert today," her young friend said, "but now I think I may need the energy. Waitress, I'll have the chocolate soufflé and some more coffee, black."

P.S. There is no moral to this little story, either. I just thought, like Evelyn, you might need to be reminded that bachelors can be evasive sometimes, and you have to be a little firm.

The Girl Changers

A young friend of mine complains that she is having a very tough time trying to be the wow of a woman her boyfriend would like her to be. It wouldn't be such a problem, Gale says, except that her guy changes his mind every five minutes.

While she is still trying to be the lovely, serene, charming, dignified, placid pool of a girl he says men find most attractive, he'll start raving about a sexy girl he saw at a party who danced on top of the table, drank champagne from a slipper and was about as serene as a boxer puppy. She says the man loves her but makes her feel inadequate because she can't ever be all the women he wants.

Gale's beau is an idiot, of course. All she has to do to keep from feeling inadequate is to realize it isn't she he's dissatisfied with. It's himself. *He* can't be Cary Grant, Leonard Bernstein, Lyndon B. Johnson, Elvis Presley *and* Jonas Salk so he's going to try to package her as Deborah Kerr, Jill St. John, Margaret Chase Smith, the Marchioness of Blandford and Mrs. Winston Guest.

A man who is sure of himself can have the limpest little duckling by his side and will indicate to everyone that she is to be treated like a princess because *he* picked her and she's *okay*.

Most people try to impose their philosophies, prejudices and tastes on others to a certain extent. A newspaper columnist even gets paid to do this.

Women alone are particularly vulnerable to character-changing attempts by men. You are, in fact, sitting ducks for this kind of treatment. No man would try to make over another man's wife, and most husbands finally give up trying to make over their own wives, but a single woman, well!

Even if she's thirty-five, a man will still consider her raw material from which he is going to mold a goddess, according to his own ideas of what a goddess should be.

I have to laugh when I think of the last man who tried to make *me* over before I got married (and it wasn't my husband). He had probably the most beautiful legs of anybody in the world, male or female, in Bermuda shorts, and I would have been happy if he had suggested exercises toward having legs like that, but no, our area was fingernails. Really feminine women, he said, did not wear polish. He got a load of teeny-tiny little nails without polish one time only and said, "Put it back on!"

He also said no girl with any character would ever go out with a man just for the sake of getting to see a great play or eating a wonderful dinner. If she didn't like the man for himself alone, she should never see him. I think he had been used to dating rich girls.

We know that certain men can have a good influence on a girl, but usually you emulate the man himself because he is kind, smart, has superb taste, great style or cooks well. Also, if a girl is in love with a man, she tries to get to like the things *he* likes, whether it's trap shooting or shooting dice.

Trying to force you into a new mold doesn't work, however. Maybe you ought to quit wearing those drab grays and browns and pop out in cyclamen, but if the change would make you miserable, be incompatible with your psyche, the changer-in-your-life is bound to lose.

And although you're willing to emulate an admirable friend, no girl is interested in trying to be anything like another *woman* whom a man has picked out as utter perfection. He should go worship at the feet of the original and leave *you* in peace.

She's Hard to Get, But Is She Worth It?

Two very attractive young women met for lunch recently. Both were well dressed and probably in their mid-thirties. The one with the plain little gold band on her left hand said to the other:

"Joe and I are going to have some people in for cocktails Sunday. I certainly hope that you can come."

"Sounds very nice. Who's going to be there?"

"Several people Joe works with and some of our neighbors."

"Any eligible bachelors?"

"Yes. One of Joe's poker cronies—the one who always wins. He's definitely a bachelor and I'm dying for you to meet him."

"What does he do?"

"He's in real estate, I believe. Anyway, he has something to do with land and houses."

"Does he sell them on commission or does he own the land and houses and collect rent?"

"My word, Sue, I really don't know. I think he probably just sells them and gets commissions. Why?"

"Well, most of the real estate brokers I know starve to death about half the year. It's either feast or famine. I'd much rather have the man own the property. What kind of car does he drive?"

"I don't know. The night they played poker at our

house, I was asleep long before the game broke up and so I didn't see what he drove away in."

"Will there be any other bachelors at the party?"

"Let me think. Oh, yes, one of Joe's co-workers got a divorce recently and I think he'll be there. He's a darling. Of course, he's still a little shaken up about his wife getting custody of the children."

"Children! Good heavens! That means child support and emotional attachments. Don't you and Joe know any really eligible bachelors?" (Here the single woman dimpled and smiled—all charm.)

"My goodness! I'll have to think about it. Anyway, I hope you'll come to the party, Sue. We always like to show you off to our friends and we love you, too."

"I'm not sure I can make it, Carol. This friend of mine who flies a plane said something about taking it up on Sunday. He pals around with a lot of wealthy men, and I think maybe he's going to introduce me to one of them."

"Well, come if you can."

The married woman seemed to grow quieter and quieter after the foregoing conversation and let her companion do most of the talking. I'd venture to say that if she and Joe ever chance upon a "really eligible bachelor" they wouldn't be sure their idea of eligible and her idea of eligible would coincide. Besides, they might also figure the guy deserved somebody who could go to a party just to have a good time—not to stake out the wealthy *possibles*.

Parting Is Not Sweet Sorrow . . . It's Pure Pain!

When do you leave a man who is making you miserable . . . whom you also can't live without?

There *isn't* any good time!

My personal rule is that when he is costing you more anguish and pain and ego-damage than he is bringing you pleasure and enchantment, it's time to say adieu. I also think when you calmly weigh his debits against his credits and finally one day resolutely send him packing, there's no more chance of having it stick than when you unex-

101

pectedly lose your temper one night, bang him with an iron skillet and, amid screams and recriminations, give him his walking papers.

Either way, your parting will only be permanent if the thought of having him back fills you with more dread than the thought of keeping him banished. Put it this way. If New Year's Eve is approaching and you'd rather grit your teeth and watch television than whisk him back only to face more weeks of his special brand of torture, your farewell will take!

I guess girls with this kind of man sound like raging masochists to girls with nice, loving, manageable men around, and they wonder how you could ever have got mixed up with such a creep. Never mind! Your creep may be only the most exciting man alive—at least to you he's not a creep, just difficult.

Don't worry either if you postpone your farewell to him long after friends and family say you should. It may be you are getting more from this relationship than they can possibly understand. It isn't easy to give up somebody who melts you down like wax when he makes love to you and makes the world an exciting place to be just because *he's* in it.

When the time does come to call a halt to your friendship, your own insides will tell you . . . not anybody else.

Now He Loves You, Now He Doesn't

If you and I were sitting around exchanging notions as to who are the most difficult men in the world, I'm sure we'd be busy yappetying from breakfast through dinner and maybe take up again the next day. I personally have known some lulus.

I just heard about a new species of monster—new to me at least. A married friend tells me her husband gets the pouts and doesn't talk for a week at a time. He comes home, has dinner, plays with the dog, gets into the same bed with her, but never talks. He's angry over some minor grievance.

Well, I'd like to submit as my entry for the *most* difficult man who ever happens to a woman alone, the Man

Who Cools Off. (It was a toss-up between him and the Don Juan—who doesn't necessarily cool off, but keeps you miserable—and the cooler-offer came out with a slight edge.)

You meet. You're pretty and charming, but your heart isn't in it because you're halfway in love with somebody else. This fellow (we'll call him Freddy), however, seems to flip for you without a grain of effort on your part. He just sits there and goes quietly ape. You agree to see him again. He's really rather touching, and of course flattering. Everything you say is so funny and dear to him, Jean Kerr must be writing your dialogue. Everything you wear was stitched up in heaven. You're his angel, his goddess; and his toes, when you finally kiss him goodnight, curl right up like carrot curls.

You start seeing more and more of him. Perhaps the real love of your life has finally done something so exasperating that you've sworn to go ice-skating in a red union suit in the park before you let him back in your life. Meanwhile, Freddy is still sending you one perfect rose to your office every morning and banks of flowers to your home.

How long does it take? Two months? Three? One day you're chiding Freddy about being so ridiculously smitten with you, and the next you're wondering just how would it be to spend the rest of your life with Freddy. He does adore you. He most assuredly would cherish you. Your toes do not remain exactly uncurled when he kisses you goodnight, either. It's even possible that when "the love of your life" called last week, he struck you suddenly as being kind of a boob.

You can almost trace it to the hour, the minute. On the occasion when you wholeheartedly begin to like Freddy and say so in every way, Freddy begins to act funny. Three days go by when he calls only once a day instead of the usual fifteen times. By now you are buying him little presents—a record, a paperweight—which impress him so much he forgets to take them home from your apartment.

On your birthday, incredibly, he has a poker game in the evening and can only see you at lunch. He admires you still in his favorite yellow chiffon, but you couldn't believe your ears last night when you were sitting on the couch and he asked whether you thought Daphne (your best friend) was attracted to him. "Not that I'd ever take her out or anything, but do you think I'm her type?" he wanted to know.

If you've really let yourself fall (and I for one don't think there's any such thing as not letting yourself fall once you're falling—it's like jumping off the roof and trying to stop at the fourteenth floor), you are now beating your palm against your temple. "Am I out of my head or something?" you ask yourself. "He adores me. He must adore me. He slew all the dragons to get to me. What am I doing wrong? How has it all changed? I must be going mad."

I haven't any explanation for Freddy, though I suppose a psychologist would have. My own half-baked analysis is that he must not really like himself very much. As long as you don't like him either, that makes perfect sense to him. The minute you change your mind and like him, he's got to think there's something the matter with *you*, otherwise what would you be doing fooling around with *him*?

If you "un-fall" for Freddy—but it's got to be real, not just a pretended disinterest because he's shrewd—you can probably get him back again. The mere keeping score in playing games with Freddy, however, is so time-consuming, there are few hours left over for work or friends or peace of mind.

Pavanne for a Don Juan

I received an interesting letter recently. It says: "You once wrote about the most difficult man in the world (the one who loses interest in you the minute you get interested in him). My 'most difficult man' was interested in me from the day we met and very devoted in his way.

"He just never cared as deeply as I did and never wanted marriage. Perhaps he was afraid or immature or heaven knows what. He's never married to this day. Anyway, I loved him to distraction. I really think I was a bit out of my head the whole three years we were together.

"After we'd spent a wonderful Sunday with each other, I was in a trance most of Monday. By Tuesday, when he hadn't called, the trance would start turning to terror. By Wednesday, I was certain he'd been made off with by some glamorous creature. I never doubted for one moment that he could have any woman he wanted, because so many women in our own crowd found him attractive. Of course, he always called eventually, but I never accepted his not calling daily.

"Another difficult thing for me was his admiration for girls. He'd stare at a pretty girl in a restaurant until she'd blush. One summer when we took a vacation together, he brought back presents for seven Toronto girls, and I thought my life was over. Occasionally I'd see him at lunch with another woman and could hardly get my work done that afternoon. Nevertheless, I couldn't anymore give him up at that time than I could hold my breath for twenty minutes.

"My purpose in telling you all this, Helen, is really not to describe this man. I don't know whether he was more difficult than other men, but I do know the effect he had on me. And if I had our friendship to live over again (I'm happily married now), I would play it differently. I would love him more and worry less.

"I should have realized he was one of those people who can't change, and, instead of waiting for phone calls and searching his eyes like radar for messages of new loves and all that, I should have tried to enjoy what we had more. I might even have taken time out to wonder and ask if he was healthy and comfortable, whether he was worried about his job, whether he was on good terms with his brothers and sisters.

"Seems incredible, but I literally never concerned myself about those things, because I was suffering so myself. I missed a very important aspect of 'love' in what I supposed was the love of the century—the ability to give generously and selflessly."

That's quite a letter. Of course, this vision usually comes only after a "sufferer" is safely in love with someone else. In the middle of a grand passion, you can't feel the "giving prospects" for the "wounds being inflicted." Still, it *might* be something to strive for.

If there's an impossible man in your life, but one you must have with you for a while anyway, it probably would save a great deal of wear and tear on your system if you didn't insist he be different and refuse to face the fact that he isn't going to change.

This acceptance may then free you to love him with more real concern. (Possessiveness and terror about losing are not necessarily love.) Never mind whether the man you've picked is deserving. It's better to have had a love affair in which you loved fully, than one in which you acted like a rabbit cornered by a bloodhound.

How Green Is the Green Green Grass?

"Why is it the men I'm attracted to are very cool and casual about me and the ones I couldn't care less about are always hanging around like puppy dogs no matter how I treat them?" wonders a young secretary who works for a television network.

First, I think you have to ask yourself if—preposterous as it sounds—you enjoy being treated coolly.

Unfortunately some girls feel so unlovable and inadequate they automatically seek out men who corroborate their opinion of themselves. They think—unconsciously, of course—that any man who adores them has rocks in his head. Any man who adores this girl obviously *does* have rocks in his head. Loving her is a bed of neu-roses.

It isn't always true, however, that the girl whose fancy is captured by someone unattainable is perverse. She may be only human.

There's a certain amount of allure to anyone or anything we don't know intimately. People who live in California ranch houses look with wistful envy at the dwellers in sleek, satin and damask Manhattan penthouses. The penthouse people yearn to go ranch house. C'est la discontent.

Even millionaires long to be billionaires. The world's richest man, Jean Paul Getty, once complained, "A billion dollars isn't what it used to be."

But let's talk about girls who are reasonably content with their apartments, jobs and incomes, but have a tendency to be fascinated only by unattainable men. There are two types:

The girl who wants to move up to quality when she

marries (Frank Sinatra would be nice) before she has even proven she can fascinate the boy next door. I won't say cats can't look at kings, but if you're going to land one, you had better see what you can do about turning into a queen. Better bring your looks, education, charm and social graces up to the class you hope to enter. (Plenty of determined girls have done it.)

The second type of girl isn't so much interested in quality or even marriage, as she is everlastingly in love with the chap who puts her down. It's a rough life, but it can be less rough if you recognize this devastating pattern in yourself and stop blaming it on capricious fate.

There are so many wonderful nonboring people who need you and will love you back, it's criminal to wear yourself out loving the ones who won't. How do you beat this self-destructive tendency?

If only the men who won't let you get too close fascinate you, by hook or by crook get closer. You'll find they perspire, are lousy losers at bridge, fight with the landlord and have head colds twice a year just like the rest of us.

See a psychiatrist. I'm always packing people off to the psychiatrist, and, if that isn't feasible, I suggest you try some self-probing and self-analysis. Popular books on the subject do help. My two favorites are: *Neurosis and Human Growth,* by Karen Horney, and *The Art of Loving,* by Eric Fromm.

Talk to some happily married women and ask them if they too were not at one time fatally attracted to a hopeless man. (There's usually one in every girl's past.) Ask them how they beat the racket and married somebody nice.

Be the intriguing one yourself. (The lure works both ways.) The minute you are the one who doesn't need or cling, they're after you like bloodhounds. How do you bring this off? Let me say first that phony tactics won't work. If you put on your "hard to get" act and pretend to be busy all week, it hurts you much worse than the man you hoped to punish. As for staying aloof and mysterious, how can you be mysterious and have a warm, intimate friendship with somebody at the same time? I'm convinced the only way to be intriguing is to have your life so full of so many people and projects you literally haven't time for them all. You certainly won't have as much time to torture yourself about what your difficult young man is doing night and day. If you're legitimately busy, you just may have him "torturing" a bit about you.

The Possible Man—For a Little While

"I just out and out picked him up," Fay said, recalling her week-end trip. "He was buying a paperback novel and I was looking for a gift to bring my nephews. We were both at the cash register at the same time and I said, 'Oh, I've heard that's very good' (referring to his book). 'I've intended to read it for about a year,' he said. We walked out of the store together and he asked if he could drop me somewhere. I said I was staying with some people just a few blocks down the street. 'Then I'll walk you home,' he said.

"We had a lovely talk. I told him that someone had loaned me a car for the weekend and rather than waste it driving around the city, I'd just decided to toot off to the country. He was staying at his mother's house with his two young daughters. In those six blocks I learned that he was divorced, had custody of the children and that his mother was loaded.

"He didn't actually say she was loaded, but I could tell from her address in the country and the fact that she had a town house in the city. He was a tax attorney, a prominent one. He told me his name and I remembered reading about him in connection with several cases.

" 'I'll have to have dinner with my family tonight,' he said, 'but would it be possible for me to see you later —perhaps around 8:30?'

" 'I'd love it,' I said. 'I'll be ready at 8:30.'

"I was in a happy fog all afternoon," Fay said. "I walked around the shore and watched the seagulls. Then I did my nails and wrote a letter and washed my hair and all the time I was thinking, 'He's one of those fantastic men you dream about meeting and maybe if you're lucky one comes along every ten years.' Aside from his good credentials, he was wonderful looking—

108

about forty-five, I would say, and handsome-ugly—my cup of tea in every way.

"I was Jello by the time the doorbell rang and he looked even more beautiful than he had that afternoon. I'd never seen such a sports coat.

" 'I'm sure you haven't had dinner,' he said. 'Why don't we go someplace where you can eat and I'll sit and watch you.'

" 'I'm really not hungry,' I said. 'I had a snack earlier. Let's go someplace where we can talk.'

"We drove to a quiet little bar that looks out over the water and there, within an hour, do you know my beautiful dream fell apart? He didn't turn out to be married or a werewolf or anything like that, but the dream crashed. He had been drinking heavily before he met me. By ten o'clock he was loaded. It wasn't the drinking or even that he became morose and moody. It was everything.

"We told each other a lot about ourselves and he said finally, 'Fay, dear, it won't work. You're a beautiful girl. You're smart. I think it's great that you hold the kind of job you hold, but it won't work. I drink too much. I don't really want a girl like you. I'm trouble for a girl like you. I want an uncomplicated woman who won't give me any problems.'

"There wasn't anything to argue about. He was being perfectly honest and brushing me off. I think only a school girl would have said, 'No, no, no. We can work this out. I can *help* you.'

"He took me home and kissed me goodnight on the forehead. I wept in my pillow."

Every girl knows them—the divine men you seem to have waited for all your life only to have them dissolve in a vapor before your eyes. They come along again, however, and sometimes it doesn't take ten years. Finally one is just right for you. He is so *possible* you even marry him.

The One You Love Belonged to Someone Else

You've started to date a divorced man. The situation looks promising. At least he's *single*, which is a step in the right direction. He's also attractive and interesting. What are the special ground rules?

1. On your first few dates assure the man that marriage is the furthest thing from your mind. I am ordinarily against lying, but in this case I think it's either put him at ease (with the lie) or drive him right out of your life first thing by confessing that you are almost frantic for a husband.

2. Don't bear down on him about *anything*—where you go on dates, whom you visit, which movies you see. He's been borne down on quite a lot recently, it's very likely—otherwise he wouldn't be a divorced man. For the time being give him freedom. You are a tolerant, nonthreatening friend.

3. Listen sympathetically as he tells you he isn't the marrying kind. He made a mistake once that will do him a lifetime. Or—and this will require more patience—show forbearance while he tells you about the qualities his next wife is going to have to have, and he doesn't seem to be talking about *you* but some mythical girl whom *nobody* could be.

4. Be understanding if he has the shorts. He's probably cleaning up legal fees plus learning how to support two households. Later he'll be better organized—or bankrupt—and you can decide where to go from there.

5. Don't run for the cyanide if he continues to see his ex-wife, especially if there are children. He'll taper off, but you must get used to the idea that he was married and once in love with this woman. She'll be part of his life forever at least in thought. Weren't there men in your life who creep into your thoughts almost daily, good or bad? Ex-wives are really no threat. That's *over*.

6. Don't expect to be a mother to his children. The most you can hope for is to be their good friend, but this will take patience and understanding on your part. They have a mother of their own and it may be hard for them not to resent you on their real mother's behalf, unless she is an angel who tells them it's okay to like daddy's girl friend. (Very unlikely.)

7. Once you've sunk into the man and there's talk of getting married, expect a great deal of backing and filling. You will have the date set one day only to hear the next morning that he's come up with twenty good reasons why the marriage could never work out. "Better we found out in

time," he'll say. You have to patiently haul him back to the starting line again.

If you should *get* this man, he'll probably make quite a good husband. I married a divorced man and wouldn't have any other kind. Some patient woman has smoothed out all the rough edges and left you a polished jewel!

No Fool Like an Old Fool—Or Is He?

There certainly was a lot of clucking and clacking when Justice William O. Douglas, sixty-four, married a twenty-three-year-old Buffalo secretary. I remember one woman saying, "It's not that I would deny any person a chance at great happiness, but this marriage depresses me on behalf of widows. If a man in his sixties won't even settle for a woman in her forties, but has to go all the way down to the twenties, what chance is there for us mature women to find husbands?"

Before we answer that, let's examine unemotionally what a sexagenarian (no, that doesn't mean oversexed) might get out of a marriage to a much younger woman.

1. Having a young girl in love with him is flattering to his ego like nothing else could be. She makes him feel half his age. Wouldn't *you* like to feel half *your* age sometimes?

2. The libidinal drive of certain older men is terrific. So is their emotional content. This person is just as capable of falling blindly, passionately in love as a young person—and with the same object a young person falls in love with.

3. He may be able to manage a mere girl better than a contemporary. Sure, it might be a father-daughter relationship, but it must be nice to have somebody do exactly as you say, especially if you've ever been married to a nagger.

4. A man may figure he deserves a fling—why not a young wife? "I may not be here ten years from now," he says, "or *one* year from now."

Before you score the man, let me say I think it is the girl who usually promotes these marriages. I believe any intelligent older man resists a long time before marrying a child, knowing exactly what people are going to say. A woman—even an eighteen-year-old one—is by instinct a marrier.

So far I've probably just succeeded in depressing you further. But there's a brighter side. Marriages with such an age difference are not numerous. This one received a great deal of publicity, because the groom was famous. Sixty-year-old men marry sixty-, fifty- and forty-year-old women every day without fanfare. I believe in most cases a man of sixty is simply not comfortable with a woman two generations his junior. Think how bored you'd be married to a teen-ager! (And the Douglases later divorced.)

If there's anything helpful an older woman can learn from this May-December marriage, I think it's this: Although some men marry for comfortable companionship (to be nursed and taken care of), many men simply do not want to be reminded that they are getting older.

Instead of bringing them their slippers and shawl and saying, "Now don't sit in a draft, dearest," you might consider reminding them they are very much men and treat them with the same womanly interest you use to treat younger men.

Stylish European women know a great deal about this technique and become more fascinating and alluring with every passing year. A young flibbertygibbet girl couldn't begin to compete with them.

He Who Scatters Your Bobby Pins

He arrives to take you out for the evening. Five minutes later all indications are that you are going to be squeezed to death or at the very least have your arm broken. As you try to quietly sip a martini, your skirt gets twisted and your blouse comes out. Bobby pins fly in every direction. Your perfectly applied lipstick is now partially applied to your cheeks and nose. What happened?

Sometimes the lunging doesn't begin until later. A friend of mine said she and her date did get as far as the restaurant but during the vichyssoise he slipped one arm around her, grabbed her about halfway between her waist and her neck, if you know what I mean, and she thought she was going to have to yell for help.

112

Why do they do it? Could you have given the man the idea that you're an easy mark? Has he not been alone with a girl since he played post office in grammar school? Is he recently out of an institution? Probably none of these things is true. As for the impression you may have conveyed, every girl who agrees to go out with a man is usually saying tacitly that if they like each other and things go well he may surely kiss her good night. If a man is physically revolting to you, you don't see him, do you? You may have given the impression that you are a warm, loving being who likes men, but I doubt very much if you did or said anything to give the impression you wanted to be bulldozed. Then why *does* he do it?

I don't know for sure. If you ask one of these fast movers, "What's the matter with you?" he's apt to say, "What's the matter with *you?*" He just can't figure out what he's done wrong. Girls were meant to be hugged, weren't they?

I'm going to hazard a guess that the lunger lunges because he is frightfully unsure of himself. He is a little or maybe a lot hostile toward women and society in general. He is also dumb. Most women love to be held and petted and patted. A man who botches the whole thing by rushing and using strong-arm methods obviously is dumb. Yes, occasionally a man is able to overpower an unsure-of-herself girl. *Most* girls are offended by such methods and the man's cause is lost.

The man who lunges usually displays other signs of insecurity. He brags. He is a terrible listener. He often thinks women should be segregated. He's keen for men's bars and men's grills and men's golf clubs. Let's face it. He's uncomfortable around women and is their deprecator and nonappreciator.

No, you shouldn't avoid *all* blind dates or go out only with men you know well to avoid bulldozing. Most men you *don't* know are too smooth and intelligent to strong-arm a girl. When you get one who isn't that intelligent, console yourself that from time to time *every* girl meets this sort of man. Remember also that you, too, sometimes blunder and are hostile. You just have different ways of showing it.

How's Your Love Life?

Everybody knows the course of true love is not necessarily a smooth one. The question is, how much stormier is your romance than anybody else's? If more than three of the following statements apply to you I'd say you're in trouble, and you might be due for a change of beaux.

You feel more anxious after you've talked to him on the phone than before he called.

You're under the impression you're his steady girl but his friends don't seem to have heard about it.

You spend more time at the party checking to see who he's talking to than talking to whom *you're* talking to.

One of his men friends is jealous of you.

He spends as many evenings with his ex-wife as he does with you.

His divorce proceedings haven't started yet.

He gets telephone calls when you're in his office or apartment and says, "Let me call you back."

He's more attentive to you when his mother is around and calls you his girl only in her presence.

He drops you cold when his mother is in town and dates only her.

Every time the subject of marriage comes up he manages to get it changed and you aren't quite sure how he did it.

You're expecting his call but let the phone ring and ring in the hopes he'll think you're out with somebody else.

One of his friends goes along with you about as often as you go out alone.

You haven't a firm commitment from him about your birthday, New Year's Eve, and the next two Saturday nights.

He says, "No, I don't think you should come to Chicago with me. I've got to get away by myself and think for a while."

He's been in psychoanalysis ten years, or he thinks analysis is for crazy people.

You go to a party together but it's hard for anyone to tell who his date is.

You've had three good cries in the last two weeks.

He has been able to keep his hands off you several nights in a row.

You check every car that looks like his not only to see if he's inside but who's inside with him.

He tells you he's invited to a cocktail party to which they asked him not to bring a date.

Every so often you feel as though you'd been kicked in the stomach by a heifer.

Fifteen Ways to Reciprocate

It's your turn. He's taken you out several times and now you want to reciprocate. This is very important. With the competition what it is, nice girls shouldn't be takers only. How do you go about it?

You can, of course, play it sneaky and just "happen to have" two theater tickets for Friday.

If you both have a sense of humor, however, I think it might be more fun to be forthright and say something like, "Phillip, it's my turn to take you out, and I want you to be my date (for a particular occasion). I hope you'll agree."

You can make quite a production of picking him up at his apartment, helping him on with his coat, seeing that he doesn't trip over curbs. But *only* if he's a fun-and-games person. Otherwise, you may prefer to stay in your traditional role and just quietly pay for the evening (out of his sight). Here are some other projects you might plan.

1. Reserved-seats movie. Buy the tickets in advance. If it's a regular movie, you could stop by the box-office ahead of time, too. Surely he'll let you buy him some popcorn. "This is *my* treat," remind him.

2. Play, concert, lecture, opera, art exhibit. Buy these tickets in advance, too.

3. Dinner in a restaurant. Pick out one noted for charm, not grandeur. If it's a foreign meal, you might order in advance and arrange for the musicians to play your date's favorite songs. Most maître d's love romance and intrigue and will help with your plans. Have the bill mailed to you or sneak out and pay it during coffee.

115

4. Lovingly home-cooked little dinner. Invite another couple over to play Monopoly later.

5. Cocktail parties of friends. Show off your nice friends and their nice homes to your nice beau whom you want to be impressed and stick around for a while.

6. Sports event—tennis or boxing match, baseball, basketball, hockey game. Hopefully, you don't hate the sport too much yourself.

7. Picnic. Prepare a divine little lunch. Include a bottle of wine and take your date to the beach, the park or the canyon to relax.

8. Surprise birthday party for him. He doesn't have to be the love of your life for you to make this effort, and what man doesn't like to have a fuss made over him on his birthday? Don't let anyone blab and spoil the fun.

9. Outing with his children if he's divorced. Or an outing with both your children. Circuses are grand. So are carnivals or an animal show.

10. Outing with him and his mother, or both your mothers. Might be nice to have a girls' tea party in honor of them both, then let the beloved son come over to help eat up the sandwiches and have cocktails later.

11. A long drive to see the wildflowers or Indian reservation or rock formations or historical monuments.

12. Business party. You may have occasion to go to fairly important banquets and dinners. These aren't the most scintillating but may impress him with the kind of job you hold.

13. Scenic daylight train trip. These are marvelous. Trains are fun. Buy the tickets in advance.

14. A weekend at your parents' house. A boy without parents of his own close by may love being adopted by yours.

15. A weekend at *your* house—if you are widowed or divorced, have a large house party and plenty of chaperones.

FOUR | # MAMAS' GIRLS— AND BOYS

or,

Can They Ever Escape The Tie That Blinds

We all have one—or had one once—and I don't think the psychiatrists exaggerate when they say this dear little person, your mama, had a tremendous, sometimes even horrendous effect on you for good or evil. It may not be the way she actually treated you but the way you *thought* you were being treated. Whatever the case, mothers require special handling by a woman alone. If you're not careful, you two are apt to get stuck together like a batch of taffy, and it can take quite a bit of doing to get you unstuck.

Don't think I'm always on the side of the daughter either. There are some mean, ungrateful grown-up little girls who need a *spanking* for the way they treat their mothers.

Naturally there are a few words about *his* mother too. The second article in this group, incidentally, "Making a Liar Out of Baby," got more yells and screams than almost anything I've ever written.

Care and Feeding of Mothers

This is my code of ethics about mothers. After a daughter is grown and if her mother is in good health, I think the daughter deserves a life of her own and a house or apartment of her own if she wants it, even though the daughter is unmarried. No mentally and physically healthy person would fasten herself on another and say, "Here I am. I am going to be your companion, roommate, adviser and millstone the rest of your life and how could you even think of refusing? I am your mother!"

During those years of independence, however, I think ideally a daughter stays close to her mother by mail, telephone and personal visits. Hopefully both mother and daughter continue to grow in grace and wisdom.

While I believe that a mother should give her daughter independence and a shove out of the nest after the daughter is grown, I also fervently believe that a daughter should help support her mother if the mother requires this and should physically take care of her when the time comes that the mother can't manage alone, even if it means taking her back home to live.

A friend of mine has just brought her eighty-six-year-old mother, an independent old lady who ran a boarding house for fifty-five years, back to her own home. It was the right thing to do, but now it seems to me the daughter is undoing all the good by treating her mother like an invalid. (I have *nothing* if not strong opinions as to how people should run their lives.) When I was over there the other day, Marian, the daughter, was talking about driving up to see her own daughter and grandchildren. (That makes Marian's mother a great-grandmother.) The old lady wanted to go along. "Mother, it's a nine-hour-drive," said her daughter. "You'll just get too tired."

"No I won't," snapped her mother. "If I get too tired, we'll just stop and rest a bit."

"I wouldn't want to be responsible for you getting ill," said her "solicitous" daughter. "I'll have Mrs. Weiss look in on you while I'm away and you can just have a nice rest here."

"I don't want a nice rest," said the mother. "I want to see my great-grandchildren."

"Remember you got sick the day we drove out to the national park," the daughter reminded her.

"But I ate blueberry waffles with jam that day," said her mother. "I won't do that this time."

How could there be any question about her mother going along, I wondered. She wasn't asking to be included on a man-woman date but only to see her own kinfolk. I was so moved by the old lady's determination I wanted to shake her silly daughter.

Day after day I see *young* women alone who don't participate—won't try for the better job, won't call up the bachelor whose phone number they have from a friend back home, won't give the party or take the piano lessons. When I see an eighty-six-year-old woman who has get up and go, I want to hand her the *croix de guerre* and also hand her a more understanding daughter.

Making a Liar Out of Baby

A friend of mine met a man recently when she was in Europe. (Gives us all hope in planning our next vacation.) They were on a sight-seeing bus together in Turin, Italy. Both were traveling alone and, well, things developed.

Although Ginny lives in Seattle, by coincidence her sight-seeing friend lives in Indianapolis, which is her family's home. Instead of going straight back to Seattle, Ginny has stopped off in Indianapolis to visit her family (as she had previously planned) and also to see her new friend.

"I've met a lot of men in the years since my divorce," Ginny says, "and I may be wrong, but I think he's going to be special."

In Europe, Ginny and her friend entered into what might be called an adult relationship. While in Indianapolis, Ginny, who is thirty-eight, would like to continue their friendship on the same basis. It isn't possible, however, without telling her mother a pack of lies. In order to be with her friend for long periods, as has been her custom, she has to say she stayed with a girl friend and have her girl friend cover for her.

Her mother believes, as many mothers do, that nice girls only kiss men good night until they get married, even if the nice girl has been married before and is pushing forty. If Ginny does go out with her friend, her mother gets anguished and suspects *the worst* (with good reason, of course) even if her daughter only stays *out* terribly *late*.

Ginny admits the immediate problem isn't the worst. She could be with her friend on a platonic basis during their stay in Indianapolis and it wouldn't be the end of the world. She could shorten her visits and be home by midnight. Still, their hours together are precious, Ginny feels. Her friend will be unable to visit her in Seattle or she to return to Indianapolis soon because of their respective jobs.

"I think probably we'll get married," Ginny says. "It looks promising, but I'm not eager to rush into anything. I spent some pretty miserable years married to the wrong man, and I want to be sure this time."

The thing that actually depresses Ginny to the core is

that she can't level with her mother, who basically still sees her as her baby-dumpling, thirteen-year-old daughter. At age thirty-eight, Ginny is unable to behave like a mature woman around her mother, capable of making serious decisions involving morals.

This is the situation with many mothers and daughters, I believe. Even a mother who does not treat her daughter as a child still hopes her daughter will be guided by the same standards as those by which she herself was raised. This is only natural. The fact is, however, that between Ginny's mother's day and Ginny's own time, the regulations have changed somewhat. There weren't any divorcees to speak of in Ginny's mother's time—nor many thirty-eight-year-old spinsters who had not retired from the manhunt.

Whether you approve or disapprove, the change in mores has indeed taken place. I, for one, think Ginny should try to be frank with her mother in a kind and patient way. No mother is too old or too unmalleable to be denied the chance really to know her daughter, in my opinion. For a daughter may only love truly someone who accepts her as she really is.

The Old Maids

Some things you don't see around much anymore are pot-bellied stoves, open cracker barrels and old maids! It's almost as rare to run into a pinched, sallow spinster as it would be to pile head-on into an ostrich-feathered madam! I'm sure nobody rues their demise.

It struck me as fantastic, therefore, to encounter two old maids in the space of one week recently. Incredibly, both were under thirty!

The first one was the assistant to the producer of a network television show. I dropped by for an interview, we chatted for half an hour and then she began to tell me something about herself.

She was twenty-seven and living at home with both parents. Her older brothers and sisters had all married, and her folks, she admitted, still called her the baby! She rarely had dates, but would be glad to, she said, if she could just meet the right kind of young men.

"How about the men here at the station?" I asked. (The place was swarming with attractive men.)

"Oh, they're all married or else they're wolves," she said.

"How about the chap over there?" I asked, indicating a clean-cut lad who looked somehow too studious to be wolfish *or* married.

"Who, Freddy?" she said. "He's kind of a nut about mythology—besides, he's a mama's boy. I'd rather stay home and read a book than go out with Freddy."

Freddy, I'm sure, was glad to let her do just that!

I shared a table with the second old maid in the dining car of a train traveling east a few days later. She was accompanied by her mother and couldn't have been more than twenty-two.

"These scrambled eggs are too well done," she told the waiter who brought her breakfast. "I ordered them moist." He took the eggs away and left marmalade for our muffins.

"I thought they were supposed to have honey in Pullman diners," she said. "This marmalade doesn't look very fresh."

At that point, the conductor came through and announced we were passing Devil's Slide, a kind of crazy rock formation in the middle of Utah. Everyone but Miss Fuss looked out the windows. Miss Fuss was now fussing with the newly arrived honey which she reckoned didn't look any fresher than the marmalade!

Heaven forbid that an old maid should not have her honey, her eggs, her clothes, her dry-cleaning and her life arranged precisely as she orders them. Heaven forbid that an old maid should get involved with a dud of a date even for an evening, although she hasn't had a date with *anybody* for six weeks.

Non-old-maids, of course, take chances on going out with just about *any* single man *once* so long as he doesn't look like a strangler. Non-old-maids, at least until they are seventy-two, rarely make a fuss about breakfast while they are passing scenic wonders of the west.

It's good to know there are so few old maids!

Mother's Precious Darling

"My mother is driving me absolutely nuts," states a nineteen-year-old girl who's a member of a rock 'n roll singing group.

"Even though I've moved away from home, she wants me to bring all my laundry over on Saturday so she can do it. She's given up on my coming there to dinner every night, but she still bakes a lot of stuff for me to take back to my apartment. She treats me like a helpless baby."

Poor darling daughter. Poor clinging mother. I admire them both for certain traits of character they show and sympathize with each, too.

I think it's wonderful for working girls to move away from home and "live their own lives." Nevertheless, it takes guts to move out when somebody is willing to wait on you like a princess if you stay. It takes even more courage to leave when somebody you're as emotionally attached to as a mama is insisting you're making a dreadful mistake.

In defense of the mother, however, it must be said that baking and ironing are acts of love. Anybody who performs either chore knows it's a lot easier to read a book. Also, this mother may not so much be trying to keep her daughter from having an independent life as she is trying to continue to find meaning for her own. She was needed and useful when her daughter was home. If Baby Jane would just accept the starched blouses and lemon meringue pies with enthusiasm, she could still maintain her independence.

Dear Nineteen-Year-Old (I'm writing her): She's your *mother*, and as the saying goes, you owe her. You'll find out when *you're* a mother that along with the joys of watching baby gurgle goes quite a lot of dull, boring, exasperating labor.

Even a mother who is currently a bit of a pain in the neck (and I can see your point—what girl with a good figure needs it flumped out of shape with lemon meringue?) once saw to it that a helpless, "give-me, give-me" little creature was fed, warmed, clothed, burped and bathroomed for a long time without so much as a thank you.

Perhaps it will be easier to treat your mother courteous-

124

ly if you pretend she isn't related. One thing psychiatry teaches us about dealing with difficult relatives is that you sometimes have to stop taking them so much to heart and view them a bit more dispassionately—as you do other people.

If she won't be reasoned with about the pies, take one home occasionally and give it to the landlord. Let her iron your dresses and keep your private wrath to yourself. (You'd play it that way with a difficult *boss*.)

I don't mean to sound as though you should "patronize" your mother, but going through the polite motions may be the only way of keeping an important relationship intact. Meanwhile, try to encourage her to get a *job*. Baby-sitting for example is dignified, and they *pay* for her loving care.

Sometimes a nineteen-year-old has to be the mature one and take a parent firmly by the hand.

Daddy's Girl

An attractive young woman interviewed me on a television show in Europe recently, and after our professional chat we had an informal one off the air.

"I miss the presence of anything romantic in your writing, Mrs. Brown," she said. She was referring to my first book, *Sex and the Single Girl,* and the next one, *Sex and the Office.* I said what I usually say when confronted with this accusation, which is often. "I don't think I need to tell girls how to be romantic," I said. "Most females are utterly romantic from babyhood on—once they have somebody to be romantic *with*. What with the shortage of men, I feel my greatest contribution can be toward helping a girl get some men into her *life*. She'll know what to do with them after she gets them there."

"I don't think I could ever do what you call 'getting men into my life,'" said my young friend. "Perhaps I'm incurably romantic but I know there will be one man who is everything I want and he will be the one. Until then I'm quite happy not to go out with men just to be going out. I'd rather wait for *him*."

"I'm sure he'll come along," I said, and in her case I meant it. She was about as pretty as a girl can be and I judged her to be about twenty-three. There seemed to be no reason for her not to expect to be swept off her feet sooner or later by *him*.

"I don't know," she said. "I'm twenty-nine (and that surprised me) and I haven't met anyone who interests me yet."

"What do you do with your time?" I asked, "aside from this job, which is marvelous, of course."

"Oh, I have quite an exciting life," she said. "My father conducts an orchestra here and we have many friends in the theater and in music circles. A lot more of them come down from town on the weekends and stay at our country place. We entertain quite a bit."

"That must keep you and your mother busy," I said.

"It's just my father and me," she said. "My mother died two years ago. Actually, my mother and father were divorced when I was very young and I never saw my father again until two years ago before my mother's death. After that I was alone, and since my father had never married again I decided to keep house for him. He's an enchanting man and not the least bit strict. Maybe because we found each other late in life we appreciate each other more than if we'd had a close father and daughter relationship all those years."

"Probably," I said.

"Shall we go take off our make-up?" she asked. We were quite heavily made up for the television show.

"I think I'll leave most of mine on," I said. "I'm going to a reception and it won't hurt to look a bit dramatic."

"Well, I shall take mine off," she said. "Or Father will say I look like a hoyden." And she did indeed scrub her face clean with theatrical cold cream until she looked about thirteen instead of twenty-three, or rather twenty-nine.

"Does it ever occur to you that you may not ever find anyone in life quite so romantic as your father?" I asked, figuring I knew an Electra complex when I saw one.

"People have said that before," she said. "But that's quite foolish. This is just a temporary arrangement until I meet the man I can really fall in love with."

I didn't say this but I certainly thought, "Want to *bet?*" A daddy's girl is a daddy's girl whether she's in old-world Europe or stationed somewhere in the United States.

Is Mother Private Enemy Number One?

Here's a well-described situation between many mothers and daughters. This girl is a librarian. She says:

"Helen, I'm single, divorced and twenty-nine. Each of these factors is no big deal to anyone except my mother. Single to her is a big tragedy. Divorced is a social disaster. And twenty-nine, well, if I were a battleship, she'd figure me ready to be scrapped. I *love* my little five-foot mom *dearly* and she loves me, but she's a 'nudnick' —a long-play record.

"All middle-aged mothers seem to have the same dialogue. I think they hire the same script writer. Here's some of the patter. 'All the neighbors say you're such a pretty girl. Nice figure, wonderful personality. How come the homely girls are married?' Or (note the contradiction) 'You know, kid, you're not exactly Elizabeth Taylor. Who are you holding out for?'

"Apparently thousands of worried mothers like mine are stepping out of store windows all over the country badgering their less-worried daughters. The best thing to do, I find, is not even answer. If you do, you're in for a real crackerjack fight. If you suggest they're being rather insulting to the one they're supposed to love best, namely you, they tell you these speeches are for your own good. After all, Momsy doesn't want you left alone in the world when she is gone. She wants to live to see you married. (We want to live to see us married, too, but please, Mother, we'd rather do it ourselves.)

"A young man takes me out. The next day I announce that he is 'outsville.' Mother whines, 'No one is good enough for my neurotic prima donna!' 'He was fresh,' I say mildly. (Little does mother know this nice boy tried to tear her daughter's clothes off.) 'You're too stand-offish,' she says. Warmer I can always get, Mother dear, but you may get to be the grandmother you want to be sooner than you'd planned.

"Occasionally Mother Perkins will give my phone number to a nice lady down the street who knows a sweet boy. Good luck with this boy. He turns out to be a left-over who wasn't cooked very well in the first place —a misfit.

"I belong to a drama group and a writing circle. I also play tennis. Dear heart wants to know, 'Who are you going to meet at these pursuits?' Must I always have my telescope trained?

"I *do* make the effort boy-wise. I go to public dances. They're one big Arabian market—merchandise being looked over and rejected. Same thing with cocktail parties for 'singles.' Pay $3.50 at the door to find wall-to-wall look-alikes inside. Tight, knit dresses and black continental suits. Girls are all looking for Rock Hudson, the fellows for Sophia Loren. Meanwhile, back at reality, the boys look like shoe clerks, the girls look like stenographers—which they *are*. Not bad but nothing to grab up like it was your very last chance.

"No girl in her right mind wants *not* to get married, Mother, but I'd like to like the chap a *little* first. I know your motives are paved with loving cement, but desperation is mostly on *your* part. Believe me, my biggest problem isn't finding a boy I can marry. I'll find him one of these days or he'll find me. My biggest problem, Mother dear, is *you*."

The Lukewarm Boys

What do you do about a boy who is not as all fired up about you as you are about him in the person-to-person sense? You like to hold hands. You get the distinct impression he'd just as soon cuddle with your German shepherd. You like to be kissed goodnight. Christmas Eve he finally got around to a peck on the cheek and it was like Tess of the Storm Country meets the North Wind—a pretty chilly sensation.

Is the man a homosexual? Not necessarily. He may be someone who just doesn't like any kind of physical contact with another person, heaven help him, a completely inhibited and possibly neuter sort of man. Sex and everything leading up to it will never be important to him.

But how come he's so damnably attractive to you—maybe the most attractive man you know—slender but muscular, beautifully dressed. When other men look a bit crumpled and seedy after a hard day's work, he's still as impeccable as a *New Yorker* ad. He's successful. He entertains beautifully, contributes to charities. A first-rate citizen really but you seem to affect him like a klieg light. When you're in the room there's no romance.

Most women who stay single for any length of time have such a man in their lives. Since neither of you is married, people tend to bring you together. You may also have interests in common like work, a charity or club or your families are old friends.

If this is the only kind of man you ever go for, I think you may be just as nutty as *he* is. Although denying it with your last breath, you're afraid of a man with hormones. You feel safe and happy with somebody you *know* is never going to ask you to his apartment for any reason other than to see his new beagle puppies. You're not really much for hand-holding either, though you claim to be.

If this particular man is just one of many different kinds you've been attracted to in a lifetime, no problem. There probably isn't much you can do about him except take him on his own terms and stop expecting him to give what he isn't able to give—ardor. You'll finally say to yourself, "I could have loved him madly but it wasn't in the cards" and go on to a hardier breed. You may even keep this man in your life as *your* beagle puppy.

It takes many different kinds of friends to make a satisfying circle. I pity the single woman who feels comfortable only with one homogenized type—the just-alike-as-grapes group she meets through work or through church or family, all having to have the same social, ethnic, political or religious background *she* does. One of the joys of being single is that you *can* have people in your life of such diverse backgrounds. When you're married, you're much more apt to have to specialize. The men in your life, in my opinion, should be as *un-alike* as snowflakes and can even include some lukewarm men without your ego being done any harm.

Little Girl in the Great Big City

How much money does a girl need to move to a big city? What are the things she should look out for? How does she go about it?

Here are a few suggestions:

Money: If you're moving to New York, Chicago, Los Angeles or any major city, you need enough money to keep yourself going for three months, figuring $200 a month minimum. Usually first and last months' rent are required for an apartment or room. Also you may pay twice as much for certain items—rent, transportation, even clothes and food—as you've been used to paying.

Put your money in the bank when you get there. It's good to have a bank reference. Purchase a round-trip bus, train or plane ticket and save the return portion against an emergency.

Housing: A YWCA residence is a fine place to begin life in a new town. Don't be snooty. The rent is reasonable, locations are convenient, rooms attractive and the residence managers are kind and helpful. Some YWCA homes even have counseling service for girls with problems.

You'll meet friends here with whom you may eventually want to share an apartment. Write the YWCA nearest you and ask for residence address in the city to which you plan to move.

Jobs: Shorthand and typing are a girl's best friend. Everybody's hunting for good secretaries. Department stores also employ lots of girls, but the pay is generally lower. Airline offices are a good bet. When you get to your new "home town," answer the classified ads, fill out job applications in major companies, check with employment agencies.

If you're after a career in show business, you may want to take another job while you're knocking on doors. If not, better plan on more than three months' living subsidy for yourself.

Clothes: It's generally a good idea to buy one new outfit in the new city after you've had a chance to look around and see what smart-looking people are wearing. Ask your new friends the best places to shop for clothes, food and drugs. In large cities, you can pay three different prices for exactly the same merchandise.

Friends: Of course you've come to town for an exciting new life, and you'll have it, but I think the thing to do is keep your curiosity at a maximum and your actual participation at a minimum the first few months or even a year.

A girl who will get hit in the head at eighteen will get

hit in the head at thirty-five—she just doesn't have good sense about what people to get involved with. Nevertheless, there are some pretty funny men around who rather fancy "adopting" naive young girls. If you aren't grabbing for instant glamour and gazing out of cotton-coated eyes, you can spot them.

Until you get your bearings, stick with the safe new friends you've found in business or in your girls' residence. I guarantee that if you look pretty, are bright and interested in other people, you'll eventually have a wonderful full-fledged life in your new city. I envy you this adventure.

Cheer Up, Mother and Dad, All Is Not Lost!

A while back I provided you with some answers to give to people at parties who ask, "How come a nice girl like you isn't married?"

A young lady I know says she thinks the answers are funny, but I am missing the real issue, which isn't what to tell people at parties but what to tell your parents. Her own mother and father, she says, have been bearing down pretty hard because she is unmarried at twenty-one.

True, parents' minds must be put at ease before anybody else's. If you've used the standard arguments—you haven't met anyone you'd like to spend the rest of your life with; you're crazy about your job and would like to concentrate on it for a year or two; girls can have babies in their forties, so what's the rush—and made no impression whatever, I suggest that more ingenious reasons may be required when you encounter the following dialogue:

FATHER: I just can't understand why you haven't found yourself a husband, Barbara Jean. All the girls you went to grammar school with are married. Your four cousins are married. Even Princess Margaret Rose finally found a good man.

MOTHER (*interrupting*): That's right, Barbara Jean. Your father and I had hoped to have grandchildren by now. Why have you let us down like this?

At this point you (with your best method-acting technique) can use one of these answers:

131

"Listen, Mother and Dad, naturally I want to get married, but I've decided to become a movie star first. I met this man the other night. He's a talent scout or something, and he's promised to guide my career just as soon as I can save the money to get to Hollywood. I've already given him $100 as a down payment."

"Daddy, I think it's time you knew. I've been in love with Mr. Spencer in your office since I was twelve years old. We plan to get married as soon as his children are through college."

"Darlings, I've been chosen Playmate of the Month for August. Naturally, I couldn't think of marrying anybody before my picture appears because after that I'll have so many offers I can't even sort through them."

"How can I get married, for goodness' sake? I've been too busy working on my novel which is going to tell all about our family life, Aunt Rhoda's ups and downs in that institution, my early childhood traumas—well, just everything."

"Look, you have nothing to worry about. I'm secretly engaged to a foreign exchange student at the university and we're going to be married as soon as he breaks the news to his other wives."

"How can I get married? I'll never love anybody but Richard Burton and I have to wait for him to get tired of Liz."

"Honestly, Mother and Dad, things are going to be better from now on. During my vacation this summer I'm going to have a complete face lift. The doctor was a little hesitant at first, but I've promised to grow a double chin by then so he can remove it."

"Your fondest dreams are coming true. Listen! The Bide-a-Wee Foundling Home is sending over a selection of babies for you and Mother this afternoon. They've even agreed to let you have two, if you see a pair you like, to make up for my years of shillyshallying."

"I'm joining the Foreign Legion. I understand they have *nothing* but men."

"I'm going to Vietnam to fight with the guerrillas. There are even more men there."

P.S. You may finally confess you haven't done *any* of these things but if they don't stop bugging you about getting married, you *will.*

We Save Rent, She's More Like My Age, But . . .

In most cases, it is hardly justifiable for young and not-so-young women to live with their mothers.

I know I have an awful nerve poking my nose into this problem, because it involves someone who loves you dearly and to whom you owe a lot. If she's ill and there's no one else to look after your mother, fine and dandy . . . do so until you can afford professional care for her which will free you to live a more normal life.

But if there's nothing wrong with this nice person except that she doesn't have enough friends her own age, enough money or enough guts to let you live your life and she hers, it bears looking into.

I know five girls between the ages of twenty-five and forty who are living with their mothers, and all are among the few single women I would label with the unfortunate and denigrating title of old maid. Even for the young ones, the pattern has been set. Their mothers did it!

Lovely as these women are and they *are* often intelligent, attractive, gracious people, they have noiselessly and without its ever being discussed pre-empted this girl-child to be their dutiful, devoted companion and frequently support with no cut-off date. Sure, the daughter is free to date and have men over and that sort of thing, but the atmosphere is wrong. It's faintly Glass Menagerie.

I believe every able-bodied woman should work, and that goes for women over fifty. My own mother went back to teaching school at age fifty-seven after she had been away from her profession thirty-four years. Classified newspaper sections list plenty of jobs with no age limit for women. It takes time for a girl to ease away from her mother, because this is one of the most delicate of all partings—and one which makes you feel guiltiest when you take the step. I believe, however, that in nine cases out of ten, it is justified.

What I have just written goes double for living with mother *and* father!

FIVE | WOMEN ALONE— SECOND TIME 'ROUND

or,

Especially for Widows and Divorcees

The other night at a dinner party we counted up seventeen marriages among eight of us and since one of us (me) had only been married once, that meant the other seven had 2.43 marriages apiece. This wasn't a meeting of divorcees anonymous either, just an ordinary dinner party. I think the guests' collection of divorces and remarriages is an indication of the direction things are going these days. Any "bachelor" you're interested in over the age of twenty-two is just as likely as not to have a wife in his past. Heaven help you, if she's still in his present and they have two-hour conversations every night "about the children." You yourself may have a husband in your past. Here are some thoughts on the subject, gleaned from widows and divorcees themselves.

Rules of Survival For a New Divorcee

Divorcees usually have to start doing some of the things single girls have been doing for years in order not to be lonely and enjoy a full, satisfying life. A new divorcee I know lists these possibilities:

"1. If you're lonesome, get a pet. The upkeep of a puppy dog or pussy cat can cost a little money, but it's worth it. Walking a dog in the city or taking him to obedience class is a great way to meet people. If you can't have this *much* of a pet, consider a cockateel (small Australian parrot). They're lovely—gray with a white face and bright orange cheeks—very cheap and no trouble to speak of. They're also very affectionate and have individual personalities. Few landlords object to a bird as a pet.

"2. Enroll in a night school class. Pick something you've always wanted to learn. Surely there's *something*.

"3. If you can afford them, give parties. Then people will have to ask you back and you'll meet new people at *their* parties.

"4. Don't be pitiful. It bores your friends. And don't be vindictive. If your ex-husband was at all nice, and you wouldn't have married him if he hadn't been, your friends like him, too, and are sorry this has happened. They don't like being put in the middle. Chew on your handkerchief, if you have to, but if you can't say nice things, don't say anything about him.

"5. Don't try to be vivacious to the point of carrying on nonstop dialogue and dancing on table tops to show that you don't need a man and one of you is as amusing as two of anybody else. Just being serene and pleasant and a good listener will do more to make you a welcome addition to the party than anything else.

"6. Start a self-improvement program. Show him what a glamour girl he lost. Work on your clothes, hair, body. If you drink, you may drink more at this time and those extra calories must come off with an exercise program. Again you can join a class for this and maybe meet some more new people. Or do it at home yourself, but *do* it.

"7. Tackle something you've always been afraid of. For me, it was getting into the ocean. For years breakers terrified me and I had nightmares about them. Two weeks after my divorce, I climbed down those 236 steps to the Pacific Ocean and put my toes into the little breakers. Now I've got up to the waist. I feel like Portia Faces Life, and I like it.

"8. Don't fret about finding a new boyfriend the first instant. He isn't the answer. Although he's nice to have around and will probably listen to your problems by the hour and agree with you about how horrible *he* was, he may also want to marry you. If you succumb to *that,* you'll have another divorce to face in a couple of years, if not sooner. This is because when you are geared to one man, miserable though he may be, another man's intimate habits are all wrong and different. You may find yourself having to make adjustments even further when you have no room left inside you to adjust to another person because you are still trying to get adjusted to *you.*

"9. If at all possible, do not see *him* at all. Ideally you would move to another town. It's depressing to be with an "Ex" while you both point out what might have been

138

and bewail what is *now*. With distance between you, you need not be reminded of your unhappiness."

This Little Widow Went to Market

One little widow I know took part of her $10,000 insurance money, plowed it into clothes, hair-dos and a $500-a-month apartment in a New York suburb in which millionaires are supposed to reside. "My aim is to get a rich husband," she said, "and I'm willing to make the investment."

Another little widow I know bought an old Dodge, loaded her children, dog and household possessions into it and drove to Santa Barbara, California, for the same purpose as widow number one—to establish residence near some wealthy men and land one. This widow didn't have as much money to invest in her project as the first one—only a modest monthly living stipend—but she had lots of determination.

A third widow of my acquaintance stayed put in Pittsburgh, Pennsylvania, and opened a dress shop. I don't know whether she was after a husband or not—she had to support herself and be quick about it because she was left penniless. Two friends of her husband helped her get backing and got the shop started.

Where do the girls stand today, two years later? Widow Number One met and married a millionaire. I could kick her for lousing up my theories like that. I'm always saying it can't be done—marrying handsomely when you have no other interest in life and just standing there like a cupcake saying "I'm available." She did it, however. Her fellow is very definitely well-heeled and they are very definitely married.

Widow Number Two lived up to my "expectations" and got absolutely nowhere with the manhunt in Santa Barbara! She didn't work or do anything while she was there, of course, but keep her big blue eyes trained on the horizon for eligible men. Apparently not many showed up, and the ones who did were looking for wealthy girls. She finally moved back home to Boston and isn't doing much of anything.

Widow Number Three had her ups and downs in business because she'd never so much as paid a gas bill by herself before. The shop is doing beautifully now, however, and the proprietress is being written up in *Women's Wear Daily* soon. Widow three hasn't married, but she's had offers. She meets lots of men in her work—salesmen who call at the store and manufacturers whom she sees on buying trips.

If all widows interested in men could track as well as the first widow, I'd pack you all off to the wealthy suburb and say have a go at it. To my knowledge, however, the outcome is more usually like that which befell Widow Number Two. The men disappear between cracks in the walls and under closet doors like summer night creatures when somebody's after them in earnest. (Why should a man be any less fleet than a lightning bug when his future is at stake?)

I still think that finding some kind of work to do is the *most* satisfactory answer for a widow or divorcee even if she has money. If the men come along, fine—you can marry one of them. If they don't come along, you can still have an absorbing interest in life. Usually the men come along sooner when you're employed.

Is Divorce a Status Symbol?

"He was pretty terrific," Natalie said. "And I just couldn't tell him the truth. I said I'd been married and divorced several years ago. He bought the story, of course, and didn't ask a single question."

"Haven't you ever done that before?" Lila asked. "I never tell a man I haven't been married. I always say I'm divorced, and then he relaxes."

"What if they ask questions about your ex-husband?" Natalie wondered.

"Usually they don't," Lila said. "Men don't like to talk about other men. If the subject comes up, I just describe somebody I once went with very seriously whom I *might* have married. I say he lives in another city and we're never in touch."

A third girl in our little luncheon group joined the conversation then.

"Isn't it funny," she said, "we've all done the same thing but never talked about it before? When I was about thirty-three, people began to act so funny when I said I'd never been married, I felt I had to put their minds at ease, and I invented Ralph. Ralph and I have been 'divorced' going on eight years now, and I've almost begun to believe there really is a Ralph."

At this point, the fourth member of the group, little me, asked for her smelling salts or maybe it was another double old-fashioned (I can't remember) because she felt herself growing weak with anger.

"Are you serious?" I gasped, hoping against hope they'd tell me it wasn't so. "Do you all really invent ex-husbands?"

"Doesn't everybody?" Lila asked.

Well, no, everybody doesn't, as a matter of fact. At least I never did—never could, never would and don't believe in it. At the moldering age of thirty-seven I was still shamelessly confessing that I had never been married, not even once.

If pressed, I explained it was not for lack of opportunity, though I don't think anybody ever believed me. The husband I got was absolutely enchanted that I was unencumbered with anything but beaux and often said so.

These three attractive, man-loving, good-citizen-type girls at the luncheon gave me the shudders with their ectoplasmic Ralphs and Tonys and Toms. Can things really have got to a state where divorce is considered more honorable than spinsterhood? Perhaps it has, but I'm not buying.

Confession in your thirties that you've never been married says certain things about you. You're afraid of men, you've been too choosy, you didn't want responsibility. A divorce in your background says certain things about you, too. One of them *may* be that you married the first man who asked you so that nobody would ever be able to accuse you of being an old maid. *This* is a *status* symbol?

Now really, if you're going to invent anything to impress a man, I would suggest a noble ancestry, a fake fortune or possibly a doctor of philosophy degree—something with a little prestige.

Ex-husbands are, after all, common as crab grass!

Don't Invent an Ex-Husband—
Invent a Dead One

"I know what you think about girls who invent ex-husbands and I'm surprised that *you're* surprised," a friend said to me. "I've invented ex-husbands for years but recently came across a better plan. I now invent a husband who has passed on."

"Fascinating," I said. "Tell me about it."

"You'd be amazed at the marvelous effect being a widow has on the male sex," she said. "It makes them tender and gallant. If you're in your thirties and say you've never been married, men say 'What's wrong with her?' If you're divorced, they figure you can't get along with men. When you're a widow and profess to have been divinely happy, they fall all over themselves trying to live up to the standards of manhood set by your departed hero."

"But it's so dishonest," I said, "making up a dead husband."

"No more dishonest than the rating system itself," my friend said. "If you're single, you're automaticallly a spook. Men even denigrate other *men* who are single or divorced! 'Bad risk' many a man has said of a particular guy who's never been married. 'Difficult—immature' they say if he has an ex-wife. Yet a man or woman whose mate has passed on is automatically endowed with noble, lovable, honorable qualities regardless of his real personality. I decided I wanted to have those qualities, too, instead of being thought creepy."

"Did you just make up dear George out of whole cloth?" I asked.

"Actually it started at work," she said. "One of the girls was getting married and was being so patronizing and insufferable about it I told her I had been married myself. 'Divorced?' she asked. 'No, widowed,' I said. Since then I can almost feel the respectability waves circling around me. As a matter of fact, this girl recently asked my advice on how much insurance I thought her husband should carry, just in case."

"But don't people ask a lot of questions about your dear departed?" I suggested.

"You know how men are about talking about the other

142

men in your life," she said. "They hate it. If they do ask questions, which isn't likely, you can just say you don't wish to talk about it. If things get to the point where you are planning marriage, you can always tell the truth at that time and it won't make any difference."

"It seems to me it's better to be the one who tries to prove them wrong and shows them a single woman without a husband dead or alive to her name can still be quite stable and attractive," I said.

"Why fight uphill?" she said. "Just as you set the stage for men with the right apartment and lovely cooking, why not set the stage with the right emotional attitude on the part of the man?"

You can do whatever you think best, of course. It seems to *me* if you're going to leave the impression that you're a widow and you aren't, you can't complain too much if he decides to leave the impression that he's fallen madly in love with you, wants to marry you, never looked at another girl before you and never expects to look at one again. While we're telling lies, two people ought to be allowed to play at this game.

Do You Let Him Move In?

"I have been going with a guy for a year," an attractive woman informed me. "Both of us are divorced and in our late thirties. His children by a former marriage are over twenty, so he has no child-support problem. I have a son, also by a former marriage, in primary school.

"Obviously our marriages were not happy ones, or we wouldn't have ended them. Don, however, is very bitter about marriage in general. I am not. I think once you have found the person you'd like to spend the rest of your life with, family responsibilities and 'loss of freedom' are nothing to be frightened of.

"My problem is that Don will come to live with us and support both my son and me, but he will not get a marriage license or, as he says, 'sign any papers.' He doesn't want to feel tied down. He says if he lives with me because he wants to and not because he has to, we will have a happier life together.

"I, too, have seen many unhappy couples remain together only because there were marriage ties that 'must not be broken,' but I am a conformist at heart. And there's my child to think of. Could he be hurt? Now? Or later?

"Don is a good guy, really—courteous, thoughtful, very kind and above all the best father I have been able to find for my boy. I do not want to lose him. I am happy with him and miserable without him. I have held onto him for a year, hoping he would change his mind and marry me, but no luck so far.

"What would you do if you were in my shoes? Would you wait to see if he changes his mind? Would you live with him? The world would be told we are married.

"Don't tell me to date others. I've tried, and it doesn't work. Don't tell me to join groups or have outside activities. They don't work either."

I would continue to wait it out a little longer. It's always tempting to advise someone whose beau isn't going along with her ideas about marriage to dump him right over the bannister and as quickly and unceremoniously as possible. I'm for that if the man is making you miserable. But that doesn't seem to be the case with you, I said. Unless there are problems I don't know about, perhaps your friend is worth "saving" and being patient with a bit longer.

He's cuckoo, of course. You'd make him a wonderful, undemanding wife. And someday you may want to try "unconvicting" him of his convictions by offering an ultimatum of marriage or no more friendship, but I don't believe you're up to that yet.

I don't see any reason for living together. There's little advantage in it for you except the offer to support you and your child. If you need help financially, perhaps he can supply that without moving in. As your permanent "guest," there will be more cooking, more cleaning, more laundry, etc. but alas, no more security for you.

Your child would probably learn of the relationship between you someday. And yes, I think it would hurt him.

As long as you don't live together, there is a better chance also of keeping channels open to the outside world. I promised not to tell you to date other men, but I didn't say a word about not keeping other friends in your life —as many as you can. You're going to need them to hold your hand while waiting for the ultimatum to work —or to cheer you up if it doesn't.

The One You Love Belongs to Somebody Else

Many, many girls ask, "I'm in love with a married man. What shall I do?"

Why don't they just give the guy up? Well, it isn't always that simple. For example, here is a very touching letter I received from a young divorcee:

"I am twenty-four years old with three small children," she writes. "Please do not think of me as a young, flighty girl who does not know her own mind. I fought very desperately to save my marriage, and when the situation became totally unbearable for me and my sweet babies, divorce became a necessity.

"One more thing you should know, I am a God-loving, God-fearing woman. My problem is this: Not long ago, I met a most wonderful gentleman. I use the word gentleman because he is just that. Paul and I attend the same church and participate actively. Our friendship has grown to the most extreme love. No, Helen, this is not the sexual desire of a woman alone. He is all things I respect, admire and love. Paul is kind, gentle, understanding, tender and most loving.

"He is also very married, is thirty-two and has two sons eight and seven. You should also know he is not 'on the make,' so to speak. I can, in all truth, say that he returns my love and devotion twofold. So you see we are not wild, immature lovers.

"This situation worries me greatly. I would not for the world hurt his children. They are precious to me, just as mine are. Yet, we live for each other and cannot stay apart. Don't think we haven't tried in every possible way. We feel very deeply that we are shaming our God and society. We want our love to be good and right in God's eyes, but we are endangering the hearts of those we love. As you can see, we are very conscious of these things. Still, we are together. Divorce, for him, is impossible right now."

This girl is no hussy, and I feel deeply for her. It would be unrealistic to say, "Give him up instantly," because obviously she can't.

The fact is, however, eventually these two will probably

145

have to part. Life has a way of popping little darts into this kind of love idyll.

The girl will fall in love again with someone she can marry, because she is a loving person. Her friend will return to his family, who, in my opinion, will be lucky to have him back. This isn't a puritanical view or perhaps even a popular one, but I feel those who love—however hopelessly and no matter *who*—are always better for it —even when they lose.

Another young woman writes of less serious involvement . . . but more vexation. "I've been seeing a married man for several months now, and we usually have cocktails after work at my apartment or sometimes he drops by Saturday morning. I don't mind his being married, because I don't wish to marry anybody just now (I'm recently divorced). What bugs me is that he always wants me to help him figure out things to tell his wife so that he can get away to see *me*. Isn't that his responsibility?"

Well, yes, I suppose it is if you're dividing up disagreeable chores. Any married man who thinks a girl friend should be his co-conspirator in doping out a painless double life is very dense and naive indeed. I don't believe this girl will have her problem very long, however.

Whether she's interested in getting married or not, I think she can find a more worthy companion . . . somebody she won't have to see at such restricted times . . . someone who isn't constantly running the risk of hurting innocent people—as well as herself, and probably both.

Alimony Turns Women into Bums

When I was a columnist, several times each year I wrote a column on the subject of alimony. Because they were all fairly sputtering with invective and also named names, they were checked out with the legal department of the newspaper and, instead of running, were put quietly to rest! *They* are put quietly to rest, but *I* am left sputtering like an old Ford operating on wood alcohol. I'm against alimony.

In one "Speaking Out" column of the *Saturday Evening Post,* writer Alexander Eliot managed in an article entitled "Let's Abolish Alimony" to make a number of good points, apparently without being libelous, so I am going to quote him!

Mr. Eliot says, "Alimony isn't a help to anyone. It's an acid which corrodes those who give and those who get and those who are deprived (the man's new wife) because of it." Mr. Eliot, a divorced man, feels child support should be mandatory—"One can be an ex-husband, but never an ex-father." He feels, however, that permanent payments to an ex-wife turn her into a very disagreeable and unhappy person.

How can that be? She's getting all that nice money every month and in some cases will never have to work to support herself again if she manages carefully. The reason she isn't too sunny over this arrangement is that she's in the position of "punishing" somebody (through making him pay in cash). Jailers, executioners, disciplinarians are not known to be God's happiest creatures. Does he deserve to be punished?

According to Eliot, the real reason for nine out of ten divorces is "mutual incompatibility"—not a husband throwing over an "old wife." Eliot quotes New York Justice H. Hofstadter as saying, "The great majority of divorces occur within the first five years of marriage, and sixty-five percent do not involve minor children." How wronged is the wife?

It takes two to divorce.

A wife getting a monthly dole also isn't happy because she often postpones getting a job and making herself into a self-supporting, full-fledged citizen. If she did that, she fears her husband might figure out some way to get the alimony stopped. So she stays forever in the shallow end of the pool with the life preservers, the rubber dolphins and the toddlers—no place for a grown, strong-limbed woman to be swimming. A woman's alimony does stop, of course, if she remarries, and the alimony may virtually keep her from making a second marriage.

In a more perfect world, it seems to me the financial arrangements of divorce would be these—based on the supposition that women are equals of men in every way, can have all the material rewards men get if they'll work for them and, therefore, do not need to be babies and coddled.

1. Divide up all the money and property that have been acquired while the couple is married.

2. *Not* divide up the money or property each partner brought to marriage. These revert to the original owner. (While married, a woman deserves all the "spoils" that come with old J. B. or young C. W. I think it is unfair and unrealistic for her to want permanent spoils when she is no longer putting up with old J. B.'s snoring or young C. W.'s pinching girls at parties.)

3. Child support based on the father's present income, to be increased somewhat when the father starts to make money.

4. Temporary alimony for wives who have no way of supporting themselves, the alimony to last longer if the marriage is of long duration or the woman is over forty. *No* alimony for wives who are independently well-off or who have jobs. This penalizes the working woman, but, in my opinion, her life is so much better than that of a nonworking woman, she can afford to give up the temporary alimony.

Do you suppose I've lost every last divorcee-reader?

Are You a Problem Girl?

A divorcee sometimes has problems to contend with which are not faced by any other woman alone or married girl either. Here are a few with their possible solutions:

Problem: An ex-husband is not paying child support, which the court has awarded.

Solution: Take him back to court, if you can find him! Most courts are pretty strict about enforcing these payments and will even arrange extradition of nonpayers who flee the state. I once heard a judge say to a man who reluctantly confessed to nonsupport of two batches of kids while a third batch waited on the bench, "You'd better take care of the kids you've got before you have anymore or we'll have to think about putting you some place where you can't have anymore." He meant it, too.

You should have a job yourself so that the nonsupport isn't so serious. Working divorcees (even if they don't need the money) usually have a better life.

Problem: Your ex-husband is such a mess (according

148

to you) it's hard to speak civilly about him to the children.

Solution: Make the effort! I know a girl who, left by her alcoholic ex with thousands of dollars' worth of bills to pay off, entertained him most charmingly one evening, inviting other people in to help take the pressure off, so her seven-year-old daughter wouldn't know there was anything wrong with daddy until she was grown up enough to face the knowledge. A child's peace of mind comes first. Right?

Problem: There are no children but you can't forget how badly the bum (your definition) treated you all the years you were married.

Solution: Don't forget, but don't make bitterness a way of life. Acid corrodes the vessel, you know. Think about this: Did you or did you not say yes when this man proposed to you? Could you or could you not have walked away instead of marrying him? Okay, you got yourself *into* the marriage. Show a little class! Suffer and hate for a little while if you like. Then get on with a better use of your time, like finding a steady beau.

Problem: Your ex-husband threatens violence whenever you date another man.

Solution: Don't try to cope with him by yourself. Women are killed every day by jealous ex-mates. You can get a peace bond against a man who is violent or threatening you with a gun. Then he is on the police books as a kook, which can be quite a deterrent. Talk it over with your doctor or attorney.

Problem: You're getting along better with your ex now than you ever did when you were married. You think perhaps the divorce was a mistake.

Solution: Maybe it was and maybe it wasn't. People who aren't married can accept another's grievous faults quite well if they aren't locked up with them twenty-four hours a day. Be glad you have such an amicable relationship with the man. Perhaps now you can be good friends the rest of your life. Don't jump to the conclusion that things would be even better if you got closer. You *tried* that. Remember?

A New Wife Speaks Out About an Old One

Let's face it. If you marry a man who has been married before and whose last wife gets sizable child support and alimony every month, you as a new wife may just have to pitch in and help out. Let's hear from a new bride, until recently a woman alone, on the subject:

"Al writes his first wife a semi-monthly check for $250 out of our joint checking account," says Roberta. "Since we both put our salaries into this account, you can either figure that I'm supporting the household and he's paying the alimony and child support, or I'm paying the alimony and child support and he's providing for the household.

"That $500 a month has to come from someplace, and together our salaries just cover all our expenses. If Al is out of town or busy, I write, sign and send the check over to his ex myself."

"Do you feel very much resentment about this?" I asked.

"I knew what I was getting into when I married him," said my friend. "And as a matter of fact I feel sorry for his ex-wife. She's got the idea she's getting revenge on Al by not getting a job and helping provide things for herself.

"She isn't hurting Al or me, heaven knows, but he's sick about what kind of life she's providing for the children. I doubt if they even get sent off to school with breakfast."

"Why don't you see about getting custody of the children yourself?" I asked.

"We're trying to," said Roberta, "but usually custody remains with the mother if that's the way it was decided in court. Of course, this girl doesn't want anything changed because her monthly payments might be cut."

"Will you have children of your own?" I asked.

"I certainly hope so," Roberta said. "And even if I have to keep working after the children are born, I'm strong enough to do it. You don't have to be with children every minute yourself in order to have them healthy, secure, well-mannered and well-educated. Love and discipline and caring are the main ingredients."

"Do you have any tips for girls marrying men who have been married before?" I asked.

"Don't grumble about the alimony," Roberta said. "Tell him constantly that he's a bargain at any price. If you let him know he's priceless, not worthless, he'll live up to what you think he is.

"When his children come to visit you, don't worry that they've been told you're a hussy. Children usually observe pretty closely and evaluate things as they see them. If they see love and plenty of it left over for them, they get the right idea.

"As for your husband, I think you say 'I love you' and never ask 'Do you love me?' Meet him at the door every night when he comes home. Drop whatever you're doing when you hear the car drive in or the door open.

"Tell him how much you appreciate him and how happy you are. Don't complain. Don't say you're tired. Remember that sex is terribly important. Learn how to do a good strip tease. Surprise him some night with an outfit that would put the burlesque girls to shame. You can do it. No censors at home. Be interesting and fun to be with. Have some exciting new ideas every once in a while, it doesn't matter on what subject.

"And be enthusiastic."

The Divorcee's Fine-Feathered (But Not Too Sensitive) Friends

Divorcees tell me that some of their married-couple friends are not the positive little helpers they might be.

"I don't expect them to take over and manage my problems," one newly single girl told me, "or to spend hours entertaining me, but I could certainly manage with a little more understanding on their part. People who *know* that Sam (her ex-husband) was an alcoholic who never faced a problem, including alcoholism, act as though a woman of forty-seven who gets a divorce is out of her skull. *Any* husband presumably being better than none."

Here are other divorce complaints.

"Some of my girl friends believe all I think about is taking their husbands away from them. I wouldn't *have* any one of their husbands. I'm only interested in one of my own."

"My friends are concerned about me and I appreciate that, but they can't seem to think of a man for me unless they can see him with a wedding ring through his nose that can be taken off and put on my finger. I don't want to rush into another marriage, but I *would* love an occasional date, phone call, walk in the park, things like that. It would be wonderful if everyone weren't so desperate to marry me off and would come up with somebody I could occasionally just spend an evening with."

"At least five friends have told me they know a nice man for me, but they never come up with one. I think they just want credit for having me in their thoughts but the actual work of calling the man and getting us together would be too much trouble or too much of a responsibility."

"One couple I know is perishing for me to get married. If some unattached man at a party happens to pay some attention to me, they're on the phone first thing in the morning to know what developed. They could be a great deal more help if they'd introduce me to some men in their rather large circle of friends and not be so passionately curious about the ones I happen to meet by myself."

"I've had two married couples who were friends of both my husband and myself over to dinner several times since the divorce. Neither couple has ever asked me to their own dinner parties. I think they feel I probably wouldn't fit in since I'm not married anymore and that they are cheering my lonely hours by letting me entertain them. It's rather aggravating!"

There's nothing to do about these complaints except to realize that you aren't alone in having them. If and when these smug friends get their own divorces and you're married again, you can be a little more understanding and helpful than they were.

Friends of the Divorcee

"I want to talk to you about the time you wrote how mean a divorcee's friends are to her," a lady whom I had just met said to me.

152

"I'd be glad to," I said.

"The divorcee with the alcoholic ex-husband whose friends said she'd be better off with *anybody* than not being married—I think what the friends actually said was, 'Get the divorce!' In the first place the woman probably drove the man to drink and then drove her friends to distraction complaining about him. So now she's finally divorced and she has a new problem. 'I'm lonely and I don't have a husband,' she complains. Since her friends *suggested* the divorce, they're *responsible* for her loneliness, she figures. The *least* they could do is find her another guy, and this is *all* she talks about. She can't understand for the life of her why no one has asked her to dinner lately. Funny thing, too. Ever since the divorce her husband doesn't drink as much."

"What about the girl who says her friends always think she's trying to take their husbands away from them?" I asked.

"Yes, and now whatever do you suppose gave them that idea?" my friend replied. "After all, what's a little hug and kiss among friends when the girl arrives at the door? Not to mention sitting on the host's lap, tweaking his ears and blowing down his neck during the party because she decides Old Bob hasn't been getting enough wifely affection. A girl like that can cause trouble among happily married couples. They decide for the good of the group not to invite her anymore, and she can't understand it. She is hurt, hurt, hurt, and they are mean, mean, mean!"

"What did you think about the girl who said her friends promise her a man but never come up with one?" I asked.

"Finding an eligible man is tough," said my new acquaintance. "Any single girl will tell you that. Maybe her married friends just don't know anybody, or the guy they had in mind for her is being fixed up by five other couples with the ravishing divorcees on *their* list. Sometimes you have to wait in line."

"Do you have any excuse for the married couple who never invite a new divorcee to their house after she's entertained *them*?" I asked.

"I surely do," said my companion. "Dining with her could just be an ordeal. It's possible the whole time they were together, the girl was either brightly and metallically gay or else aired every problem she's had since the last time they saw each other and since she was ten years old. Also, why didn't she have someone to be her partner for the evening? There's always some guy who'll sit in on a dinner party. So maybe he's dull or hasn't hit it big in business yet or he's your brother or even your sister! My landlord is my best sit-in. He bores everybody to death, but at least he's a man."

"You mean you are a divorcee?" I asked.

"I certainly am," my friend said. "But I'm not a complaining one. They're the biggest bores in the whole world."

That's one girl's opinion anyway.

The Not-So-Merry Widow

A young widow going out on her first date since her husband's death reported the pleasant excitement of getting dressed for the evening, the great fun of sipping cocktails with a man who *wasn't* a friend of the family and then, gradually, the dawning of the awful truth. The chap's interest in her was decidedly physical.

After saying no with some vehemence, she escaped his clutches and went home to cry into her pillow all night.

Poor darling. I can imagine this run-in with a wolf may have set back her desire to return to the world of men by several months.

She probably feels guilty, too, on behalf of her late husband who, she's pretty sure, would want her to be happy, but who would frown like the thunderbolt god at the thought of her being dragged off into the bushes!

The widow's experience is in no way different, however, from that of thousands of divorcees and single girls looking for husbands who come face to face instead with lust! I would say to a widow what I would say to any woman alone. Men with strong libidinal drives are not necessarily ogres . . . like this woman's dinner date, some are just a bit gauche and in too much of a hurry.

All *good* men are interested in a woman physically, while a woman may be more interested in companionship, fireside chats and someone to help her bring up her children. Lust, yes, but later. Much, much later!

I'm no psychiatrist or philanthropist, but I would implore the widow or any single woman to be tolerant of men and

154

try to understand that their needs may be different from hers. The bachelors are a bit spoiled these days, because there are so many more of us who want them than there are of them to go around.

It's like Madame Curie plowing through pitchblende to find radium! You may have to plow through dozens and dozens of wolf-types to find the one good man for you. It only *takes* one.

Living with Ghosts, And Learning to Live Without Them

This is a poignant story I heard from a divorcee the other day:

"Karl and I have been divorced for two years," she said, "but I was no more divorced emotionally than if I was still cooking his breakfast and sending him off to work every day. When you're married over twenty years, it's hard to think of yourself as 'single.' I always referred to Karl as my husband and managed to talk to him on the phone several times a week. Even though I had the divorce papers in my dresser drawer upstairs, there were certain of my neighbors and relatives I let think Karl and I might be getting back together any day. I even believed it myself.

"When Karl was transferred to another city, I just moved the children and me to the same city on the excuse that the children deserved to see their father as often as possible. Actually as teen-agers they led a pretty active life and didn't see much of their father even before the move. In a new neighborhood it was easier than ever for me to tell people my husband was out of town on business and had to travel a lot.

"Since Karl didn't know too many people in the new city, he sort of let me back into his life. I got in the habit of going over to clean up his apartment twice a week and look after his laundry. I also cooked dinner whenever I was there and made things and left them in the icebox for his other meals. This went on for about six months, and I was fairly happy. Then one day I went to Karl's apartment with a cake I'd just baked and there was a girl there— quite young and pretty. She said she'd just stopped by to pick up her glasses, which she'd left the night before. I told her I was Karl's wife and she said, 'Oh, yes, his ex-wife.' I started to correct her but I couldn't. Technically she was right, although I still thought of myself as his wife.

"When I got back home I called Karl at work and asked who this girl was. He said he's been seeing her for about six months and they were probably going to get married. I went completely to pieces and said I had to talk to him. He said there was nothing to talk about. We were legally divorced and both had our own lives to lead. I said what about the cleaning and housework he'd let me do and he said he'd never asked me to do it, that he'd begged me not to. This was true, of course.

"I went into a decline after that and didn't even bother to get dressed in the morning. I drank a bottle of port wine every afternoon and would be fuzzy when the kids came in from school.

"One day one of my neighbors came over to borrow some eggs and stayed to chat. She noticed some painting on my wall and said she's always wanted an original oil but had only been able to afford prints. I said the thing to do was paint them yourself. That's what I had done. She couldn't believe the stuff was mine but I said I was quite a good painter before my divorce. It was the first time I'd ever admitted to anyone that I was divorced. She said she'd like to commission me to do a painting for her.

"I guess that was the turning point. I went to work on her painting. It's one of her children, and he comes over every afternoon to pose for me. She's thrilled and I've finally realized I really do have something to offer the world as myself—not as somebody's appendage.

"I was a long time waking up. I'm glad I'm finally out of the woods. I don't think it was Karl I minded losing. It was my married state."

SIX | **BRINGING UP BABY**

or,

Women Alone—
But Not Quite

Many a dating girl nowadays has a little something dating girls in the past didn't have . . . a baby . . . or several babies. Again, not having been a divorcee (with or without children), I gleaned my information on this subject from friends. The article that says kids should mop the bathroom floor got howls and protests when it first appeared.

Mommy's Dating Again

Is there a recommended procedure for divorced or widowed women to use in integrating children with beaux? I asked several divorced mothers exactly how they handled this situation.

A chic divorcee of New York City states, "I would never marry anyone my children didn't like or who didn't like them. However, though I want to get married, I find, just like single girls, that every man you date isn't husband material. Until you meet the man you want to marry, I see no reason why children and beaux have to be forced on each other. I spend my days with my children and don't feel I'm doing them an injustice not to include them in all my grown-up activities. They are often fed and tucked in bed before I go out."

A divorcee from Rockford, Illinois, has similar thoughts. "Although I'm very fond of Jim, I know we aren't going to be married. He has just about told me he could never feel the same way about my children as he does about his own. (He's divorced, too.) That settled it. I have him over to dinner with my boys perhaps once a month, but I don't insist on their going out with us."

A St. Petersburg, Florida, divorcee says, "It depends on the man whether you all do things together. Some men adore children and want them included on most of your outings. If it's a bachelor who isn't used to being around children, I think easy does it. If he doesn't feel forced to like your children or they to like him—in other words, you aren't a bundle of anxiety when they're all together—I think they gradually grow on each other. I do think everybody ought to be introduced right away. Never make the mistake of not telling a man you have children because then he's really shocked when he finds out."

And a mother from Providence, Rhode Island, says on the subject of skitterish bachelors, "Children can be pretty great. After a couple of miserable evenings when Gloria and Rocky, my five- and seven-year-old daughters, bounced all over my friend and said, 'When are you gonna marry Mommy?' we had a little talk. I explained they were being my worst enemies, but that I really needed their help. Since then they have been absolute little dolls. Of his own volition, Chester asked them to go to the movies with us last week."

None of this is conclusive, of course. I'd be interested to hear from any of you regarding your own dating situation.

One thing all the girls I talked to agreed upon. It should not have to cost you to go out with a man. Therefore, your date pays for the baby sitter. One of the girls suggested that when he brings you home from a date, you enlist him to drive the sitter home. Then in his presence you say, "How much do I owe you, Mrs. Clompkins?" While you are searching in your purse, any gentleman who is one will take care of the bill.

Smother Love Versus Mother Love

A widow of my acquaintance recently told me this story: "When Tom died, the children were only seven and ten, and we had been a very close family. Every Sunday we went on a picnic or outing and on holidays we usually took a trip. Tom was never one of those men who played with his children when the mood struck. They could bother him any time they chose. I spent most of my time taking care of the needs of the family and was perfectly happy.

"The first few weeks after the funeral I used to look at Timmy and Claudia and weep my heart out silently. They were so young to be without a father, especially since they had always been so close. I made up my mind to be both father and mother to them to the best of my ability. I don't mean to sound immodest but I think I succeeded pretty well.

"I put them before everything else, unlike some mothers I know. If there was a circus, an art exhibit, an animal show, a children's movie, a stamp exhibition we were the first in line. Sometimes we took other children along but often it was just the three of us. We had wonderful times together and though I missed Tom desperately I felt I was living up to everything he would have expected of me by developing a fine son and daughter.

"In the beginning people used to try to fix me up with blind dates, but they were always so disappointing I decided if I couldn't have a good man I'd rather not have *any*. I certainly never did the things I've seen other widows and divorcees do to bring men into their lives—picking up men in bars, flirting with strangers and that sort of thing. I really didn't need a man anyway because I was too busy with the children's lives and their special activities.

"Timmy is one of those boys who knew exactly what he wanted to become when he was eight years old and he's had painting and drawing lessons ever since. Claudia is more the out-door type and I guess the boating, skating and horseback-riding excursions we've been on would number in the hundreds. Sometimes I've been in the grand-stand rooting for her hockey team and also wound up taking the team home after the game. Our station wagon was always available for taxi service.

"The years went by. The children are now fourteen and seventeen respectively, and funny things have begun to happen. Just last week I was passing a department store and saw a painting of some sunflowers with a blue ribbon attached to it in the window. Underneath was a placard with my son's name on it saying he'd won first prize in a city-wide high school competition. I didn't know he'd even entered the contest. When I asked him about it he just said, 'I wanted to do something by myself, Mother,' and that's all he said. The very same week Claudia came home wearing one of the most horrible-looking dresses I've ever seen in my life. It was purple crepe with a very low neck. I didn't know whether to laugh or cry. Claudia wasn't laughing, however. She said, 'I wanted to pick out my own clothes for a change, Mother. Don't worry. I didn't charge it to your account. I saved my lunch money.' And she flounced out of the room. I guess these must be what you'd call hostile symptoms, but I'm absolutely bewildered. With all the teen-age drinking and delinquency brought on by parents who didn't take enough interest in their children, I don't see how mine could possibly be anything but grateful for the kind of attention they've had."

161

Anybody want to bet? My own money would be on the possibility that the hostility gets worse. Many child psychologists agree that one of the finest things a mother can do is develop a life of her own with loving friendships among people her own age. A job is great for a widow. Having a man in her life after the mourning is over is great. How else are children supposed to learn what is "normal" if mommy lives in a world peopled only by her children?

Do Children Keep a Divorcee From the Rich, Full Life?

So many young divorced mothers seem to be sorry for themselves. The problem, they say, is money and time.

How can they give the children what *they* need and have any funds or time left for themselves? Many say they can't go back to work, because there'd be nobody there when the children came home from school.

To give you an idea of what's possible for the Mother Alone, I've asked a young divorced friend, who is raising children and still has a mighty good life, to write down her credo.

Writes Martha: "The child comes first. *You* had him, with assistance from your husband, of course, and you are responsible for him. You didn't just find yourself pregnant!

"If you had your child in love and happiness, which later turned sour, then you *may not penalize the child.* If you had your child to cement what was already a bad relationship, you were being very foolish indeed, because that's a trick that's never been known to work. Once again, you *may not penalize the child* for your own stupidity. How would *you* like to pay for somebody else's mistakes?

"Even if you 'found yourself pregnant,' you could have put the child up for adoption. Thousands of people are begging for babies.

"So don't complain if there you are, with a child or children on your hands. Remember, you asked for them.

"Fortunately for divorcees, small children don't know or care whether you are rich or poor. All they really need is food and love, the latter a commodity that nobody seems to get enough of ever.

"You may die to see your little muffin in a thirty-dollar

organdy party dress, but she'd be just as happy in a three-dollar one if Mommy made it for her.

"Of course, the money must go for the child's needs first, and if there's any left over it's for Mother. There's no such thing as a mother with so many child and home responsibilities, however, that she can't work, especially if the children are school age. And if you work hard, as a company is only too pleased to have you do, you can get better and better and make more money. Some of your grown-up fun is at work.

"Many girls hire teen-age baby sitters to care for their children after school until mother gets home. Sometimes a neighbor will agree to keep an eye on them and check on their play and homework. Most people are kind, love children, recognize you have special problems and will help as long as you show you care more about the child's welfare than your own. This means no stopping at a bar for 'happy time' after work or the neighbor arrangement will end. You also can't ask a neighbor to feed your children except in dire emergency—*never* because you've picked up a date.

"After you're home from work, the children are fed and loved by Mama until bedtime. *Then* if Mama wants to go out, she arranges again for a sitter. Often your date will pay if you simply say, 'I can't afford a sitter.' One girl I know literally charged a man for the food she cooked for him, and he was delighted to pay. He adored her cooking, and she explained she simply could not afford three more lamb chops for his dinner. They just celebrated their fifteenth wedding anniversary.

"If you're going to a friend's house for dinner, the children can often be brought along, tucked in a bedroom to sleep until time to go home. Generations of children grew up without baby sitters.

"I guess you can tell from my writing sniveling mothers make me sick!"

"Lift That Mop!"

Like many another divorcee, a thirty-one-year-old girl we'll call Joan, supports not only herself but two growing children as well. "I'm supposed to get fifty dollars a month from their father," she says. "If it arrives one month in four I'm lucky." So much for outside help!

It is admirable that Joan is able to cope with financial responsibilities on a Comptometer operator's salary—"We have thirty-seven different ways to spend Saturday without spending any money," she says.

Even more noteworthy perhaps is the fact that most people who know her two boys say they are two of the best-disciplined, most-popular and well-adjusted children they have ever met.

Joan's methods of child raising are not exactly orthodox for 1966. "There's precious little permissiveness around our apartment or doing what comes naturally at chore time!" says Joan.

At ages eleven and seven, her boys make their own beds before school. When they come home, they wash the breakfast dishes and occasionally rinsed-off dinner dishes from the night before. "If they aren't washed when I get home from work, they know they don't get dinner," says their mother. "Stevie was drying dishes when he was three."

Joan hasn't used the vacuum or scrubbed the bathroom in five years. "That's their department," she explains. And she doesn't carry in groceries. "That's for the men!" (Joan has them put in medium-sized sacks.)

A relative once told Joan the children had entirely too much responsibility for their age and persuaded her to see a family counselor. The counselor, after a number of separate meetings with Joan and her boys, said, "They seem like pretty happy kids to me. They'll make somebody wonderful husbands!"

It's possible people who criticize this woman's "sharing-the-household-chores" approach to child raising haven't the stamina for it themselves! "It's much easier to scrub the bathroom yourself in the beginning than send a child back to do it five times until he does it right," says Joan. "I probably wouldn't have played it like a general if I could have played it soft," she adds. "It was a matter of freeing me to make a living."

It sounds to me as though this woman alone has admirably combined discipline of her children with love and good management. I wish I had a daughter to marry one of her sons!

Fun and Games with the Kids

A young mother has these suggestions for entertaining children without spending any money:

"1. *Bicycle Riding:* It's one of my personal favorites because it's great for *my* figure. I can have fun with the boys and get a beauty treatment at the same time. And its the only form of exercise I know that doesn't *seem* like exercise. We ride about 30 minutes every afternoon when I get home from work during nice weather, and they seem quite proud of the fact that their mother can stay on a bike without breaking her neck.

"2. *Horseback Riding:* I found some people with a ranch near here who raise and train horses for show. They have a ring on their property in the stable area and welcome someone who will exercise the horses because it has to be done every day.

"3. *Beach:* We've always been lucky in that we've lived near the ocean and we love squatting in the surf and drinking up the sun. The boys swim quite well (something they learned at the YMCA, not from their mother), so while they're swimming I sun. Then we all do sand sculptures, catch little crabs, collect rocks and shells—all that sort of thing.

"4. *Indoor Games:* I've always asked relatives and friends to give the boys educational or thinking-type games for birthdays and Christmas so that I can play, too. We have Scrabble, Monopoly, checkers and Chinese checkers. We also paint by numbers, make mosaic pictures and put together models. We have quite a collection of monster models at the moment—Dracula, the Wolf Man and others.

"5. *Nature Hikes:* If your feet can stand it, kids love to hike around the woods. You find an area as isolated as possible and look for various insects, leaves, flowers and ferns. Then bring them home and see if you can find the same objects in the encyclopedia.

"6. *Field Trips:* We visit art galleries, museums, historical points and national park or monuments (any place that's open to the public with no admission). It's a good idea to read up on the place you're going to visit beforehand so when the children ask questions you can give a reasonably intelligent answer.

"7. *Tours:* An ice-cream plant is a wonderful place to tour. The nice manager always gives samples. Kids also love to see things made by assembly techniques so a tour of most any manufacturing plant would interest them, and tours of newspaper offices—from the press room to editorial—usually rate high with kids.

"8. *Farms:* This one is an all-time favorite with my children and I imagine would be with any youngster living in the metropolitan area. First you find the name of a farmer or dairyman in your area. Then you write a nice letter explaining that your children have never seen a cow close up and would he please let you bring them to his farm some afternoon just to look at the animals and see what goes on on a farm. You'd be surprised at the kind of reaction. We've been invited for lunch. And the farmer will let the kids try to milk a cow and ride a tractor. This one is even fun for me.

"9. *Tree Hut:* If you have a backyard with a tree but know absolutely nothing about carpentry, don't let that stop you from building a house. I acquired some lumber and it took the boys and me one whole week end to get three planks into that tree. Eventually a neighbor man took pity on me, repaired my shaky job, and the kids had a tree hut that was still up when we moved away.

"10. *Cooking:* I was surprised to find that little boys like to dabble in the kitchen as much as little girls. You can spend an entire afternoon teaching them to make fudge, a cake, Jello or cookies. Just make sure they understand they have to clean up the mess.

"11. Friends of mine who have little girls tell me that in addition to the things I've mentioned, a favorite with them is making doll clothes, doll beds and doll houses."

Pamela Speaks

From time to time, I like to interview well-known women alone to find out what they are doing and thinking that could help us. Their lives and our lives are different, of course, because they have more money and more fame, but you'd be surprised how much we have in common. I

166

had two talks with Pamela Mason, a glamorous, talented woman in her mid-forties who divorced actor James Mason after twenty-four years of marriage. Pamela has two children and so many refreshing opinions that my short-hand broke down completely, but these are some of the things I *think* she said.

Raising children alone: "It doesn't hurt children not to have a man around the house. Children have practically always been raised by their mothers and it may be better for them *not* to be confused by conflicting orders."

Protecting Children: "If a child is old enough to drown, he's old enough to be taught to swim. I started teaching Portland (her daughter) when she was four months old. The same thing is true of problems. The day a child bursts into the world, he starts having problems. That's life. He should learn from *you* the world doesn't go 'round just for him, but life can be wonderful, regardless, if he plays it right."

Teaching children about divorce: "The important thing is to explain that the relationship Mommy has with Daddy is different from the relationship Daddy has with his daughter or son. One is his wife of many years, the others is his child. The relationship can't possibly be compared. Though Daddy is not going to live at home any more, it doesn't mean he adores his children any less."

Meeting men: "The women who complain there aren't any men give up too easily. A realistic woman knows she has to go from 'failure to failure' to find a man she can date. There's only one prince charming in every forty or fifty men you meet, and you have to keep circulating."

Where the men are: "It's no good going someplace because men are there. If sailing is what a man likes but you loathe the water, you'll never have anything in common. So forget it. Do something that interests *you*. Take French lessons, art classes or something you enjoy. If you love to dance, go where they dance."

Having fun at parties: "I don't think I ever opened my mouth until I was thirty. I finally found the best thing to do is throw yourself on people's mercy. Don't be afraid to be self-deprecating. You may get people interested right away if you can say, 'I know I'm the last person you'd want to sit next to, but at least you can relax. I don't mind silence. I'm used to it.' Or, 'I'm not much of a conversationalist, but I'm a great cook. I do wish I'd sent

167

a pecan pie to the party instead of coming myself.' Don't bone up with a news magazine. If you really know anything about anything, you're *bound* to be unpopular. Just plunge and the more idiotic you sound the better. For instance if you say, 'I read that the Duke of Windsor is getting a divorce to marry Gloria Swanson,' everybody will gleefully try to straighten you out."

Career girls : "Cleopatra proved back in 39 B.C. that it pays to have something going for you besides looks. A little Egyptian cutie-pie swinging her hips along the Alexandrian streets wouldn't have got a nod from Caesar or Antony. Cleo with her brains, her cunning, her ships, her grain, her armies made the grade. When you get close to a man, it's okay to be smart. It also helps if you have grain and ships."

How to Live on Your Income

A lady recently cornered me and said, "The love-stuff advice is fine, but let's get down to business. How does a woman with two children, no child support and good taste live on a stenographer's salary?"

My dear, you have come to the right person. Having lived on a tiny income for many years, when I was single, I know something about it. You can do it and in style, but you have to scheme. People who aren't smart about money are broke on $25,000 a year. A woman alone can often put them to shame with her shrewdness. Here are the rules:

Guiding principle #1: Don't dribble. Never spend money on anything you don't need badly or that is not going to bring you considerable pleasure. This rules out every last border-line purchase like kitchen gadgets, movies, going out on the town with a girl friend just because *she's* in the mood. You must be ruthless.

Guiding principle #2: Never consider the saving of five or ten cents beneath you. If you can walk the ten blocks and save carfare, walk. You have to be a little stingy about money, but it won't go on forever.

Specific rules: Bring your lunch. Don't get caught in that "ordering something up from the coffee shop" routine. A hamburger and malt is 99 cents plus tip. A carton of cottage cheese or tuna sandwich from home (the highest of protein and good for you) are 25 cents apiece.

Learn to like kidneys, heart and liver—the most nutritional foods you can eat and a fraction of the cost of steak. Plan menus for the week and buy only what is on the list. Don't keep too much food around and eat everything up. Use only fresh fruits and vegetables in season. Skip potato chips, corn chips, soft drinks, candy, olives, pickles—any type of snacks.

Use skim milk instead of whole milk. It's cheaper, less fattening and has all the food value.

Give up smoking and cocktailing for a month. Then stretch it to a second month.

Conserve on gas and lights. Turn off lights when leaving a room. Don't use a full tank of hot water when showering or bathing. If you aren't watching TV or listening to the radio, turn them off.

If the television set breaks down, let it stay broken down and skip the repair bill. What are you missing?

Welcome hand-me-down clothes. Remake them into something chic or get a seamstress friend to help you.

Have only black leather shoes and purse in winter, black patents in the summer. Too many colors and kinds of accessories run into money and are no more chic.

Have the cheapest kind of phone service—party-line or limited calls.

Wash your own hair and do your own nails. Use the cheapest shampoo and hand lotion. There isn't much difference.

Use the cheapest cosmetics. They're all good.

Make your own Christmas cards. They can be a post card with your special poem.

Economy may be the making of you. When we don't have a husband to depend on and to support us, we are forced to be more dynamic and self-sufficient. As for your children, money to burn never built a child's character or even made him any happier so far as we know.

To Sit or Not to Sit—
One Grandmother's View

How much free grandchildren-sitting should a widowed grandmother do?

None, according to a friend of mine who runs the book department of a large department store, has three bubbly grandchildren and has been widowed since 1942.

"You pitch in when an emergency arises and everybody else has konked out," she says. "And your son or daughter should know they can depend on you in times of real trouble, such as illness, but for day-to-day baby sitting I think your kids have to accept the fact that their kids are their *responsibility* and hire a professional sitter when one's needed."

"Isn't that a bit hard-hearted?" I asked. "I understand some young couples depend almost entirely on their parents for baby sitting."

"It's a bad setup for a grandmother," said my grandmother friend. "You've raised your own children as best you know how. In my case I did it without the children's father the better part of their lives. It isn't fair to be pressed into service to care for a whole new set of children. As long as both parents of the grandchildren are living together and have an income, baby-sitting fees should be budgeted in just like rent and clothing."

"But don't you want to *see* your grandchildren?" I asked.

"Who said anything about not seeing them?" my friend said. "I see them all the time, but it's at my invitation. About once a week or at the least every two weeks I take one of the children out for the evening, then back to my apartment to spend the night. The kids take turns and it's considered a real treat to spend the evening with Grandma."

"What do you do when you go out together?" I asked.

"We usually go some place fancy for dinner," she said. "I call up from the store during the day and say, 'If he isn't doing anything, please get Jimmy or Larry or Bob ready and I'll be by to pick him up.' When I arrive the child is all spruced up and chomping at the bit. We go to one of the two or three best restaurants in town and have a really nice dinner. He is allowed to have as many as three Shirley Temple cocktails and the waiter or waitress really makes a big fuss over him. After dinner we go to a big drugstore or variety store and he can pick out any present he pleases up to three dollars. Usually he picks something less. Then we go home and play games. Before bedtime we have ice cream and ginger-ale floats or toasted cheese sandwiches and hot chocolate. Next morning I fix waffles with chocolate syrup and deliver him home to his parents. That's about as much visiting with a child as I can absorb at one time."

"Wouldn't the children enjoy the outing more if their brothers were along?" I asked.

"I don't believe so," she said. "When you're one of three children, you usually enjoy being *the* one who's singled out for attention and you like not having to share the adult with anybody else. Anyway that's my approach to baby sitting and I think it's a good one."

Apparently her grandchildren think it is, too.

SEVEN

FRIENDSHIP, FRIENDSHIP

or,

A Girl Needs a Girl Sometimes

You've heard girls say no doubt, "I'd much rather be around men than women," or "All my best friends are men . . . they're *so* much more interesting." Now what kind of nut-girl is *that*? True, men as a class (as a sex?) are often more interesting because they're out in the world *doing* things that smart but lazy women should be out doing *themselves* (that's a whole other *book*), but a girl can love men only if she is able to have loving friendships with women too, don't you agree? A few words then about friendship with both sexes.

Friendship, Friendship!

Old friends are the best, they say. And I say old friends and frequent bumper crops of shiny new ones are absolutely *de rigueur* for a woman alone!

Her friends often serve as her family. They haul her to and from the airport when she goes on vacation and to and from the hospital if something suddenly goes plonk that should be going plink, plink, plink.

If it weren't for friends, I'd be the first to admit the life of a woman alone could be dismal. With them—and the more the better—it can be great.

These are some rules for upkeep and preservation of old friends, wooing and winning new ones:

OLD FRIENDS

1. Even though your life has changed radically, keep a foot in the past by keeping tabs on one or two old buddies. The older you get, the more pleasurable it is to chat with somebody who remembers you as a cute, pigtailed little girl. (I still correspond with two playmates

from Little Rock Pulaski Heights Grammar School whom I've rarely seen since 1936!)

2. Telephone old friends on birthdays. You can keep up with more that way than if you send cards.

3. Write personal notes on Christmas cards.

4. When old friends seem to be cool or "acting funny," give them a second, third and fifth chance to shape up. It may have been something they ate, or psychiatry is bringing out the "real them." You have to love friends through crises!

NEW FRIENDS

1. Collect them any place you can *track* them—at work, at church, in night school, on trains and buses, on vacations, through contacts (hometown pals should have people look you up who are visiting or moving to your city). I'm not even against bringing home a proper-behaving stranger from a concert or the public library if you're over twenty-five and have been conversing pleasantly. The way you start them talking is to look straight in their eye with a startled-fawn look as though expecting them to say something. Nine times out of ten they will!

2. Ask employees of your company visiting the office from another city to come by for cocktails. (Ask early in the day if it's a man!) You can also include one or two other office folk if you don't want to look too predatory.

3. Into every small or large party you give, pour somebody who's never been to your house before.

FRIENDS TO DISCARD OR NOT CULTIVATE

1. Those who give you the "wish I were somewhere else" fidgets the first minute you're with them. Life is too short to be bored.

2. Friends who don't need you as much as you need *them*. If they're snooty or *always* too busy to talk, take the hint. Other prospects are waiting.

How Are You in the Tact Department?

Good friends are often the loved ones in a single woman's life between beaux, so of course *they* deserve to be treated with loving care. A woman alone also depends on charming and pleasing *new* people, however, to enlarge her social life and so it doesn't hurt to be tactful with strangers either. (It doesn't even hurt a *married* woman to use tact, but somebody else will have to look out for *her*. I'm only concerned with *you*.) Very well then, let's have a little chat about words not to say or write to a new or old friend or even an acquaintance if you want not to bug him.

Never say to anybody, "I think you're confused," even if he is. "Confused" is a "see-red" kind of word, implying the person you call it is muddle-headed and woolly-brained. You can say, "You must be wrong about that," or "Explain it to me again—it doesn't sound quite right" but never just out and say he's confused.

Why tell anybody he looks tired? You really aren't the concerned mother fretting over a frail child. Your friend needs you to *overlook* some things. If he's tired, he hopes it doesn't show. If he *isn't* tired, all the more reason not to put the idea in his head.

Skip saying that a person is the spitting image of somebody else. If you must bring up the resemblance you can say, "You and Jane Fonda remind me of each other," or "I have a friend who's a little bit like you." The person you're *talking* to is the original. The other one is the carbon copy.

I know you wouldn't verbally tear up a girl friend's boyfriend because she loves him, but what about her more casual friends? If she's seeing a lot of certain people, they must have things in common. If you say her friends are creeps, that implies you think she's creepy, too, because she and they blend and fit.

Somebody says, "This is a lousy picture of me." The last thing she wants to hear is that you think it's good and looks just like her. (She hopes she looks *better* than it.) "It really isn't *bad*," you can say. "But I don't think it does you justice."

The most dangerous and least-called-for-analysis I know is that of a girl friend's financial picture, winding up with your telling her where she's going wrong. "For the money you're spending on this place, you could move to a decent neighborhood." (Maybe she's happy in the neighborhood she's in.) Or, "You ought to be able to save at least a quarter of your income if you're careful. The way you're going you'll die broke." Maybe the girl pays an analyst or has a child living with relatives whom she supports. Even if she manages her money abysmally, it's very little business of yours.

Don't send people magazine articles, snapshots and cartoons in the mail and say, "I'd like to have these back, please." Who asked you to send them? If you insist she get a look at them, enclose a stamped, self-addressed envelope.

I think mimeographed letters for the purpose of knocking off all correspondents at once is for the Local Bird-watching Society. Only if you've just returned from Russia or have some mighty lengthy and important developments to report should this mass-production system be used. Almost anybody would rather have a nine-line personal letter than a nine-page mimeographed document directed "to all my dear friends." If you want to read a magazine article, you can always buy a copy of the *Saturday Evening Post*.

Care and Feeding of Girl Friends

An old friend was visiting the other night. We were single girls together and our friendship goes back about fifteen years. In a moment of reminiscing she said, "Do you remember that Valentine's Day party Carmel Jones gave and we made valentines and played charades and all that? Well, I don't think I ever told you this because you were so crazy about him at the time, but Joey Luke gave me a big pitch that night. I just changed the subject and got away from him as fast as I could."

Lo these fifteen years later I felt a catch, a clump, a scrunch in the old rib cage. I know Joey wasn't the most true blue, but I had cared very deeply for him. Instead of a latter-day confession making a woman feel "Aren't I lucky never to have married him, he's even worse than I thought," it may ruin whatever pleasant memories she has left of that period.

Ruth only told me this because I'm happily married now. As a matter of fact, she introduced my husband and me and considers herself the matchmaker incarnate. I do, too! Nevertheless, I am moved to jot down a few rules for the handling of girl friends who are, after all, one of a single girl's dearest possessions.

1. Never gratuitously tell a girl friend any of her beaux has been after you. Chances are he'll never say anything, so there's just no reason for the subject to come up. If he's a rat, she'll find out soon enough. You may think you're trying to bring her to her senses sooner, but it's more likely you're a bit proud and smug. If she's through with him and he's asked you out, that something else. Then you talk.

2. If a friend discusses a boy she's considering marrying and you can't stand him, leave yourself an escape hatch. Don't castigate him vehemently, shudder at her plans and it's going to be impossible for all of you to be friends if the marriage ever takes place. You can say there are some things you don't like about her friend but you can understand his great appeal. It's always safe to say you think she'll be good for him and that she can help him a lot.

3. Never tell a girl friend anything anybody has said that is derogatory about her. You may think you have the soundest of reasons, but getting your guts poked at by listening to second-hand criticism isn't really very good for anybody. If she says somebody doesn't like her, is causing her grief at the office or whatever, you don't have to be a goody-goody and tell her she's imagining things. People know when others don't like them. Your best help, instead of adding more horror tales, is in advising how she might cope with that person and get on with him better.

4. You've heard a rumor that a girl friend in the same office is to be fired. Think carefully. If there's any possibility that she might save her job by talking to her boss before the ax falls, tell her. Chances are it's only a rumor, however, and those fly about everybody, or the decision has already been made and she can't unmake it. Your telling her prematurely will only cause her agony sooner.

5. If you really don't want the story to get around, don't tell it to anybody in the first place. I never can understand girls who say, "I told her about Mary but I told her not to tell." Obviously you couldn't keep the secret yourself—why should you expect more of a girl friend?

Be a Fair-Weather Friend

Despite copious propaganda to the contrary, I think it's often easier to love a friend who's in trouble than a friend who's making good. When the poor darling is down and out you can be Lady Bountiful, Sigmund Freud and Little Mother to her. It's fun. To shower sympathy, wisdom and sisterly advice on a girl who's lost her beau, her job, her husband can be the making of your day. It isn't that you really hate your friend or wish her misfortune. It's just that you're in so much better shape than she for the moment that a wave of well-being practically washes you out to sea. The master wordsmith De La Rochefoucauld described it this way: "In the worst disaster of our friends, there is something not unpleasant to ourselves."

What about a friend who's doing well? As long as she doesn't do better than *you're* doing, you can usually handle the situation and be pleased for her. You are both, so to speak, still skimming around in the same canoe, taking turns paddling ahead. But what if the girl leaves the canoe to get on a yacht? (These metaphors!) What if she's voted Miss Texas, gets a contract with a recording company or marries a millionare? You've got trouble, my friend. I remember a friend of mine winning a contest which netted her not just an ordinary trip to Europe but a beautifully gowned, pampered and petted celebrity-treatment one. I tell you it was Bad Day at Black Rock for little me. It wasn't so much a case of my begrudging Yvonne the trip as it was a case of my asking the fates, "What about *me*? Why didn't it happen to *me*?" (One reason it hadn't, of course, was that I hadn't even entered the contest.)

Eaten up with envy as I was, I gave my friend a new four-leaf clover and a luscious silk stole for her trip. Then I counted the days until I could enter the same contest a year later. I won it, too, as it turned out (this is a true story), although that year they had ten winners and we each got a less fabulous trip than Yvonne's. Still travel is travel.

I think it's phony to claim that such things as jealousy, envy and something close to hate can rage in your soul when a dear friend suddenly zooms to fame or wealth. Once acknowledged, however, I think you jolly well have to make yourself rise above these emotions and be a friend through *thick* as well as thin. Your friend needs you just as much then. You not only pay her the surface compliments and happiness-wishes, but also try to wish her happiness in your heart. Meanwhile, back at the snake pit (your own ego), you set the wheels in motion toward getting to the enviable position yourself. And phooey to that old muck about recognizing your limitations. As far as I'm concerned, you haven't got any. You may not always get as far as your good-luck friend, but you always get *something*. From the lofty vantage-point of my forty-three years, I *know* you don't have to envy a friend's spoils past the initial green-spasm period. Your own spoils are right there for you to take provided you're willing to work exactly as hard as your friend did to get what *she* got.

Do be a fair-weather friend even though it's *much* easier to be the other kind!

The Hilton You

A suffering hostess entreats: "Please give us (women who live alone) your opinion of week-end guests—mostly relatives—who descend without warning. They usually have small children around whom their own lives revolve.

"When they show up, we immediately cancel all engagements (unbeknownst to our unexpected guests), rearrange our furniture to accommodate baby paraphernalia, find sleeping arrangements for all, let our guests rest after their long journey and while they are resting, find something we can do quietly so as not to disturb them, then have all our suggestions as to what to do for entertainment met with a firm, 'No, maybe next time. We thought it would be nice just to visit.'

"So there we all are—we sit and look at each other for a couple of days. Of course we love these people and they mean well. Half the time they've probably come to cheer up the dull existence of the 'lonely old maid.'

"Still, there must be something short of a fifth of Scotch (after they have departed, of course) to alleviate the strain on the nerves of the hostess. Any suggestions?"

Yes, a few. First off, I think this nice-sounding girl probably deserves a whole new set of not-so-obtuse relations. Short of that, it seems to me there's less strain if you don't wistfully expect there not to *be* any.

Strain almost inevitably sets in between people who love each other dearly, but have little in common currently. If you prepare for a day or two of junior-grade self-consciousness and fidgets, they won't depress you so.

As for planning activities which they put the kibosh on right away, what could be simpler than not to plan? Have a little leveling session when they arrive. "Donna Mae, dear, it's just so wonderful to have you and Al here, and I'd be grateful if you'd tell me the truth about something. Would you like me to plan two or three things we could do this evening and tomorrow—I was thinking you hadn't seen our new municipal auditorium, and there's quite a good folk music festival there now, or we could go on a picnic to the lake tomorrow. Or would you just rather stay here and visit?"

If Donna Mae says stay here and visit, think of the wear and tear you'll save on the picnic hamper, to say nothing of the family budget (yours, of course).

As for people not announcing themselves, that is absolute maniacal thoughtlessness and calls for a bit of retaliation. If whoever it is, no matter how blood-related, shows up on your doorstep without warning, I see no reason to cancel any plans you've had—at least not big ones. Visit with the visitors for several hours, then go keep your engagement, explaining that there simply wasn't time to call it off. If you're a real coward, you can embroider whatever is taking you away to be more important than it really is—your date is the nephew of the boss and offending him could spell disaster. Or it's a baby shower at which you're co-hostess—how can you not show?

This bachelor girl didn't mention this problem, but as for visitors who become "stayers," a friend of mine has this solution. After the allotted time is up, but nobody's packing, just announce that the next registered guests are arriving that evening. If that doesn't get action, have two girl friends come over with three suitcases each.

Are You a Girl Who Can't Say No?

If you can't say No to a man, probably you don't want to. I think men and women are quite equally matched—except possibly in Indian wrestling or shot-putting (and how often does a man ask you to do that?). In the more usual contests of strength and will power, you're capable of refusing—just as *he* is if *you're* the aggressor. Men, too, sometimes have to say No.

The kind of No I think it's often hard for a woman alone to say is to an invitation for a social outing that's going to bore the screaming daylights out of her. Then she is often as soft as butter and weak as water because to refuse might hurt somebody's feelings.

Because you're single, people sometimes think they are doing you a big favor to ask you to the begonia festival (when plants in close proximity actually give you hives) or a chamber music society of local businessmen whose effort sounds only slightly better than the neighborhood kids humming through tissue paper and combs.

Now you know I'm for doing everything that might fetch you some new acquaintances or a new outlook or a new interest. And I'm for helping. If somebody needs you to hold the Great Dane while he scrubs it down with detergent, put on the closest thing you have to armor and go hold. But social torture is something else.

A secretary, age thirty-two—long a never-say-no girl—told me about a project she recently had the strength to turn down. Her boss and his wife asked her to come with them to a banquet in a hotel at which achievement awards were being made by a local merchants' group. The tickets were twenty-five dollars a head, everybody was to wear evening clothes, and a lot of civic leaders were going to be there. Big deal!

She didn't have an evening dress (though she possibly could have borrowed one). She didn't know a single civic leader or consider most of them attractive enough to want to sit and gape at across a crowded room. As a working girl, she'd attended plenty of business banquets and knew all about sitting at a table locked in a death grip with the same two people all evening.

"No," she said. "I'm sorry, I can't. I have some girl friends coming over to play bridge, and I'm afraid there isn't time to uninvite them."

It's a shame she had to lie—a shame people put you in a position where you must because they can't imagine how it will be for you.

A wealthy widow asked me to spend the weekend at her home in Lake Arrowhead, California, a few years ago. The scenery was spectacular, the house was beautiful, but the widow was a bore. Her idea of a good evening was going from bar to bar picking up men—or trying to.

I told her the truth. "Dora," I said, "I'm a dead washout at picking up men in bars. It's really torture for me. Why don't you invite somebody who'd be better suited?"

"I wasn't planning to do that at all this weekend," the widow said. "I've got a more interesting project."

We stayed out of bars all right, but our project was taking the loose rugs out of her nine-room house and airing them in the Lake Arrowhead breezes after beating them with a rug mallet. (Her temporary help had refused, and she said it would be good exercise for us.)

I went along with the rug-beating, because I figured it was exactly what I deserved for being such a sucker. A straightforward "I'm sorry, I'm busy" lie would have got me off the hook.

Don't feel guilty when you say no. Reserve the guilt for being too cowardly to refuse. The people with their begonia festivals, musicales and Lake Arrowhead weekends can often find somebody else who would be delighted to join them anyhow. One girl's rug-beating may be another girl's idea of real fun.

Let's You Be a Real Good Guest

"I have to get it off my chest," a very tired lady told me. "An old ex-girl friend of my husband's came to visit us this morning and has just driven out of the driveway at three in the morning. We're ready to climb the walls.

"My husband has an early golf date with a client tomorrow morning. I have the children to get off to Sunday school and had saved all my gardening for then.

"We are both fond of this girl. I don't even mind that

she and my husband have a tremendous rapport based on their past friendship, and sometimes I just sit and listen. But this gal doesn't know when to go home. She was asked for lunch and we were even delighted she could stay for dinner, but enough is enough."

I've gone over this letter with a magnifying glass to see if there isn't a secret cache of venom lodged between the lines, but I can't find it. Sounds like a very tolerant dame to me. I'd have thrown the old flame out right after lunch if I'd been magnanimous enough to have her at all.

A single woman is dependent on her friends, of course, especially her married friends. Two wonderful solid couples more or less adopted me when I was single, and I can't count the holidays and birthdays I was fished off the streets by one or the other to be cheered and entertained.

But let's review the rules for being a good guest. It goes without saying that you have to be more considerate than the girl mentioned in the letter and know when to go home.

Dinner party: Wear something pretty, and don't make it too casual (unless they positively specify). I'm against "when in doubt, underplay it." A girl who's dressed up in chic black when she *could* have got away with her little beige knit is very flattering to the hostess.

Bring a little present (fresh lilacs, thin mints, a bottle of wine). It's old-fashioned, but nice.

If the dinner companion they've selected for you is ninety-three, be the divinest dinner companion that ever happened to him. Sure they should have given you somebody better, but being a living doll to him will convince them you can handle a prince next time.

Conform. No, it won't kill your immortal soul. Diplomats do it. You're a swinging, off-beat Greenwich Village type, but the party is square. Tone down the "real you" for the evening and at least be square enough not to make everybody uncomfortable. You're a country girl among the sleek and sophisticated. Don't put on airs, but refrain from discussing the trouble you had with the clothes dryer this morning and just listen if necessary.

Help with the chores, but only those that show you off nicely. No, it isn't selfish. You really shouldn't be grubbing about in the kitchen before or after the party, but you can certainly pass sandwiches to guests on the terrace or mix a highball for the thirsty.

Feel out the situation between host and hostess. If he's far too fond of girls already, don't flirt. If he's a bit paunchy and run down, nothing could flatter his wife more than for you to find him absolutely fascinating.

If the man who brought you to a party knows everybody, but you don't, and he deserts you, concentrate on the women. If they like you, they'll see that you get a whack at conversation with their husbands.

Weekend guest: Stay with the host's schedule. The girl who insists on sleeping just that one more hour (after all, doesn't she work all week and deserve it?) or who wants to eat a tiny bit later than the others can drive everybody mad—and not ever get asked back.

Making your own bed and straightening the bathroom makes a huge impression on the hostess. If there's help, the gesture is even more touching and appreciated.

Resist the impulse to bring nineteen changes of clothes. Girls who are always disappearing for their next change are considered a bit of a bore by more seasoned guests.

Even if you'd rather take poison than row out to the lighthouse or watch the apricots being picked, go along with the plans. The people who thought them up thought you'd enjoy them.

Dear John or Dear Just Anybody

Listen, there's something I should have told you ages ago that can brighten up your life, and I forgot. It's writing letters.

I can see you sniffing and turning to the next page without further ado. All right, sniff, but I tell you you're missing out on a gold mine rewardwise if you don't let letters into your life.

What kind of letters? Who to?

Well, they should be to people who have done something you admire, to whom not many other people probably will be writing. If you write them a sweet letter, they will usually write you back, and you have all this activity going on in your mailbox.

Everybody likes to get mail, now admit it. Yet I know some single women who faithfully pad down to the mailbox every day hoping for mail, but the good fairies would

186

have to have sent it because they forgot to plant any letter seeds.

It isn't a major thrill getting a letter—unless it's from *him* or from the bureau that tracks down missing heirs—but it is a minor thrill and can be a continuing one week after week if you do your homework.

These are the people you can write to:

The man or woman who has written an article or book you particularly liked.

A local store whose windows give you pleasure every day you drive or walk past them.

The grocery store whose box boys or check-out people are particularly friendly and honest and helpful.

Anyone who is contributing toward making his community or the human race a little happier—a research team, a civic leader, a doctor, a charity worker. (It might not even be someone concerned with the human race. You could write to the society that finds homes for pets or a person who is supporting fifteen brindle strays herself.)

A dress designer or manufacturer whose clothes have made you feel prettier year after year.

An architect who has designed a stunning house or office building. (The name will usually be on a sign outside during the construction.)

The hotel where you had a nice visit. Or somebody *in* the hotel. "Dear Gino: My hairstyle was so pretty I considered staying up all night so I could sneak it back to Des Moines unrumpled."

The restaurant where the food was fantastic.

It's easy to find prospects. As you read, drive around, listen and observe. Certain people will strike you as extremely admirable and turn on a big yes in your head. So reward them. The least-likely answerers will be movie stars, recording artists, famous politicians (with the exception of your congressman, who can be quite attentive). Most of the people just get too much mail to respond personally.

I think my happiest letter exchange was with a paper box company in California. Its owner had painted all the smokestacks pink, lavender, turquoise, green and butter yellow. It was simply uplifting. You'd be stuck in heavy traffic getting in or out of L.A. on the freeways —there's one stretch where it's always bad—and at the height of your pique you'd look over and see these cuckoo smokestacks and have to laugh.

Well, I got the name off the side of the building, looked up the address in the phone book and wrote the president a letter. He wrote a letter back saying he was framing *my* letter (nobody had ever thanked him before), and it was enough to give you the sniffles.

What about writing pan letters? Well, sometimes people need criticizing, of course. You probably won't get a letter back, however, and you'll miss the inside thrill of having made somebody happy.

There's usually some way to track down an address. Most public libraries, train, bus and air terminals keep a complete file of phone books from other cities.

In writing appreciation, keep your letter reasonably short—the idea is not to pour out your life's story, but to pay a compliment. Type if you can, but legible writing is fine. Don't worry about saying it fancy.

Gifts and Loans for Men

How big a gift should you get a man you are head-over-heels in love with?

It would depend on your income, of course, but I don't think extravagant gifts for men are ever called for unless you're married to the man.

I didn't dare bring this subject up before Christmas, because people would have accused me of being anti-healthy-economy if not downright negative.

Nothing could be further from the truth. I'm all for gifts for everyone you feel like giving them to—the oftener the better. I just don't think big, expensive, put-you-in-hock gifts for men are a good idea. (Don't fuss, Mr. Merchant. I think they're indispensable for women!)

This brings up the subject of money in general in connection with men. If you're more solvent than a man, how many restaurant checks do you pick up? In most dating situations, I think a man pays. He takes you where he can afford to go, and that settles it. You *go*, too, if you like the man.

It's all right for a girl to take a man to dinner in a restaurant occasionally if she feels he deserves it. Arrange to sign for the check or pay it away from the table so you don't embarrass your friend. Certainly you reciprocate restaurant dinners from him with home-cooked ones by you. That's a lovely arrangement, and I hope it never gets to be the other way around—you have to take *him* out every time he barbecues a hamburger for you in his apartment.

About loaning money to men, I take a very dim view of that altogether, though perhaps I am more cautious (and stingy) than a girl needs to be. All I know is that *I* managed without borrowing money through all the lean years when I helped support a family on a secretary's pay.

Therefore, when a man suggests borrowing money from you, I can't help advising you to say to yourself:

How come I am in a position to have this money to loan him, and how come he is in the position of having to borrow it? Granted, there are emergencies, but how did he get into this emergency? If he had been as careful and frugal and practical as I have been most of my life, would he now be in this pickle?

If the answer is that he hasn't been as careful, why should you now give him the benefit of your years of thrift? Obviously you gave up things to have the money. Why turn it over to him who didn't give up a thing regardless of his present straits?

If you want to make the loan, at least know your borrower, as they say at the bank. Know where he works (he *does* work, doesn't he?). Have a specific schedule as to when the loan will be paid back—not just some vague, indefinite future.

If it is a sizable loan you're helping him with, I should think you would co-sign a note at the bank. That means he pays the bank back and you only become involved if he fails to meet the payments. If he can't *get* that kind of loan, we're back to my original suspicions! How *come* he can't? Banks love to loan money, and if his credit isn't good enough for *them*, who are you, Lady Bountiful, to take the chance they won't?

They're All Married but You

There are all kinds of loneliness, and one of the

189

loneliest kinds I know of is that which is sometimes experienced by a single woman in a particular group of married people.

Most married couples are marvelous with their single-girl friends, but I'm talking about a situation in which perhaps a man has taken you to a party at the home of people you don't know. You would think he had brought them a garbed-in-feathers aborigine for all the effort that's made to get to know you.

The conversation swirls and eddies around you by the hour without touching a single subject on which you could possibly discourse. The group thoroughly masticates several parties you haven't been to, doings at the country club you don't belong to and housing problems that couldn't possibly be yours because they only concern people who live on five-acre lots.

Perhaps there's a slight conversational nod in your direction toward the end of the evening. The Gracious Hostess finally says, "Oh, yes, and what kind of work do you do, Miss Applebottom?" By that time you almost can't remember what kind of work you do, but as you gather your strength and explain, you realize you might as well be talking to a Maypole. Anybody who doesn't do what she does (care for children, home, husband—in that order) isn't doing anything at *all*, in her opinion.

Abject loneliness can also be expressed by a married woman who's a stranger at a party. I went to a very chichi one the other evening. I didn't know anyone and joined a group of three girls. (That was my first mistake. There *were* men there.) They were talking about girls' finishing schools when I joined them. That would have been fine for a while. But after fifteen minutes, I'd used up every dab I knew about Finch and Miss Chapin. There was still no acknowledgment that I'd joined the group or any effort to find out who I was.

Another married woman told me of being at a "strange party" the other night at which a little group of women was discussing wigs. My friend and another girl confessed they were wearing them. The hostess, without batting an eye, said to my friend, a stranger, "I'd rather presumed yours was a wig, but I'm surprised to pieces about *yours*, Madie. It looks so natural."

Why are hostesses and guests sometimes rude? When they are rude to a married woman, I can only assume it's because they don't have good manners. In the case of "including out" a single woman, I think it's often that they just don't know what to make of little unmarried you.

Some women still feel it is a little immoral for a woman not to have a husband. They may possibly think you're after their husbands, which is so rarely the case. (You wouldn't *have* them.) Sometimes women and even men subconsciously pick on you because they are "pickers" on what they consider the underdog. They must have somebody to feel better than.

My only suggestion for getting through such an evening is to smile a lot and keep listening as though the conversation *mattered*. People can't really tell how bored you are from the outside.

You Have a Guy—She Doesn't

One of the most delightful young single women I know told me a rather horrifying tale of her treatment at the hands of a "generous" single sister. It went something like this:

"Ginny Ann called and asked if I'd like to have dinner with her and the boy she's been going steady with. He got on the phone and asked me, too.

"It was very sweet of them, of course, and I said yes. Well, they picked me up, and it was one of the most wretched evenings I've ever lived through. I had to sit there like a lump while she patted his face, squeezed his arms, rubbed against his shoulder and talked baby talk. He buttered her bread, cut her meat, kissed her ears and seemed to be about to gobble her up.

"When we walked along the street, she kept bumping him with her hip. I'm younger than both of them and no fuddy-duddy, but I honestly didn't know which way to look. It was all so Braille. I really was angry, and it wasn't envy. I just resented being put in the position of being a captive audience at love's young feast."

Another young woman told me of being invited to the movies by her roommate and her roommate's date one evening. The date let her stand in line and buy her own ticket. In the movie, he put his girl friend in the center, the roommate on the aisle, and he and the girl friend became entwined like ivy. "I couldn't figure out why they'd asked me," said the roomie.

Married couples are sometimes guilty of "showing off" for a single girl, too. A wife will positively ooze affection as her husband lights her cigarette. A husband will act as though girls had just been invented as he ogles his wife.

Possibly their motives are unselfish. They may think they should present a picture of ostentatious wedded bliss so the single-girl guest will be encouraged to want to be married herself. They should realize, of course, that a single woman can spot true love and affection without having the greatest little show on earth performed for her benefit.

"I've noticed a great deal of knee patting and hand holding just before the divorce plans are announced," says one caustic single girl. "Maybe it's some last-ditch stand to keep it from happening," she adds.

Married couples may have forgotten how it feels to be the third person. Single women themselves have no excuse for gauche behavior. Here are some ground rules:

If you like another girl well enough to include her in your evening, like her well enough to see she has a wonderful time. Explain to your young man, if any explaining is necessary, that you are *both* his date. This is a threesome, not a twosome plus an extra girl.

In the capacity of host, he will pay for whatever you both eat and drink and for all the entertainment. If you want to help him, that's your business, but don't do it in front of the guest. If the other girl offers to pay, she should be refused hands down. If she's really sincere about repaying, she can have you both to dinner later. There are occasions when everybody goes dutch, but we're describing a more formal evening.

Whatever gallant gestures the man is making toward his own lady love should be made to the other girl, too. He brings you both a single yellow rose. He lights both girls' cigarettes and butters bread for both.

He should walk with both of you on his arm, if that kind of walking is to be done. He can even hold both girls' hands briefly if he's the affectionate type. If you can't trust him, what are you doing bringing another girl into the scene anyway?

As for love stuff, keep that down to a simmer. It won't

kill you. Obviously, it's you who have the beau. You don't have to climb all over him to show he's yours.

May I suggest another bit of behavior if you're on a date with or without a girl friend in tow? I think the sexiest-looking couples, if you want to be thought of as positively maddening to men, are the ones who sort of smolder, but never ignite into a full-fledged conflagration (at least until they get out of sight).

Looking into your eyes when you talk, touching hands occasionally and the whispered word betoken greater esteem from your man in public than having him clasp you to his chest like a life jacket.

Tell Them How to Mix and Match You

So they have a man they want you to meet. Hooray! Before they gum everything up by arranging an awkward meeting, why not turn over the ground rules to the fixer-upper? You could mail them to him/her in a plain envelope or slip them under the apartment door some rosy dawn so you don't actually have to confront the date arranger with your demands.

RULES FOR DATE ARRANGERS

1. If you're a married woman turning a bachelor who has been your long-time friend over to me, search your soul and be sure you really *want* to turn him over to me. Be sure you aren't giving him to me because you secretly have a crush on him yourself and feel it would be less awkward if he had a girl friend with him when you, he and your husband all get together.

2. If you're a single girl delivering me one of your old beaux, please search your motives, too. Now I'm not saying yellow teeth which habitually have a toothpick dangling from them will revolt me. We may have *chemistry*. I just want to be sure you aren't giving me someone you're still latently fond of and the minute you find he likes *me* you'll want him back again.

3. Is the man you're fixing me up with married by any chance? I may *like* him. Married men can be quite wonderful unfortunately, but I just don't want to spend any un-

193

necessary time daydreaming about the possibility of our going on a Bermuda honeymoon together.

4. Please don't tell this man anything silly about me and don't tell me anything silly about him beforehand. I mean don't build me up as Jayne Mansfield (that would take *some* building) or him as Rock Hudson when we're actually just two average people. When you've expected too much from a blind date, the shock and let-down are horrendous. Play it cool with advance data. All you have to say is that you have a nice man you want me to meet and tell him you have a nice girl. We'll find out about each other later.

5. Don't worry if we have little in common. Two schoolteachers may absolutely hate each other. I may *flip* for a man who is fifteen years older than me, born in the wrong zodiacal sign and who makes a living doing something I can't understand even when you draw *diagrams*. If we're both friends of yours, that gives us enough in common to go on. It's assumed you wouldn't have a friend so revolting I couldn't get through an evening with him, *would* you?

6. If you could let me know in advance when the meeting is going to be, that would be dandy. I could have clean hair, uncircled eyes and get a good grip on myself. If you can't give me any advance notice, however, I'll show up anyway.

7. Your quiet and gracious living room might be a better meeting place than a crowded cocktail party or noisy restaurant. If it *is* your living room, perhaps your four exuberant little children could have been put to bed first. (Who can compete with kids, noise-wise and charm-wise?)

8. Don't brag about me in this man's presence. I'll manage to let him know all the things I'm good at and know a lot about, never fear.

9. Don't be too cagey about what we're all doing getting together. I mean you don't have to pretend it's an *accident*. The purpose of this evening is for your two friends to meet. It's very much like sending someone to be interviewed for a job. He *knows* it's an interview. Be happy and feel perfectly at ease about the fact that you know two people you can introduce who might come to like one another. If there's any way to let us be alone for a few minutes, that would be a good idea, too. Maybe you

can have him walk me to my car or something. A girl alone with a man usually is at her best.

10. Don't be on the phone with your "What did you think of her?" and "What did you think of him?" before sunup the next morning. We'll both clue you in in good time. The first meeting may not have been decisive and more time may be needed.

P.S. I hope you don't think I'm being too hard to please. If this man should by any chance turn out to be the answer to my prayers, I'll remember *you* in my prayers every night for the rest of my life. I may even send over a ruby and diamond bracelet.

Hot- and Cold-Running Friends

We've talked about hot-and-cold-running men who need you desperately one week, but a week later you might as well have galloping scrofula for all they seem to want to be around you.

We don't know for sure what happens. It is almost never anything you did, wore, said, cooked or played on the hi-fi. The young man just got over his great need, but he forgot to tell you.

Some of a girl's girl friends and some of her married friends can be almost as confusing as her beaux. It's now-they-need-you, now-they-don't, but they forgot to tell you. Naturally you worry about what you did wrong.

Someone told me this story recently: "This young friend of mine has been almost slavish in her devotion to me, although she is happily married to a charming boy, and heaven knows I adore men. The girl and her husband are six years younger than I.

"Madelyn used to do everything but sit at my feet to hear my pearls of wisdom about life. On my birthday she gave me not one present, but a whole basketful, gorgeously wrapped. Whenever I went to dinner at her house, she cooked a Lucullan feast.

"I've never thought there was anything peculiar about her devotion. She was just as lovely to my beaux when they visited me. Nevertheless, she used to stick so close to me, it was like pulling off adhesive to get loose.

"Then two weeks went by when I didn't hear from her.

She always called oftener than I, because I was simply too busy at work to have the long conversations she liked. I finally came to and got on the phone, figuring she must be ill.

"Everything was fine. She'd just been busy. I didn't hear from her again for two more weeks, so I called again.

"Same routine, only this time she wasn't home. I left word, and it took her four days to return the call.

"For somebody who's complained that a friend was sticking like adhesive, I realize I'm being a little inconsistent to worry about what has happened, but I can't help wondering.

"We talk seldom now, but when we do I could swear nothing is wrong. I haven't offended her. She isn't mad. It's just hard to understand why she's gone from avid admirer to cool cookie practically overnight."

There's probably a deep-seated, cuckoo reason for this young lady's on-and-then-off devotion. I'm not even going to take a stab at it except to say the younger girl obviously doesn't need her older friend anymore and may have gone on to another crush.

The new crush could be literature, music or this time even a man. Don't think a thing about it. People's needs, especially immature people's needs, change hourly, and they never call up to explain. You can only counteract this by being constant with your own friends.

Sometimes you, too, want to see less of a girl friend, but don't know how to go about it (men are a different subject and will require space of their own).

To cool a girl friendship, I never believe in coldness or rudeness when you do talk or see each other. But you simply instigate fewer and fewer of these meetings yourself. Even though you're always a doll when you chat, your friend finally concludes, if she has any sense at all, that old Franny is just awfully busy these days. She shouldn't be deeply hurt by a gradual let-down.

EIGHT

THE AGES OF WOMAN

or,

From the Terrible Twenties to the Glowing Years After Thirty ... Forty ... Yes ... Fifty

I never believe in lying about your age unless you're twelve trying to place a two-dollar bet at the daily double window. Yet every time I've ever written that a girl should say how old she *really is* I hear derisive cries that "A woman who would tell her age would tell *anything*," etc., etc., etc. I guess you *do* have to be a bit of a blabbermouth to give out your birth date, but there's something so great about *every* age (with the possible exception of the early twenties) that I never can see any reason not to tell. People the same age as *you* are happy and comfortable when you do tell, especially if they're lying and pretending not to be anywhere near the age you just said you were. Anyway, this is about the different ages a woman goes through and how to cope during each of them.

The Terrible Twenties

Are you about twenty-four years old, insanely in love with the wrong man and unable to give him up? Is he clobbering you emotionally?

Are you twenty-two, add or subtract a few months, and spending most of your salary and half your time in the doctor's office?

Are you twenty-eight, convinced you were meant for elegant salons among fashionable people but still going to the movies with the same kooky men?

Are you in your twenties and *anywhere* certain *no* man is ever going to ask you to marry him?

Isn't it hell to be young? I don't know how anybody lives through it. I'm talking about the years from twenty to thirty, which should be the most glamorous of your life and very often are the most gruesome. In your childhood and teens somebody looks after you and you are pretty much sheltered from major burdens. In your thirties and forties you have your sea legs and can cope with just about anything.

In your twenties, usually anything that *can* go wrong will go wrong and you have not had the experience to cope with it. Also, the lovely things you *have* you don't appreciate.

You find fault with your looks—the same looks which, if you had them at forty, you'd shoot off Roman candles at high noon to celebrate. In those same twenties, your sex appeal is automatic and inexorable for most men, yet alll you do is snap and complain because men want you physically. The future is so fearful and uncertain. Will *he* ever come along so you can stop worrying about getting married? Will you ever have the lovely possessions and Harper's Bazaar-photographed life you admire so much?

I remember my own twenty-seventh year—deeply infatuated with a Don Juan, only I didn't know he was a Don Juan. I thought if a man was a bachelor he was *eligible* and if he wasn't proposing and kept chasing girls, there must be something wrong with me. Twice a week I was at the doctor's office taking tests—allergy tests, blood tests and whatever was supposed to be positive was always negative and vice versa. Money was so scarce that I ate for three days on the remains of a lavish office party. I'd been in charge and just took everything left over home in big paper cups.

Well, my friends, things get better. They really do. Somehow your body shakes down or shapes up in your thirties and stops malfunctioning. (This may simply be a matter of treating it better and not living on office party snacks any longer.)

If you keep plugging at your job, the money gets better, too. As for the men, you may not slough off the Don Juans completely, but their charm wears a little thin. One year you may even fall in love with a lovely man who can love you back.

It's so silly not to be able to enjoy what you have when you have it, but it was ever thus—youth wasted on the young and all that. I want to gather up all the "twenties girls" who write me and tell them that life isn't really that serious, that it's even a tiny bit amusing and glorious and sexy. But you can't josh a twenty-three-year-old girl. She is busy being Camille.

Since I can't get through to *them*, I will just say to *you* in your thirties, forties and fifties: Don't let me hear a word about *you* wanting your youth back! If you had it, you see, you'd also be stuck with that worried, frantic, will-it-ever-turn-out-right twenties attitude, and surely you wouldn't want to go through *that* again.

Sex and the Older Woman

Just how long *can* a woman remain attractive to men? Have they pretty much quit looking at you as an object of desire by the time you're forty?

Good heavens, *I* don't know. I know what they *tell* you, which is that women stay attractive to them forever, but it would be more convincing if, while they were telling you this, their gaze wasn't spread like taffy over the movements of some nubile creature across the room dancing the Watusi.

I'll tell you what I *think* is the case. I think a woman can continue to have men interested in her when she is forty, fifty, sixty and even older if she continues to be interested in *men*. She can't captivate *all* men but one man will get her message and that's all it takes—one good man. Most people get hooked on somebody who finds *them* irresistible. There's nothing so aphrodisiac as the sure knowledge that the person you're with can't keep his hands off you. The older woman who hasn't "resigned" from men is going to continue to please them.

I do think there are certain qualifications to have which will help you with the cause. Here they are.

1. A little money. Don't tell me it isn't *fair*, I'm not interested in your complaints. I just know an older woman who has enough money to live comfortably, dress beautifully and travel is usually more exciting to men than one who is trying to borrow a hundred dollars.

2. Great looks. That's a matter of working on your face to keep it smoothed out and fresh-looking and making up with skill. You must do your double-chin exercises and your everywhere-else exercises, too.

3. Barrels of charm. Surely you've learned by now to

say what people want to hear and to be a good listener. There are never enough good listeners to go around— especially depth ones—and you *be* one.

4. An unobtrusively good cook. Most any young thing can get up a gourmet meal by slaving for four days straight. You should be able to serve up light, greaseless, inspired meals without seeming to fuss.

5. Big interest. You must know by now I feel the *best* interest for a woman alone is her work but you can also be more attractive to men if you are caught up with a charity, school, hospital or fund-raising drive than if your only interest is *you*.

6. Elegance. This can definitely be the quality that separates the enviable older woman from the one who wonders where the men are. How do you get to be elegant? Some people say you *can't* when you're young and I would go along with that. Little things contribute to the impression when you're older. You pin a fresh flower to your blouse, carry a snowy perfumed hanky instead of the usual cleansing tissue. You have a few *good* suits and dresses and wear them often. There's a bowl of *fresh* not artificial fruit on your coffee table. You use cloth napkins at a dinner party. You know what's new in cinema, books, art, politics. Being elegant comes on gradually but you'll like it and cultivate it.

7. Quietness. A frantic, jittery, desperately-trying-to-please older woman drives people up the walls. A serene one with a serene face is a pleasure to be around. Men relax with her.

8. Children in their place. You adore them but don't live *through* them.

But You Look Ten Years Younger!

Says a female attorney I know, "I'm thirty-nine but look ten years younger and have a great many invitations for dates."

Her statement depresses me. Why do we have to pretend to be younger? In order to get married? Men marry women in their forties, fifties, and sixties every day. Many times they even marry women who are older than they are. Girls who do bounce four years off their age and never confess

202

to their husbands tell me it's a nightmare alley. They have to "remember" to have graduated from Manual Arts High School in 1943 instead of 1939 (and dodge old classmates like the plague) and not remember certain stars on the late late show and not have been old enough to vote for Roosevelt. It's a mess.

Is the reason for wanting to look ten years younger so that men will date us? The way you get men to date you is to look as sensational as you can and be tremendously interested in men. Girls of nineteen who can't do this go without dates, while women of fifty who can, have as many dates as they want.

Do you say you're thirty-five instead of fifty-one because companies aren't hiring older women? That's possibly a legitimate reason to fib but they usually outwit you by requiring a birth certificate. Or, if you aren't found out, you lose out on the start of your Social Security payments.

Chronological age is something you can't do anything about and that's why I resent having to be ashamed of it. People should be ashamed of their mean, miserable dispositions, the way they carp at the people who love them, important things they *could* do something about and *don't*. Yet I know a dreamy girl of twenty-nine who passes for twenty-two. Men like younger girls she says. How insecure can you be to start deducting birthdays in your twenties? And what kind of men are these?

A beautiful actress said in an interview the other day, "I'm forty and I don't care who knows it." The truth is the lady is forty-six and apparently *does* care who knows it. How much better to have told her real age so people could really marvel at how glorious she looks. By way of contrast, another actress I know is forty-seven and says so and is one of the most attractive women alive. When she wears her red chiffon and you can see down her neck to simply fabulous cleavage and her blonde hair and blue eyes and fair skin are all dazzling you, she is an absolute dish. Why should people patronize her by saying she looks thirty-four?

Obviously I don't mean you shouldn't look as ravishing as you can and borrow some of the other attributes of youth as well—curiosity, resilience and quickness to forgive enemies—but I think your own age will do very nicely, thank you.

Delectable After Forty

The other night at a dinner party, a happily married man was waxing absolutely rhapsodic over a divorcee friend of ours.

"She's delicious," he said. "She's so wholesome, but . . . well . . . so enticing! If I were going to leave Sheree for anyone . . ." And then his voice trailed off.

I thought we might learn a few things from this dreamboat who was forty-three on her last birthday. Tracking her down the next day, I said, "Gloria, would you care to tell me so I can tell a lot of other people *exactly* what you do to stay young and sexy?"

"I'll write you a list," she said, and did. This is the list:

Be yourself. Don't put on airs.

Be childlike in your enthusiasm.

Remember you *are* what you eat.

Walk beautifully. Don't waddle, wiggle, wriggle or undulate.

Exercise *everything* . . . toes, face, even your tongue, but not by talking.

Keep your voice young and firm.

Sit still.

Don't sprawl.

Keep busy. Get involved.

Smile.

Be sure your clothes are no more important than you are.

Wear only your most becoming colors.

Make up carefully before you leave the house, then forget it.

Love something very much, even if it's just a puppy.

Kind of an unexciting little list, isn't it? Like something a maiden aunt might give a young girl going off to boarding school! But do you know what's important about that list? Inherent in its every rule is grinding, rigid self-discipline! Yes, you must exercise. No, you must not eat mounds of corn chips and fudge sundaes. Yes, you must *care* about the work you do.

Oh, how divine it would be to have a nice short cut to physical attraction and not to have to bother with all that work and self-denial! You can skip it after twenty but after forty there very likely isn't any other way to stay sexy! These kind of dull "do's and don'ts," according to Gloria (and I couldn't agree more), are what separate the faded and "had-it" girls born before 1923 from those men still pine for!

The Friendly Forties

Every age can seem to have been the best of all possible ages to a woman who isn't that age any more. In retrospect she was so young, so glandular ("sexy"). Everything was so possible.

One thing that makes any past age seem so delicious is that *now* you know how everything turned out. The terror is plucked from the period, leaving only the charm and nostalgia. Obviously you were a princess at the time and didn't know it.

As far as the twenties go, when you actually *are* twenty-two, twenty-four or twenty-nine, you feel about as princessy as a tornado victim. The thirties, I believe, are less fraught with plagues, more filled with satisfactions, but they, too, have their bad moments. Right now I'd like to dwell on an age I think you can actually enjoy while you're *in* it— almost any year in the forties.

If my big hooray for the forties sounds like pure rationalization—after all, it's the only age I've got—you can send me a big cake of soap to wash out my typewriter! I think I'm being sincere when I say:

I like the forties because you finally have a kind of line on yourself. You stop expecting yourself to act and think like somebody else.

You are more comfortable with men than you've ever been in your life. Perhaps the opposite sex seems just a fraction less opposite, but it also seems less like "the enemy." You can now embrace men warmly as part of the race—not hedge and sniff around them in deep suspicion.

You no longer have to worry about whether a man likes you simply because you're a sexy dish but doesn't care about you as a person. You still look great, but if he's smitten, it's got to be because you have other things going for you. (You may find this depressing but I find it heartwarming!)

Speaking of loving friends. You have a passel of them, both male and female. At Christmas time when you send out cards, you run through them barefoot.

You can cook a decent meal and give a decent party. You don't worry anymore that the thing may bomb and it rarely does.

You are apt to be more financially secure.

You're helping some people, and helping them takes your mind off yourself.

When you take it into your head to take on a project—vacation in the Mexican jungle, plunge into oils up to your breast bone—invisible hands do not seem to be holding you back. You are finally very nearly your own boss.

Your figure is still good.

You know at last what kind of clothes look good on you and have stopped mucking around with the others. You're a little elegant, even glamorous.

Instead of facing every unpleasant situation and heading straight through the flames, you've discovered that sometimes the best tack is to avoid the wearing friend, the dull, loud party, the tedious club chairmanship. Instead you hide out among things you enjoy.

You believe fervently in certain causes. Though you don't take out after everybody who disagrees with a sharp machete, people do indeed consider you *someone*, not just another female.

Never Mind the Dialogue, Where Are the Men?

I've been contending for so long that if an older woman keeps her figure exercised, has some interesting work to do and is genuinely concerned about other people, the men will materialize. I still believe it. However, I no sooner get the words out of my mouth than somebody says, "Yes, but where do you meet men?"

To answer this question, I consulted a Los Angeles psychotherapist (his name must be withheld) who has had fine results in helping many young and older women find a more meaningful life. My authority says:

"The question that each middle-aged or older woman must ask herself is: What am I interested in? What do I like to do? What might I learn to like to do? Which of these activities are ones that also attract men? Solitary hobbies such as furniture refinishing or knitting are artistic but don't inspire the forming of social clubs.

"Some outdoor pursuits you might consider are tennis, badminton, golf, croquet, skating, horseback riding, skiing, hunting and swimming. (Please note: my advice about keeping your body in shape would come in handy here. You don't want to have a heart attack on the first outing.) Indoor possibilities are chess, checkers, bridge, Great Books classes, sketching, painting, sculpture, music and photography. All these have fans who have become enthusiastic enough to form clubs.

"Once you decide where you want to plunge," the doctor continues, "consult your local newspaper for club meetings or activities. If there is no other way to participate, go register in an adult class in the local high school or junior college.

"The thing to remember," he warns, "is that you cannot fake enthusiasm. Experts usually like to help a novice who is genuinely interested in their hobby or specialty, but the interest must be genuine, not phony. If you are an alive and curious person, you'll get along fine. It may be necessary for you to try several activities before finding one in which you can take a genuine delight, however.

"The catch to all this," the doctor says, "is that you may be afraid to try all these new things 'at your age.' You'd rather overcome your fear and *then* do them. Unfortunately that isn't the way it works. You must engage in the activity you select while you're still a little afraid and in doing, overcome your fear.

"As for the dance clubs, lonely hearts clubs—some are legitimate and some are not," the doctor states. "There is no way to know in advance. You have to try. Inquiries to Better Business Bureaus and district attorneys' offices can bring warnings against groups about which complaints have been made."

There now. This all sounds like very sensible advice to me. Let me know how you make out.

Happy Fiftieth Birthday

"I knew my fiftieth birthday was going to be a traumatic experience," said a very attractive divorcee friend. "I got through the forty-eighth and forty-ninth all right because they were still the forties, but this one I knew was going to be rough. I decided to celebrate it by changing a few things in my life starting that very day.

"I didn't pick big things because I could never have made them stick. I just picked small things I could be enthusiastic about and which I'd intended changing for years. Would you like to know what they were?"

"I'd be fascinated," I said.

My friend then rattled off this list:

"1. I went to the grocery store on my birthday and bought everything a different brand, different flavor, different cut, different size than I had ever bought before. It wasn't too easy because at fifty you've shopped a few times and *cooked* a few things.

"Nevertheless, I found canned onion soup and little mandarin oranges I'd never tried before, crystallized ginger and mango juice. I also bought veal kidneys and a whole fish, head and all, which would be a new cooking experience. I'm going to include something new and 'foreign' every week.

"2. I started eating six small meals a day instead of three big ones. The doctor had suggested it ages ago and I like it. For breakfast I have two scrambled eggs and coffee, nothing else; mid-morning a banana and orange-juice cocktail; lunch is one tomato stuffed with tuna; mid-afternoon I have whole-wheat bread and a hunk of cheese, dinner is a hamburger patty; before bed I have apple, carrot and raisin salad. It's fun.

"3. I weeded my lipsticks down to three shades and three only—true red, orange-pink and true pink—but I got in three sets of each. One for home, one for my purse, one for my travel case. Saves scrambling and switching every time you go out of town or out to lunch. I think at fifty you need to simplify your life and arrange to take off on outings without such a fuss.

"4. I cleaned out every last scrap of clothing I hadn't worn for two years even if it was a once-expensive evening dress or riding breeches. If I haven't worn them in two years, I said to myself, the outlook isn't good and somebody else can get the good from them.

"5. I mentally crossed three friends off my list. We go back so many years I'd never been able to stay away completely before, but now I mean to. One is a vicious gossip who I'm sure gossips the same way about me with others;

another is 'anti' practically everything I believe in and I don't see what we have in common. The third is a plain bore. I've invested enough years with them and now I only want to be with people who make me feel *good*.

"6. I quit that very day offering unsolicited advice to my kids. I can't remember either of them ever taking any of it, so who was I kidding! When my son or daughter bears down on me now about getting rid of this house which is 'too big for me,' or learning to drive which I don't want to do, I tell them the advice-truce works both ways. We are going to let each other manage our own lives and be good friends!

"I hate to tell you this, but it's one of the most satisfactory birthdays I ever had!"

In Love with a Younger Man!

A mature and charming widow I know is quite seriously in love with a young artist. He is twenty-nine, and she is fifty-four. She's awfully good to him. She helps find buyers for his paintings among her friends and business associates. She occasionally helps him out with rent money and has been known to lend him her car for as much as three days at a time (which means borrowing one for herself). Marriage is out. He is married to his work, and she realizes he's too young!

Friends who love the lady are as apprehensive as typhoid-shot patients awaiting the needle. What's to become of dear Muriel when Gauguin brushes her off? Such an intelligent woman usually, why is she letting herself be used like this?

Is Muriel being used? Muriel doesn't see it that way! Her young man is poor (she can't help but admit that). But he is genuinely gifted (even her *friends* admit that!). The dollars she contributes to his upkeep—usually by buying his paintings—bring her as much pleasure as a vacation in Majorca might bring someone else. Her eyes are wide, wide open.

She knows the arrangement is not permanent and that she is more emotionally involved than is required of a "Patroness of the arts." The lad may fall in love with a girl his own age and marry her, or, worse, he may become so successful that he no longer needs Muriel's "help."

These gloomy possibilities exist. But even though Muriel's

209

friends may be nervous, Muriel plans to prolong her special pleasure in the boy as long as she can.

Any married woman who is honest will tell you that she hasn't the perfect mate *or* the perfect marriage! The affluent businessman-husband who gives his family *everything* may spend too much time away from them acquiring the everything! The spouse who's only too happy to race home at five every day and stay there all weekend may have trouble finding the cash for Johnny's tuition. No one man—lover or husband—can give you a perfect life. You might say there's a catch to everybody (including *women*, would you believe it?).

Any single woman who wants, during some period of her life, to "invest" in a man she adores who is not at all suitable for marriage is not, in my opinion, headed for disaster. She's getting an adventure out of her system that may make her better able to make a happy marriage when the right man arrives!

Some teen-agers who think nineteen is their very last chance of wedlock could profitably slow down long enough to realize that there is lots of time to choose a husband. As my friend Muriel knows, every meaningful relationship doesn't have to end in marriage.

When Your Traveling Companion Is a Man

"I have a friend in her sixties who goes north each winter with a gentleman who stays at the same hotel she does," confides another sixty-year-old lady. "I am sure there is nothing but friendship between these two. What is your opinion of this arrangement?" (My opinion is that it's better than going with a girl friend, and I'm a little sorry it's only friendship.)

She adds: "Another friend goes on trips with a gentleman (she is seventy-two, he is sixty-nine). She says she pays her own motel, and I believe her. She says if two ladies can have this agreement, so can a gentleman and a lady. Do you think that is right?"

Yes, it sounds like a sensible arrangement to me, providing she isn't paying for both of them, and I suppose under certain circumstances—if she was very rich—that would be satisfactory, too. Most people in their sixties have been married. They certainly aren't youngsters any more, and any arrangement they wish to make about traveling together, whether it's to be a romantic or purely platonic journey, is their own business.

It is interesting and refreshing to me that older women—some in their seventies—are still very much concerned with the opposite sex. It sometimes seems to me these older girls are more interested in men for *themselves* than younger women who have in mind marriage, babies, support, status symbols, etc. Widows in particular ask where to meet these men. (Seems to be an eternal question for all single females, even those born as late as 1947.)

At the risk of sounding like the original broken record, I must say once again I don't think it's right to try to isolate men as you would the potato bug to be used for whatever purpose you had in mind. I think an older or younger woman will do better to say, "How can I have a more stimulating life?" and then the men just sort of show up. (And it's true. You do need them, and they are wonderful.)

I would suggest a woman alone over fifty do the following to get the ball rolling:

1. Get some kind of work to do, even if it's baby-sitting. (Maybe the family you sit with will have a widowed father or uncle.) Take shorthand and typing—only takes a few months to learn, and typists are nearly always needed. Try clerking in a store—they have men customers.

2. Take courses that have always interested you. One seventy-year-old widow I know has learned French (it took four years, true) and met any number of interesting Francophiles she sees away from class.

3. Go to lectures and *listen*.

4. Adopt a struggling student to help, girl or boy. Don't get "taken," but an occasional home-cooked meal and a little darning won't hurt.

5. Volunteer to help in a hospital even if it's doing the grubby stuff. It'll make you feel good, and them, too.

6. Join a political, church or social club and see how much *work* you can do. The chairmen and the workers are the ones who get out and mix with new people and have the fun.

7. Give a party, perhaps Saturday afternoon tea, and ask *everybody* you know including the young folks. Tell

them they can just stop by for a few minutes. Nothing fancy—cookies and tea will do.

8. BEHIND THE SCENES STUFF: Keep your body exercised and limber. You want to be up to all this running around.

NINE | **NATURE
NEEDS
A LITTLE
HELP**

_or,_

_Being More Sensational
Than You Really Are_

Self-improvement is supposed to be not only a dirty word in this year of "naturalness" but _two_ dirty words. "Just get out of bed and put on a dab of eyeshadow after your sponge bath is the party line for girls who would succeed with men. Don't do anything contrived or phoney." Piffle! Natural is okay if all you want is greasy hamburgers with greasy substandard men or scruffy jobs for scruffy money, but if you long to have life a bit poshier and the men a bit dreamier, there's nothing to do but shape up. I always found the shaping up rather fun anyway, and although I recently swore off ever again saying publicly some of the things I did to look better and to get what I wanted, they were all written down in these columns before the swearing-off.

Who Cares If You're a Mess? Everybody!

I'm no housekeeper. Housekeeping is about last on my list of life's cherished pleasures, but I think a flagrantly dirty car, apartment, desk, office, person indicates not only a careless girl, but maybe a disturbed one. There *is* some connection. If you care enough about *you,* you'll care about them.

Another single-girl friend says there is even a connection between flagrant messiness and losing a man. Neither of us says neatness *gets* the man—nobody is that fatheaded—but the lack of it can cool him down about forty degrees, especially if he's over thirty. She suggests these failure procedures:

"You and a man are going steady," she says. "He's practically in the bag. One day he unexpectedly stops by and catches you washing windows with a smudge on your nose, rolled-up blue-jeans, tattered shirt and no make-up. He

215

says he thinks you look cute. He's never seen you this way before.

"The next night he comes by to take you to a movie. You are in capris and your shirt isn't tattered, but it could have been pressed a little better. You meant to wash your hair, but didn't fit it into the schedule. He says you're going uptown to a show instead of in the neighborhood. You don't put on a dress because you want to be comfortable. He saw you looking worse the night before —and besides, you love each other.

"Next time he arrives straight from work and asks to use your bathroom. It has to be reached from the bedroom. You should have made the bed, but didn't think it would show from the living room. When he comes out, he's frowning slightly. It could have been all those stockings and lingerie hanging from the shower rod. The wastebasket was brimming over, too.

"You have been planning to attend a married couple's anniversary. You should have sent your clothes to the cleaner's sooner. You ask him to pick up what you are going to wear on the way over to your apartment. You are late for the party. Everyone is ahead of you in fun and ready to eat when you get there. He is disappointed because he didn't even get to taste a drink.

"The next date you cook dinner for him. When he stops by for a drink the following day, last night's dishes are still in the sink and several ashtrays are full. You aren't wearing make-up at all any more, because men in love like the natural look. At least you *think* they do. Besides, he's yours.

"One day he tells you he thinks you should stop seeing each other. He isn't seriously interested in getting married and doesn't want to monopolize your time. You cry your heart out. He was in the *bag*."

Maybe this story is exaggerated, but not *much*. And maybe the unemptied ashtrays didn't do it, but they helped.

The Flattest Tummy in Town

I've said it before, but a firm and slender body is possibly the greatest single beauty asset a woman alone over forty (or under forty) can have. After a face, it's the first thing a man notices. Sometimes he notices it *before* the face. There isn't just everything in the world you can do for sagging face muscles. They're hard to get to. But there's ever so much you can do for a too heavy or sagging figure.

The other night at a party I met an attractive man and just out and out asked him what he did to have such a nice flat stomach. He was about fifty and looked like a greyhound.

"I've been using the Canadian Air Force Exercise Plan," he said. "It takes eleven minutes a day and I've taken off maybe three inches around the waist."

"Fascinating," I said. "And how long have you been doing this?"

"About three months now," he said. "I do the exercises before I go to work every morning."

"And did you have to diet, too?" I asked, barely able to take my eyes from the stone-hard, elegant-looking stomach.

"No, just the exercise," he said.

Maybe this isn't the kind of thing you talk to a man about at a party, but I consider my greyhound conversation one of the most profitable of my life. I bought the book, of course, officially titled *Royal Canadian Air Force Exercise Plan for Physical Fitness* (paperback edition, one dollar) and went to work. It really is the best exercise plan I've ever found for getting results and being something you can live with, too.

Please don't think anyone ever pays me to endorse a product or a plan. The only reason I ever pass on a recommendation to you is because I sincerely believe something is good and might help you. The plan for women in this booklet takes only twelve minutes a day (I guess we have more blubber and need the extra minute) and starts slow and easy. You just do three or four each of twelve different exercises at first. Now you know three of anything isn't very much work and you're finished practically before you've begun. Just when you figure it's too good to be true, because it is, they up the number of times you do each exercise. This really doesn't bother you much, however, because you build so slowly. Pretty soon you're doing fourteen baby pushups, ten waist bends, 170 run and hops and all kinds of other things in the same twelve minutes and your figure is coming along nicely.

I don't suppose this brief exercise period is as good as an hour a day, but who's going to home-exercise one hour a day unless she's training for the Olympics?

You may get fed up with this little plan like all others (I've quit twice), but because it's only an innocent twelve-minute-a-day program, you don't dread or postpone slipping back into it again. "Hello, exercises," you say. "I'm back!" And they don't hold your absence against you.

There's a place in the book to record your jumps from plateau to plateau. You also keep track of your inch-loss and it's almost like having a friend watching over you. Happy flat tummy!

Be a Lazy Summer Beauty

In the summer, especially in the doggy days of August, nearly every beauty routine seems like TOO MUCH TROUBLE. That's too bad, because August is a very good month, romance-wise. Comes September and men get so preoccupied at their office. I know you have your own favorite beauty columnist but let me toss in these easy, easy, easy summer beauty plans, which are practically no trouble at all.

The cold shoulder—and everywhere else: Leave a bottle of cologne in the ice-box. After a bath, douse the cologne all over your body. Simply delicious! Don't forget to turn the shower clear down to cold before you step out.

Egg on your face: Every morning while you prepare breakfast, run your fingers inside the egg-shell (after it's broken of course) and pat egg-white all over your face. This is the best facial mask I know, winter *or* summer. It lifts and tightens the skin just beautifully. Leave the egg on ten minutes or more; wash off with cold water. Your face will feel pepperminty.

Soft and silky surfaces: Dispense with your regular creams and just use pure baby oil as a night cream or any-time-of-day cream. It's good for babies and good for you, too. Baby oil smoothed all over your body after a bath makes you velvety. The oil is absorbed into the skin without leaving a residue. Keep it in a small apothecary jar

218

and you can just dip your fingertips in—no need to shake a bottle.

Colorful hair: A beauty-shop operator showed me how to mix and apply hair-color this simple way. Combine as many colors of dye as you're using with peroxide in a plastic mixing bowl. Put colorless nailpolish on the end of a sharpened pencil and wrap cotton around it. That's your applicator. Very easy to swab color through the parted hair with the long cotton-swabbed pencil.

Absolutely electrifying: I know you don't need me to tell you how to spend money, but an electric toothbrush can eradicate bleeding gums, make them beautifully pink and healthy and your teeth feel dental-office clean. While you're at it, an electric hairbrush does hundreds of times as much brushing as you could in the same time with no energy expended.

Go straight downhill: Wrap up in a wet sheet. Then figure some place to lie so your feet will be higher than your head for fifteen minutes. It may be awfully moisturizing to the furniture which doesn't need it but great for *your* circulation.

Summer browsing: Scrub your eyebrows with a very stiff toothbrush to get the dandruff out of them.

Undress division: Sleep nude. Go without some of your underwear in the daytime.

Cool on the inside: Squeeze half a lime over a tall glassful of ice. Toss the lime in, too. Fill to the brim with any noncaloric soft drink—orange, cherry, lemon, ginger, cream, cola. About five calories to its name and absolutely gratifying.

More of You Shows in a Swimsuit . . . Including Your Insecurity

A friend of mine was modeling swimsuits for her husband and two girl friends at a beach resort the other day (she had them out on approval) and suddenly found herself doing everything but hiding behind the furniture and potted ferns.

"I was self-conscious," she said. "I haven't been in a swimsuit in three years, and I just felt my figure wasn't good enough." Actually her figure was fine.

Haven't you noticed, though, that at beaches and pools there seem to be those girls who are quite at home in their swimsuits and those who look a bit uneasy. Of course, it has everything to do with the shape of your shape as well as how much time you spend in swimming togs, but my point is this:

As a single woman, it behooves you not only to look as svelte as possible in a swimsuit, but feel happy and adequate and comfortable. Blind dates sometimes may be swimming dates. You don't want a patina of self-consciousness to mar this beginning. Even if you arrive at the lakeshore, beach or pool with girl friends, all are pretty good places to make new friends. You're certain to be continually looked over.

Here are things I think you can do to be happier in a swimsuit.

1. Rub hand lotion into your feet and massage and knead them every morning and night. Keep your toenails clipped close to the toe and manicured. *Do* something about those corns!

2. If you're a brunette and there's too much hair on the upper leg to shave, slather it from the knee up with 1/3 each of soapflakes, household ammonia and bleaching peroxide until it's blond as straw. Do your arms, too.

3. Paste a picture of a girl with an almost perfect figure inside your medicine cabinet. It will keep you inside your diet and *on* that exercise program. If you still have a pooching, marshmallowy stomach by July 4, don't go swimming. You need more work!

4. If you've been out of a swimsuit all year, wear one around your home a few hours before the day you come out!

5. Throw out the tacky beach coat or hat that used to be adorable but has had it. Notice how young people who look greatest of anybody at the beach only wear what's spare and contemporary.

6. Take swimming lessons at the YWCA.

Who Wants to Be a Health Nut?

Listen, there are an awful lot of sillier things a woman alone could be than cuckoo about nutrition! You *know* that a car runs better on ethyl than on after-shave lotion and that an electric sewing machine hardly runs at *all* on gas. Well, *you* don't run so well either on coffee and sweet rolls for breakfast, hot dogs and milkshakes for lunch and artichoke hearts for dinner!

Doctors, blood chemists and nutritionists have their differences, but you can hardly find *one* who doesn't agree that a woman needs 51 to 75 grams of protein a day to prowl about sleekly like a jungle princess instead of scurrying around pitiful and scared like a mouse.

A minimum 51 grams of protein is a lot of protein, to be sure. The only way to get it into you is to have at least one or preferably *two* things containing protein at every meal. For example, a hamburger patty with a poached egg on top for lunch and cottage cheese with slices of lean meat for dinner would put you over the top!

If you eat that much protein, there's hardly any room or desire left over for a Danish or corn chips. You can forget to diet! Calories from protein make you walk faster, breathe deeper, work harder, have lovelier hair and fingernails and lose excess weight!

It's kind of rough getting started on this love affair with protein when you've been in love with frozen pizza. Just let me say it's probably going to be more rewarding than ninety percent of the love affairs you'll ever get started on! Give it a try! Here's a little chart showing how many grams of protein are in what foods. Remember, you want to pile up at least 17 at every meal.

Lean meat, poultry, fish	1 oz.	6 grams
Tuna fish	1 oz.	8 grams
One egg		6½ grams
Milk	1 oz.	1 gram
Cottage cheese	1 oz.	5 grams
Yellow cheese	1 oz.	6 to 7 grams
Yogurt	8 oz. jar	11 grams

A word about the cost. Protein is *not* more expensive than junk. A carton of cottage cheese is 25 cents in most cities. It contains 40 grams of protein! Ground meat is from 50 cents to a dollar a pound. A quarter of a pound —say 25 cents' worth—contains 24 grams and there's your dinner! Take in some fresh fruits and fresh under-cooked vegetables and a little oil every day, and presto . . . you're a health nut! And a jungle princess!

Look Ma, I'm a Yogi!

I read everything I can find about relaxing and calming down, because I sometimes think when they made me they forgot to install any factory whistles. When everybody else is laughing, chatting and enjoying the scenery, I'm still cleaning out my desk or sponging down the ice box. I assume this perpetual motion stems from the fear that, if I stop, something out there will catch me.

If you have this problem, too, or simply have more work and responsibility than you can handle, you may enjoy trying this little relaxing routine I just picked up from a British book called *Yoga for Everyone,* by Desmond Dunne. (I hope it gets to the States soon, because it's wonderful.) The silly routine seems to work. I call it: How to Stop Everything Dead and Recharge Your Battery. Here's what you do.

1. Choose a place where you'll be alone and undisturbed if possible for the brief time this takes (five minutes minimum).
2. Lie on the floor. Dunne says, "A bed is too soft and yielding. You may fall asleep." This is bad, he says, because "ordinary sleep doesn't completely rest the body." You're busy moving around, contracting muscles and wearing yourself out from dreaming. Try not to lie in a draft.
3. Lie flat on your back, weight distributed evenly. Having assumed a comfortable position, hold it. No shifting every so often to find a more comfortable spot. This is really the crux of the routine—absolute stillness. When you first start, you think you'll go mad not being able to twitch around, but it's the enforced stillness that makes you finally crumple and relax.
4. Now, quoting Dunne, "Stretch an arm, leg or even your neck or feet—any part of the body. Stretch it hard. Make the muscles contract and study what is happening. (You'll be surprised at the way in which parts far removed from the seat of operations contract in sympathy. A strongly clenched fist, for example, will cause contractions to be felt all the way

up your arm and down your shoulders and back.) Hold the stretch while you trace these sensations in detail, then let go. This completes step one."

5. For the next step toward deep relaxation, "stretch hard again—but this time do it in slow motion. Build the stretch up slowly and observe and note every sensation inspired by it. Again, hold the stretch while you make a mental record of all that is happening. Then, once more in slow motion, 'let go.' Here is the secret of success: you must let go as slowly as possible, carrying the 'let-go' process beyond the point where you have ceased to be conscious of any physical sensation whatsoever. Continue further with this 'let go' mechanism till you reach the stage where you are no longer trying to relax, but have completely lost all feeling of alertness in the portions of your anatomy concerned."

When you start, it's enough to concentrate on one part of the body only. Later you'll begin to "let go" more generally until you stop thinking of specific areas and commence untensing the whole body as a coordinated unit.

Says Mr. Dunne, "From time to time as you relax, you will become more aware of muscle groups that escaped attention or having been relaxed at first have again grown tense; they must be newly relaxed, of course."

After a while you'll stop darting from this to that group of muscles. You'll discover it's best to begin with the head and then pass down the body, relaxing groups of muscles as you find them, easing the arms from the shoulders, the legs from the hips and so on. When you've practically blanked out all tension and alertness right down to the toes, go back up to the eyebrows, eyelids and eyeballs and start over.

Get up when you have no more time to spend. Even if it's just five or ten minutes, you should feel "all slept out!"

P.S. Mr. Dunne's book is simplified yoga, and these brief paragraphs have been simplified Dunne. Still, it's enough to get you started. You might try for two periods a day if you're a really wound-up top.

Beautiful on the Inside

Sometimes I have to remind myself that a woman doesn't need to be young, glamorous, chic or skinny. As a matter of fact, she can be downright dowdy and still attract men if she really likes the creatures. One of the non-Queens of the May I'm talking about has this to say:

"As owner of your candid and scintillating books and as a faithful reader of *Cosmopolitan,* I have frequently wondered when you'd discover that homely, pudgy, dowdy, flat-heeled old maids sometimes, quite often, have all the males they want. I do—I really do.

"I was born homely—maybe ugly, for all I know—and have never done much about it. I guess I just accepted my huge nose, small eyes, nonexistent lashes, beetle brows, receding chin, crooked mouth, knock knees and all the rest. There were always so many more interesting people and fascinating ideas to cultivate than to brood about my looks.

"As I look back, I suppose I was a very pitiable young girl and woman. I never had a date in high school or college; but, strange as it must have seemed to others, I really didn't want dates, and so I certainly didn't miss them. It seems to me I was about thirty-three before a man kissed me with anything but a duty peck.

"Well, here it is 1966, and I'm fifty-five. Middle-age spread has widened my hips and tummy considerably; there are occasional gray hairs; I am blind as a bat without my bifocals, but—

"There are four men who think I am absolutely tops. All four are eligible. Two are professional men; two are retired, and all four think they are in love with me. Can you beat it? Can you explain it? It must be chemistry!

"Anyway, you're so right. You don't need to be a Queen of the May to attract eligible men."

My word! Congratulations, and I mean it.

This girl is obviously so terrific she doesn't need glamour. I love to hear success stories as long as they're true and not embroidered just to sound good.

But I'm not backing down on my stand about making the best of yourself. Few women have the inner poise and self-assurance required to be at ease when they're totally un-chic-ed up. You can do only so much "positive think-ing," and then you need to be backed up by what you see in the mirror. The *least* prepossessing girl can look more beautiful at the right weight, in beautiful make-up and clothes that *zing*.

Let's say chemistry happens regardless, but sometimes you have to help it happen. I'll wager my correspondent has a fantastic personality or some other asset that she may not even realize she has.

The Sexy Plain Girl

I met a movie star at a party the other night—one of the "new young" actresses who is actually about thirty-two, but has been working hard for many years at her career and deserves every bit of her star status. This particular girl has been publicized as a sex symbol re-cently, which she most certainly looks like. Later in the evening I heard two men who had also met her talking about the fact that she really wasn't a "sexpot" at all.

"Pretty, yes," they said, "but she doesn't give you the feeling that you're Adam and she's Eve and you ought to go pick an apple together."

"She seemed to have a lot on her mind," one of the men said, "like whether she had all her lines memorized for the next day and whether she was doing all the things her press agent had told her."

Nobody was criticizing. The men just seemed disap-pointed that somebody who was supposed to be sexy, and who is actually quite a beauty, didn't make them feel more manly.

By contrast, a single girl came to dinner the other night (I call everybody girls but she's actually forty-four) and just about demolished my husband and two other men in the charm department. When I let her in the door, I said to myself, "My word, Lila (whom I hadn't seen for several years) is less attractive than I remembered. I'd forgotten her hair was *that* skimpy and is it possible she's just faintly *cross*-eyed?" That was early in the evening. By ten o'clock she had taken everybody in the place—girls as well as men.

For one thing she was wearing a Teal Traina dress

which doesn't come inexpensive but which was pure dynamite—lime green, shocking pink and black stripes that ran around her figure diagonally.

"Don't turn around too fast," somebody told her, "or you'll drive yourself right into the ground."

Her figure was perfect for the dress—or let's say she *made* it perfect—flat tummy, trim hips and she got all the mileage out of that little number the designer must have meant it to give. By the end of the evening the three girls still hadn't figured out what she had and the men weren't asking. They were just enjoying whatever it was. (What she had, of course, was simply a criminal amount of charm and verve.)

You *know* I exaggerate sometimes. You *know* this girl probably wasn't *that* devastating nor the movie star *that* disappointing. Still you must also know that I never underestimate the advantages of being "naturally" beautiful. I just don't think a girl can *be* too beautiful despite the fact that people are always saying a girl like that has problems. (I'll take the problems!) I do know, however, that if you're a plain girl like my friend Lila you can indeed rise above it and so *far* above it as to seem to have, whether you actually have it or not, more sex appeal than the beauty. It isn't easy. It takes a great desire, willingness to work long and hard with what you've got and the conviction, which Lila has, that men are probably the most wonderful things ever invented and you are going to let them know it! Any plain girl who's followed this route will tell you it's a lot of fun.

Young Lady Slobs

"I'm single and live in a court apartment where there are both married and single people," she said. "We run back and forth and visit one another, and it's very friendly and companionable. You have the benefits of living alone but also the friendship of neighbors.

"The other day my mother and father came to visit me and brought along my aunt and uncle. Some of my regular girl friends from the building dropped by to meet my folks. They all got along fine, but I noticed my mother and aunt looking at the girls very peculiarly during the

226

visit. My mother is no fuss-budget, and I couldn't imagine what the girls were doing so I started observing. Then it struck me. Alice was doing her fingernails on my coffee table, a gift from my aunt, with just a tiny piece of tissue separating the open bottle of polish from the table. One tiny tip-over and that would have been the end. Lois had brought a grapefruit with her which she was proceeding to peel and section and eat the way you would an orange—without even a paper napkin for the skin which she just left on the couch. I was used to my friends, but I do think sometimes that girls who live alone—even college graduates—tend to become absolute slobs. What do you think?"

I think she's right.

Girls visiting either in jeans, pedal-pushers, shorts and sandals do things they probably wouldn't dream of doing when they're perfumed, hosed and heeled and out with a date.

The following are some of the activities which you just might avoid—no matter how informal the atmosphere— the next time you visit a girl friend if you want to be really welcome.

Fooling with your toes. It's fun, but nerve-wracking for others.

Feeling your face or picking a pimple.

Scratching head, legs, arms, nose.

Using a toothpick with great verve.

Burping.

Talking about fundamentals of the body.

Sneezing loudly without benefit of covering mouth.

Using bathroom without closing the door.

Talking with mouth full.

Biting nails or hangnails.

Cleaning fingernails.

Filing fingernails.

Sniffing—very annoying habit—while tissues go begging.

Fishing out an olive with fingers when there's a cocktail pick.

Talking too loudly. Interrupting constantly.

Using profanity. Maybe it isn't the other girl's style.

Standing in the doorway to talk instead of simply saying good-by and leaving.

Bringing over coffee, using half-empty cup to dump cigarette in, leaving whole mess behind.

Refusing to take hint when the hostess is really too busy to visit with you.

All checked out? Okay, you can go visit.

How to Be Very, Very Popular with Men

When my friend Charlotte Kelly attended her company's annual sales meeting in Bermuda this summer (how fortunate can a girl employee *get*), she took along a cherry-red terry-cloth poncho—two giant towels sewed together with a hole for her head—to be worn over a swimsuit. One afternoon one of the men in the group said, "Charlotte, how about letting me try on your poncho?" What he really wanted to do probably was try it on with Charlotte *in* it but Charlotte whisked it off and gave it to him. He liked himself so well that several other fellows got in line for the poncho and one by one went whooping up and down the beach making like gauchos. At each beach party after that, one or the other of the men called Charlotte beforehand and said, "Char, be sure to bring the poncho."

One night this summer I caught a glimpse of myself at a party in my blonde wig and decided I really *did* look like Harpo Marx. (Some women were never meant to be blondes, alas.) I took the wig off, laid it on the bed and reappeared as my natural brunette self. One of the fellows sneaked in and put the wig on, returned to the party *really* looking like Harpo and brought the house down. From that point on the wig went from man to man to man. (I wish they'd taken up a collection for the fifteen dollar cleaning and setting bill!) We saw enough Mae West imitations and soft-shoe routines to bring back vaudeville.

Am I telling you this to indicate that Miss Kelly and I have depraved men friends? I don't know about Charlotte's men, but mine are mostly hard-working, responsible darlings. The wig and poncho capers just reminded me that a lot of men have a lot of play in their systems, not necessarily the kind done with girls but *play* play. The girl who aids and abets them in getting the play out of their systems, helps them come on funny and appreciates them when they *do*, is apt to be very, very popular.

One girl I know often slips her shoes off at the office

228

and works stocking-footed at her desk. Two of her male associates stole her shoes one day last week and didn't give them back when it was time to go home. Sarah sputtered and raged, padded from office to office looking for her shoes, but actually she was enjoying pleasing the men. They were very proud of themselves and are working on a plot to steal her shoes before a client meeting some day soon.

Another girl I know is frightened of unusual noises. She was pathologically afraid of the dark as a child and it's a "sincere" phobia, but she is the absolute delight of men at parties who are able to imitate owls, razorback hogs, creaking doors and Dracula. Nancy goes to pieces and they love it.

A man is not playful all the time—heavens no! But he is *some* of the time and he doesn't have to be drunk or cuckoo to be in his playful mood. The girl who is blessed with a sense of humor and the ability to encourage and respond when he's feeling playful is to my mind about as lucky as a girl who was born beautiful.

What Are You Doing to His Eardrums?

We were talking about single girls at a party the other night and one very attractive man asked, "Why is it that so many pretty and otherwise intelligent girls ignore their voices? I know at least four," he said, "who could knock me or any other bachelor right off his feet until they open their mouths. Then out comes this noise that sounds like a Damon Runyon character speaking."

The man is right about New York accents. Perfectly lovely girls sound to an outsider as though they are trying to mimic the most outrageous character actresses on television when they play the part of a dumb salesgirl or particularly dense telephone operators.

Other girls in other areas do themselves just as much harm. When I moved away from Arkansas, I was under the impression my heavy twang was a delightful southern drawl until a kind but firm friend assured me it was an assault to the ears, and I did something about it.

A regional accent may not be the problem at all, but rather a nasal, reedy or rasping quality to the voice. Or

229

maybe you just need to speak up and quit mumbling.

It seems to me, for all the harm an unpleasant voice does a girl, however, this is the area of self-improvement most completely ignored. Although a low-placed, sexy, quiet voice could probably net a girl more new admirers than the next five dresses she's planning to buy or the next five vacations she's planning to go on to track down men, how she sounds doesn't enter her consciousness from one year to the next.

Suppose you've seen the light or heard the truth? Changing a voice is not the simplest thing in the world to do, I'll admit. The most important step toward changing, however, is to listen to yourself and become aware of how you really sound. To do this you need to record your voice on a tape or record and play it back. Many men in offices have tape recorders and perhaps you could borrow one for the evening (the recorder, not the man).

A dictaphone will work, too. If it's your first exposure to the sound of your own voice, it will probably scare you to death. Good! That means you'll get busy.

To improve your voice, you can do worse than to listen to voices you admire and analyze what makes them attractive. Copy as much of the quality as you can. Obviously you can't ape anyone else completely, but actors and actresses whom you love to listen to usually have no particular accent. Certainly they don't have a phony sound. They simply pronounce everything clearly and have a certain strength in their voices.

Reading out loud every day can help. This will at least improve your diction, the tendency to slur and eliminate some of the tired, breathy quality from your voice. You may even want to work with a professional speech expert. Sometimes you can find a very good one in your local high school or college.

It's easier to practice voice improvement on the phone than any other time. You don't have to worry about how you look and can think "voice" exclusively. Many girls who "think voice" exclusively for a while, remembering to put in some beautiful highs and lows and to stop speaking in a monotone, find that men call them up far oftener than they do girls who are merely "thinking miscellaneous."

Are You Using Your Voice To Get What You Want!

Now we're going to have a little voice lesson—not singing, but speaking. Your voice is part of the equipment with which you attract men and other good things in life. Probably I should say it's part of the equipment with which you *could* attract men and other good things in life if you just knew how to do it.

Marian Rich, the New York voice teacher who has coached Marlon Brando, Olivia de Havilland, Jennifer Jones and hundreds of other famous and nonfamous people, says people's voices definitely reflect *them*. An itty-bitty little voice reflects an itty-bitty little outlook on life. Sometimes a woman keeps a weak and shallow voice because she really doesn't want to grow up.

The pathologically shy avoid even trying to speak resonantly because a marvelous voice would call attention to themselves, heaven forbid. And of course some people think any kind of voice training would make them sound phony.

Miss Rich, who doesn't sound phony but does sound wonderful, says the human voice has a range of two complete octaves if anybody wants to use them and there's not a bit of doubt that a beautiful voice can interest, influence and practically mesmerize those around you if you wish it to. Naturally, she avers, the better you sound, the more you love yourself and you know how good that is. (If you don't, who's going to?)

The most important step toward having a more beautiful voice is breathing deeply, forcing air all the way down to the bottom of the lungs instead of just breathing from the chest up. (Most voice and speech teachers subscribe to this principle.) Most of us are shallow little breathers, however—gasp, gasp, gasp.

You should think of yourself as a musical instrument. You fill your body with air, then you blow the air out through the mouth and that makes the sound. How you work your tongue and lips determines the words people hear. If you just have a shallow amount of air in your body, the sound is apt to be like tin plates scraping together. (We both know poeple who sound like that.)

231

If you've taken in a nice big draft of air by breathing deeply all the way to the bottom of the lungs, you can make rich, fruitful sounds. (Would you buy a tube of toothpaste filled only from the neck up? It's just as wasteful if you're only filled from the neck up with air.)

How do you breathe deep down instead of from the neck up? You have to learn to practice and it takes a bit of doing. Actually, correct breathing is how you breathe in bed when you're lying there relaxed. Go lie down and try it and you'll see what we mean. While you're at it, here's Miss Rich's deep-breathing exercise you can work on while you're lying there:

Flat on your back, blow out all your breath energetically with rounded lips. Relax and wait with no breath in your body. Then take a deep breath through the nose and repeat. Blow, wait and breathe. Be sure you wait as long as you can before you breathe again. You'll see your stomach go out as you breathe in, then gradually recede and become flat as you let the air out of your mouth. Most people think it's the other way around but naturally since you're taking something new into your body—fresh air—it fills your body up and makes your stomach distend.

The exercise works best when you lie on your back flat on the floor. Bend your knees, keep feet flat, cross arms over your chest, wrists at armpits. Take a long deep breath through your nose (it should make your stomach pooch out) and let it out slowly on a prolonged "shhh." The trick is this: the chest must not lift as you breath in, must not drop as you breathe out. There should be no up and down motion of chest if the breath is really coming into your body correctly and filling up the bottom of the lungs.

For phrasing and tone production: stand flat against a wall with good posture. Read the next paragraph by alternately taking a deep breath through the nose and pooching out the abdomen as you breathe in (don't talk while this goes on).

And once you've got the breath in you, abdomen pooched out, read (or whisper loudly) a phrase at a time. At the end of each three or four words, as marked, you should have used up your breath and your stomach should be flat against your back. Take in another breath (don't read while you're doing it) and expel it by reading or whispering three or four more words as marked. Here's the paragraph to read.

Mark a paragraph / in this manner / into the shortest possible phrases. / First / whisper it / with energetic lips / breathing / at all the breath marks. / Then speak it / in the same way. / Do this / with a different paragraph / every day. / Keep your hand / on the abdomen / to make sure / that it moves out / when you breathe in / and moves in / when you speak.

When you've practiced and mastered this exercise, you've actually got down the principles of deep breathing which can give you a more resonant, full-bodied, less tired, reedy or babyish voice.

For a more musical quality, Miss Rich suggests you read any material by making the first phrase go from the bottom of your voice up; the second phrase start at the top and come down; the third make a circle with the important word at the top; the fourth with the important word at the bottom.

For diction: place tongue tip on gum ridge back of upper teeth with jaw held open as wide as possible (with practice the tongue will stretch). Without allowing tongue tip to move away from ridge, say "deedle, deedle, deedle." If you can't do it at all, it's a sign that you need the exercise.

And here are some tongue twisters to try:

The sixth sheik's sixth sheep's sick. Fanny Finch fried five floundering fish for Francis Fowler's father. The seething sea ceaseth and thus the seething sea sufficeth us.

Have fun!

How to Be Cool and Daring

I just called a coat manufacturer to ask about buying a coat wholesale. Brrrrr! It can be very cold outside, baby, when you're talking to a New York coat manufacturer. The man's "no" was so resounding that both my cats crept away from the telephone and went into the linen closet to hide. I felt like going right in there with them.

Why do I suppose that like me you are just so much blubber and get your feelings hurt easily? Why do I suppose you would be tempted to try more brave, new, wonderful things if it weren't for fear of getting smacked down by the people you try them on? I think so because you're a woman. And I think a woman alone may feel *more* timid because she has no official helpmeet to go in there and take on anyone who clobbers or hurts her (not that many husbands do that either). When an unmarried woman's daring·schemes have crashed around her, leaving her among the embarrassing pieces, she feels even lonelier.

Nevertheless, you can't be let off the hook not to dare anything because daring is what gets you a more exciting life, new friends, more men and the satisfying feeling that you are, after all, not a mouse but a sleek, shiny, sinewy mountain lioness. I think the answer is to dare with "built-in safeguards." Here are the rules:

1. Whatever you want somebody to do—speak at your club meeting, let you see his famous stamp collection *privately*, be interviewed for an article you're writing, let you attend a cocktail party for press only (so you can give your twelfth-grade students a first-hand account of a particular dignitary)—*write a letter first*. Briefly, charmingly, persuasively, put down the details of your request. Say you'll telephone for an answer. This will save your getting switched from person to person on the phone (very ego-bruising). They can give you a simple yes or no when you call (I did this with the coat manufacturer but must have got some commas in the wrong places).

2. In composing your letter, figure out why they should do what you want. What's in it for them? Obviously your desire may not be enough. If you can play on the other person's vanity, sense of civic duty, love for children, old love affair with your mother or whatever it is, do it. Give them a selfish reason to do what you want.

3. Don't request favors from movie stars or sex symbols. They're just too snowed under. I once wrote to five movie stars and the President of the U.S. asking that they write a letter to my sister, Mary, who was stricken with polio in the hospital. She never heard from the movie stars. Franklin Roosevelt wrote a letter.

4. It's easier to be nervy if you make your request on behalf of someone else. You want a dreamy man to at-

tend your party? Have the party in honor of a friend of his. Your boss's twenty-fifth anniversary with the firm is approaching? Go visit the brass yourself and stir up a celebration. Maybe you'll be invited to the banquet.

5. Be where the men *are*, perfumed, chic, friendly and eager, but let *them* make the proposals. You simply create a favorable atmosphere toward being asked for a date.

6. Knowing how easily your own feelings get hurt, be compassionate and say No tactfully to the people who ask you things you can't give or do.

Legs Are In, Bosoms Are Out ...
Well, Sort of

You're probably going to think I've gone clean off my rocker, but it occurs to me that legs may possibly have replaced bosoms as a focal point of male interest. (As a woman alone, you want to know what men are *interested* in, of course!)

Now don't laugh yourself to pieces before you've heard my rationale. A man will always look at a bosom if he can *find* it, but many current styles gloss over, play down and "understate" the bosom to the point where you just have to *assume* it's there *somewhere*. At the same time, no matter how un-figure-revealing the dress, it usually falls just above the kneecap if it's fashionable, and so you have acres and acres of legs on display.

I'm not going to fuss about this shrouded-body, exposed-leg situation and I don't think you should either. I miss being able to show off my tiny waist, but nipped-in waistlines are sure to come back *some* day. In the meantime, there's always the bikini if I get lonesome for tiny-waist compliments.

If you're possessed of a lovely bosom, you can still collect the admiration due you between the hours of five P.M. and midnight. Some late-afternoon and evening dresses, unlike the daytime pillowcases, go further than dresses have practically ever gone to reveal not only bust contours but cleavage. From nine to five in the daytime, however, I think we should all wake up and appreciate that legs are in, regardless of where bosoms are, and show them to advantage. (Designers may drop skirts again any minute and we'll kick ourselves for not appreciating what we had.)

I don't think the shape of the leg is terribly important toward showing it off well. It's the spirit that counts! Some men really like heavy legs and find them attractive. Too skinny legs can always be developed with exercise. If your legs are short, you can wear high heels. There probably aren't any such things as legs too long.

Whatever your leg shape, these are tips to remember.

1. For legs to look their most sensational, the figure above the legs should be sleek and flat-stomached. Get busy!

2. Hosiery is so inexpensive now there's probably no reason ever to wear a run. When stockings get picked and snagged, retire them, too.

3. If your legs are very short or slender, stretch hose are marvelous.

4. Legs should be kept shaved, naturally. If you don't want to shave above the knee, bleach. (Two parts peroxide, one part household ammonia, soapflakes mixed up in a bowl. Slather on thighs, arms too if you like, and leave ten minutes. Re-slather a few times. Dry in the sun for faster bleaching.)

5. Many dresses are lined and don't need a slip. If you *do* wear one, sit down in front of the mirror in your dress and try on various slips with it. If the slip shows when you're seated, let it be a beautiful color, lacy and lovely.

6. Shoes can be less rather than more expensive so you can have new ones oftener. Keep all your shoes heeled and polished. Funny how we spend a mint on new dresses and pretend nobody notices scruffy shoes. Hah!

7. Practice sinking into and getting out of cars, cabs, chairs and couches to show your legs off to best advantage.

Let's Stir Things Up a Bit

I suggest, especially if you're over forty-five, that now might be the time to stop pretending that parts of you aren't really there, let alone worth bothering about, and that you pay some attention to them. I know you must put lipstick on and wash your hair often enough to concede that you have lips and hair, but I'm talking about more ordinary, run-of-the-mill parts like gums, eyebrows, heels, and elbows. Women often take these for granted or just ignore them completely.

I think you might spend at least one hour very soon babying these things, getting up the circulation, worrying them, pampering them. It won't take long and you'll enjoy it. You'll need a toothbrush, two or three dry bath towels, a lavatory, a scissors, nail file and some rich cream—none of which, save the towels, you will match up with any of the areas you have ordinarily matched them to.

The toothbrush is to scrub your face, the lavatory is to rest your foot on while you challenge your toenails, the cream is for your elbows and heels. You'll wash your teeth with your fingers, what else?

Here's the routine:

1. After you've washed your hair (which means you've been in a steaming shower a good long time and are really well done), remove yourself and wrap a clean towel around your head. Now dry the rest of you off thoroughly, really scrubbing hard with the second towel. Now, one at a time, grab the two fatty pouches at your hips in both hands and massage hard. This will at least remind you they're there and that you must do something about this dead giveaway of an aging figure as quickly as possible. The massage itself is good for breaking down fatty tissue.

2. Dry your face thoroughly, then take a soft, dry toothbrush and lightly brush all over your face, especially around the nose and between the brows. You'll probably get up some dead skin that hasn't been gone after in months. (The liquid cleansers most of us use, although gentle, aren't the rugged face cleansers that soap and water are.)

3. With your dry toothbrush and fingers, scruff up your eyebrows. Push them the wrong way. If I'm not mistaken, there will be the driest kind of dandruff lodged in there that hasn't been gone after in a long time either.

4. With your thumb and forefinger massage your gums front side and back. Go far back into your jaws (don't bite yourself) and do the roof of your mouth, too. Dentists say this is the greatest for having healthy gums.

237

5. Next place one foot up on the lavatory, knee bent so you get to this foot with your hands. Now clean the toenails thoroughly with your file and push back the cuticle with the rounded edge. Do the other foot.

6. Give your heels a good towel scrubbing, also your elbows. Now rub rich cream or oil into your elbows, ankles and heels. Smooth a little oil into your face, too.

You ought to feel like a new woman!

Bless Your Heart!

I feel so strongly about healthful eating for women alone that I'm inclined to be something of a nut on the subject. I do believe you have to sneak up on it, however. Every so often you make a fresh stab at including simple high-protein food at every single meal—meat, cheese, eggs, poultry, fish plus some fruits and vegetables. At the same time you gradually steel yourself to abandon ice-cream sodas, coffee cake, mashed potatoes and gravy and that other naughty high-carbohydrate stuff. One day you're home free (and feeling and looking marvelous).

As you probably know, some foods that are sky-high in nutritional value are pretty much snubbed. Liver, kidney, brain and heart—collectively spoken of as glandular meats—are part of this group.

In her book *Let's Cook It Right*, nutritionist Adele Davis writes of beef heart, "Since it must work continuously from the animal's birth, it has an abundance of excellent protein and the B vitamins." She also points out that mothers (and that would include mothers alone) could do their family no greater service than serving these muscle meats almost exclusively.

By the way, Mrs. Lindberg, who provided that yummy steamed liver recipe on page 244, and Mrs. Davis are both famed West Coast nutritionists and are friends.

To make the introduction of glandular meats into your life practically painless, I'm going to jot down Mrs. Lindberg's recipe for high-powered meat loaf. It is rather a large recipe—enough for company dinner and your own lunches and dinners during the week.

HIGH-POWERED MEAT LOAF

2 onions, chopped
1 green pepper, chopped
2 pounds round, ground
1 pound heart, ground
3 eggs
pinch of thyme and basil

½ cup soy flour
½ cup powdered skim milk
3 tablespoons catsup
1½ tablespoons salt
¾ cup fresh milk

If your market doesn't carry soy flour, don't substitute another kind. It should just be eliminated. Powdered whole milk may be used if you don't have powdered skim milk. Sauté the onions and pepper lightly in a little oil. Add the rest of the ingredients and mix well. Mold into a loaf in shallow pan and bake at 350° for 50 minutes.

Now, as a special reward for your having made this heart meat loaf, here is Mrs. Lindberg's recipe for

PROTEIN ENERGY CANDY

1 can heavy (Eagle Brand) sweetened condensed milk
3 tablespoons soybean (or other) oil
2 tablespoons vanilla

4 drops black walnut flavor
1¼ cups regular powdered skim milk (not instant)
½ to 1 cup chopped walnuts

Mix together condensed milk, oil, flavorings. Add powdered milk ½ cup at a time, mixing until smooth. Mixture will get so thick it will be difficult to mix. Keep adding as much powdered milk as possible. Add walnuts. Place on platter. Chill and cut in squares.

No Nose for Compliments

A Brooklyn mother says of her teen-age daughter: "Gwendolyn has a great personality, a good figure and natural red hair. Lately she has been bemoaning the fact that her nose is becoming the butt of some unkind remarks. I admit (but never to her, naturally) it is her worst feature.

"Should a girl of 15 have her nose bobbed? She is definitely becoming self-conscious, and I want to spare her as much heartbreak as possible. Could she just have her nose shortened, or must the bone be broken? I would greatly appreciate your counsel on this matter."

According to doctors, a girl of fifteen is a little young to have her nose changed, because the cartilage and bones may not yet be fully developed. Most physicians believe seventeen to eighteen would be better—and there's still a lifetime to enjoy her new profile. I took the step at age thirty-nine, and the day never goes by that I'm not grateful.

I've seen this particular operation change and enhance any number of single women's lives, and it's something you may want to sneak up on yourself if you have reason. A good plastic surgeon won't let you go into it if you shouldn't, so you don't have to be afraid to talk it over.

Yes, the bone technically is broken, but this isn't as gruesome as it sounds. The surgeon works up through the nostrils, meticulously cutting or filing away excess bone and cartilage to shorten, straighten or slenderize. Noses with too much of an indentation (saddle nose) can be built up, too.

Let me tell you more about this operation—I won't call it "my operation" because it's been undergone by so many grateful people.

Usually you go into the hospital the night before, and they give you a sleeping potion. The next morning they give you something stronger, and in fifteen minutes you could be palmed off for Juliet on her slab, though you're still conscious. Then they wheel you up or down to a room with green people all about, shoot a lot of local anesthesia into your face (procaine very often) and start to work. You're conscious, but you don't care, and of course the procaine keeps you from feeling any pain.

The operation takes from thirty minutes to an hour depending on what needs doing. You can tell they're in there filing away, but it doesn't bother you. When you come out of your rosy haze three or four hours later, you are wretchedly uncomfortable. The next day, when you usually leave the hospital, you are moderately wretchedly uncomfortable, during the rest of the week just moderately uncomfortable, but you're on your feet.

After that you're fine (anyway that's how it was for me). You wear a splint four or five days, then it's re-

240

moved. At the end of the first week, all the marvelous colors you've turned—black, blue, lime and magenta—begin to fade, and you aren't nearly so fascinating looking. The second week you get lighter and lighter, and usually two weeks after the operation or even a little sooner you can return to work looking quiet decent. Your nose stays tender and the least bit swollen up to six months—after that you're quite perfect.

Nasalplastry isn't covered by medical insurance, but if other work than just reshaping has to be done—a deviated septum that won't let you breathe right or something—they'll do it at the same time for no large fee, and insurance may cover part of that. Your policy may also cover hospitalization. Doctors are also pretty sweet about negotiating prices down for the small-budgeted.

A word about the "morality" of the thing. Whether you agree or disagree that bone structures should be tampered with, aren't we all getting to look too much alike with our straightened noses, capped teeth, wigs full of beautiful hair, busts padded and hips girdled to a perfect 36 each? Yes, I absolutely agree we are.

It would be a much more interesting world if sailors from foreign ports still prowled waterfront towns with two black teeth and a patch over one eye (my sailors sound suspiciously like pirates). Women with pocked skins or deep birthmarks certainly were more intriguing to stare at than a lot of reasonably attractive ladies who look just like each other.

But who's going to volunteer to stay exactly the way nature or disease made her and forgo having a lovely new skin or nose for the sake of keeping the human race more diverse or interesting? Not me, darling, and I hope not you, either.

Do You Dress for Him or You?

Several women in their fifties have asked for advice on dressing well, particularly on a budget. Strange as it seems, many of the same principles apply to a good basic wardrobe for a woman over fifty that apply to a woman under thirty. (As a matter of fact, they can often wear the same clothes.)

Of course, your wardrobe is determined in part by the kind of life you lead. If you go to lots of luncheons, I suppose you need hats. If you have a job, you need *more* changes of costume.

I believe, however, the following suggestions will have you beautifully dressed and pleased with yourself in everything you wear. Many of these thoughts are taken from my last book, so if they sound familiar to you, it's because I haven't found any new or better principles to go by.

1. Dress to please yourself and wear what *you* feel most delicious in (if you will pardon that word borrowed from the fashion industry). Do men really know more about what looks good on you than you do? You've had much more practice.

2. Keep trying to improve your taste so you can get away with Rule 1. Usually the people with the worst taste are most un-helpable. The whole world can think you look like a Russian wolfhound run amuck with unlimited credit at the thrift sale, and you think you look just dreamy. The way to reform is to study really beautifully dressed women and figure out why they look great—and why you don't look anything like them. Study fashion magazines, too.

3. Don't buy anything you don't adore—not even a collar and cuff set. If you're lukewarm about it now, you'll be ice-cold about it later.

4. Don't buy anything just because it's sensible. If it doesn't thrill you, find something else (also sensible if you like) with more zing to it.

5. Lock yourself up during half the sales of the year. Try to fill "holes" in your wardrobe only from expensive stuff reduced and not load up with junk.

6. Don't be afraid to return things when you've made a mistake. (I don't have to tell you to be prompt, and the merchandise must be as fresh as you received it.)

7. Don't pay too much or too little for anything. Unless you're terribly rich, there's a point beyond which a thing can't do you that much good. If it's too cheap, you'll have to buy again too soon, and it doesn't bring enough pleasure while it lasts.

8. Put the most money in the things you wear most (unless it's a muumuu). For most women, this is suits,

basic dresses, a coat. I'm wildly partial to wool for big investments.

9. Buy one complete outfit each fall-winter and spring-summer season—the suit, the bag, the hat, gloves, shoes, etc. Then you'll never be without at least one costume that makes you feel elegant and put together.

10. Wear lots of your best shade. Don't be afraid of overdoing it.

11. Stick to one or two colors in bags and shoes. One good black leather bag and several pairs of black leather shoes will get you through the winter. Same thing for bone or patent leather in summer.

12. No matter how important it seems, don't splurge for the big occasion dress you'll wear only once. Borrow, or make it out of draperies like Scarlett did.

13. Make your clothes fit. People do notice hems and pooches and sags.

14. Do follow fashion—it's your friend. If you haven't changed from "your best style" in twenty years, you're missing a chance to feel new and fascinating. Discard what's grotesque, but there's usually something exciting in every new crop that's just for you.

To Be a High Liver, It's Liver, Darling!

Not all doctors agree that women alone and other bipeds need vitamin supplements. Some doctors get quite testy on the subject and say, if you'll just eat three good old-fashioned square meals a day, like your ancestors did, you'll live to be a hundred.

The trouble is the kind of food our ancestors ate just isn't around any more! Our forebears raised vegetables on soil that wasn't *debilitated*. They picked them fresh daily off the vine or out of the ground.

Furthermore, our darling ancestors could eat up to 4,000 calories a day and burn them off. (Naturally the bigger the quantity of food consumed, the more minerals and vitamins you get.) If you and I ate that many calories without pitching any hay or tanning hides, we'd get as big as water buffalos.

Perhaps you don't want to take vitamin capsules or your doctor doesn't recommend them. I don't believe anybody could argue, however, that the more vitamins and minerals you get in you by "natural sources," the better you'll feel.

Los Angeles nutritionist Gladys Lindbergh (who is close to sixty and looks thirty-five) maintains that a pound of liver a week is imperative in the diet of a healthy adult woman.

Mrs. Lindbergh points out that liver contains thousands of units of vitamin A, which contributes to beautiful hair, strong nails and gardenia-petal skin. Liver also contains factors that help your *own* liver detoxify the harmful chemicals being taken into the body today. (If you don't believe these chemicals exist, Rachel Carson's brilliant best seller *Silent Spring* will convince you!)

Liver powder is a great convenience for girls who don't like to cook much (available at drug or health-food stores). Stir the powder into tomato or fruit juice and down it as a cocktail daily. Start with one teaspoon and work up to three tablespoons per glass of juice.

Or, here is a recipe for steamed liver that may make you positively *fond* of the stuff! Remember, a pound of liver a week down the hatch is your goal.

MRS. LINDBERGH'S DELICIOUS STEAMED LIVER

Heat in a skillet equal parts of butter and oil.

Cut up *two* big onions and sauté until they are just clear. (This is Chinese style.)

Take the onions out. Pop in the liver. (Always cook a pound at a time.) Cook it over a low flame a minute or two until the liver just turns gray. Now turn it over and put the onions back on top. Pour on 3 to 4 tablespoonfuls of vinegar. Put a lid on the skillet quickly and cook another five minutes. Turn the heat off and let the liver stand another five minutes. There'll be no liver taste or smell, and the dish is delightful.

Chop up any liver that's left over, mix with seasoning and mayonnaise, serve later on celery sticks or rye crackers with grated egg on top.

Scared Stiff? That's Good!

Some time ago I testified for two hours in the New York Supreme Court (I was suing a man about his book title), and to tell you the truth, my knees were shaking throughout the entire performance. When I stopped chattering for a minute or two, my teeth were still going strong, clackety, clackety, clackety. I may have been more scared sometime in my life, but I can't remember when. Yet, it was one of the most interesting and exciting days I can remember.

I want to ask you, my woman-alone friend, just how long has it been since you have been scared absolutely witless by a social gathering, a confrontation with an important person, a public appearance in which you had to make a talk? If it's been over six months, I am going to hold a good thought, say a little prayer and also do some plain and fancy urging you to find a nice, miserable, scary situation to throw yourself into.

Getting shaken up, challenged and scared practically beyond endurance a few times a year is one of the best things that can happen to a single girl.

These occasions keep you growing and maturing. They catapult you from the everyday you into being a little braver, stronger, gutsier person. If looking out toward the next few months you don't see anything looming that might rout you from your placid, comfortable woman-alone cocoon, I suggest you think about introducing one of these into your life to make a little trouble and eventually a lot of fun for yourself.

1. Ask for a raise. Plan your strategy. What extra things will you volunteer to do to deserve the raise? How many people would they need to replace you if you left? The more paralyzing the idea of asking, the better.

2. Make some calls to see about a new job—possibly a rung above the one you hold.

3. Join a public-speaking class. You will suffer and finally have a good time every time you make a speech.

4. Join an organization—even if you aren't a joiner. Get on some committees. You'll have to make announcements at the meetings. You may have to ask people to do things they'll hate. Hooray!

5. Give a dinner party. Ask a couple of people "over your head," or a man who's never dated you but one you'd like to know.

6. Have an honest talk with somebody who's been giving you trouble for years. Out with your feelings about what he's doing wrong.

7. Set up an easel and start painting on some public corner. If you've never painted a stroke, so much the better.

8. Go on an important vacation—Europe, Mexico, skiing—alone.

9. Join a little theater, opera or choral group, if they'll let you in.

10. Join a modeling class. So you're never going to be a professional model; people will be looking at you critically as you walk, and that's *good*.

11. Dress to the teeth and go to the snootiest, ritziest gown shop in town and try on clothes.

12. Contact some intriguing person, not too famous; tell him you want to write an article about him (or her) and go interview.

Assignment completed? Very well, you may go home and be comfortable again—for a *while*.

The Big Yes

There is a course of action for single women I feel strongly enough about to wonder how *anyone* could disagree. (Someone will, I imagine!) This is it. I think a woman alone can have a better life if she is effusive. Effusive, if I'm not mistaken, means super-enthusiastic.

A man retiles the kitchen sink. I suggest if you are going to accept his work as satisfactory at *all*, you might as well come on strong and even exaggerate your pleasure. "It's glorious. I never would have believed the sink could look like new like this."

If you accept an invitation to a friend's house for dinner, there is *nothing* in the world you'd rather do that night. If you *don't* like a plan or some work, that's okay, too. Say so or be quiet about it. If you do like it, however, I think lukewarmness should be barred from human responses.

Here's how to play the big yes:

1. A man invites you to a football game. "I've been perishing to see the Rams and the Forty-niners. I'm so glad you thought of it!"

2. The landlord has repainted your apartment (not an hour before he had to, but nevertheless . . .) "Mr. Reeves, my apartment looks simply beautiful. I'm so pleased. You're really a very nice landlord."

3. The bank teller let you make out your deposit slip at the window instead of sending you back to the table where it's supposed to be done. "You really were so nice to let me do this."

4. The alteration lady in the store brings in your suit to be tried on. "Gosh, it fits beautifully. I wouldn't have dreamed you could let out the hips so much. I'm awfully pleased."

5. Your father helps you wax the car. (He's waited on you hand and foot all of your life and you've forgotten he doesn't *have* to.) "Daddy, you are an absolute angel. I can actually see my freckles in the paint. Why don't I take you to dinner and we'll celebrate?"

6. Your mother makes you a bedjacket. "I just love it, Mother. I don't know another girl in the world who gets things handmade for her."

7. The restaurant owner is at the door as you leave. "I really think that's the best veal scallopine I've ever eaten in my life. I'm telling everyone."

8. One of the girls at work helps you with some typing. She made a few typos, but never mind. "Doris, you really were a mighty sweet girl to take all this stuff off my hands. I'm deeply grateful."

9. A man asks to kiss you and you want to be kissed by him. *Kiss* him so he'll ask you to go out with him forever.

If you're too reserved to do this kind of carrying on, practice. If you feel that enthusiasm weakens your position with the supplier, forget it. It strengthens it like mad.

The Villain Could Be You

Something came to my attention and I want to pass it

on before the idea becomes murky and I lose it. It's one of those things that make you say, "But of course. That's the answer." Then, if you don't move fast, you're back in the forest searching for mushrooms again.

This is the not-very-original thought that hit me like a ton of bricks: *You yourself are the one who keeps you from having everything in the world you think you want.* (With the exception of getting a husband. There aren't enough men to go around. But everything else is included.)

A pretty, single career girl gave me this insight. "Since January," she said, "I've had about four dates, none of which ever panned out. I've moaned and wailed about the man shortage, but that's a bunch of baloney. Girls much less pretty than I are constantly dating. I haven't attracted men this year because I didn't want to. When I broke up with Jerry (her beau for the past three years) I said it was over, but instead of sincerely wanting to date, what I actually wanted to do was go underground. So I did. Look at me. I scruff around my apartment instead of cooking up outside projects. At parties I make a beeline for the girls. I work endless hours at the office. *I'm* doing this to myself."

She gave me another flash of insight about a job she recently lost. It was a challenging job and she somehow managed to get fired from it within six months.

"Managed to get fired is just what I mean," she said. "There was only one man I had to please, and I got along with him like a hornet. That's not like me. I can get along with a whole bunch of hornets if I want to. Somewhere sunk deeply within me was the idea that this job was too much for me, that I really didn't deserve it and wasn't good enough for it. Perhaps subsconsciously I didn't want to make good. So I managed not to. Then I blamed it all on a difficult boss."

Do you think this girl, a recent graduate from an analyst's couch, is a victim of a "down to the mine" complex (the tendency of analysands to prove even their reason for wanting a peanut butter sandwich is emotional)? I don't think so.

Consider all the complainers you know with legitimate grievances who never *act:* The housewife says she's so exhausted she can't stand up. Yet she won't let her family sleep on unironed sheets. (Could it satisfy her to be a martyr?) A woman sniffles that her husband has belittled and humiliated her for fourteen years, but she makes no move to see a lawyer. (Could she feel comfortable being mistreated?) A teen-age girl longs for dates but makes not the first move to lose even five of those thirty pounds that must come off. (It's really much safer inside that wall of fat.)

I, too, have my grievances that never get acted on. How about yours? If you understand that it's *you* who are screeching on the brakes before you reach your heart's desire, it may not get the brakes unstuck, but at least you won't feel so frustrated.

To Shrink or Not to Shrink

Does psychiatry really work?

Almost everybody's heard or read about someone who committed suicide while under psychiatric care. Many psychiatrists (I know some personally) seem nuttier than their patients and seem to be making *twice* as big a botch of their lives!

Nevertheless, based on personal experience and observation of friends, I believe that psychiatry can help enormously. Several single women have told me it's the soundest investment they've ever made.

I believe psychiatry helps most dramatically in taking the joy out of punishing yourself! You may still kick yourself around a bit, but the old thrill is gone!

Take the men in your life, for example. I've noted that most women who are unmarried a considerable period of time are apt to become involved with at least one man who had to have been invented by the Marquis de Sade. (Any man who doesn't want to marry a girl who wants to marry *him* fits that category!)

Caution, however! One "difficult" beau in your life doesn't make you a masochist.

But suppose every man you ever become seriously interested in turns out to pound you to pieces emotionally. You think you meet these chaps by accident? Could it possibly be you track them *down?* A psychiatrist will *prove* you do!

Your ego may be so weak that you figure this is the only kind of man you deserve—bad, wicked, nothing lit-

249

tle you! The good doctor can help cure you of the habit of acting like a cube steak. He may even be able to get you started loving somebody who can love you back. (*P.S.* Women alone have also found "head shrinkers" a great help with death-grip parental attachments, frigidity, hating men altogether, etc.)

Treatment is expensive. And no matter how deserving but under-funded you are, practically no doctor can treat you for nothing. Usually he can see only six patients a day, and a free hour for you would be asking him to give up a sixth of his income.

Still, it's amazing how many "poor" girls have been able to work out some kind of sessions even if just on a once-a-week basis. And there's "group therapy" which I think is absolutely terrific. (You won't *believe* how hysterically funny somebody else will look to you who has exactly your set of neuroses!)

If the sun doesn't come up for you but once a month, if you're weepy half the time, if you keep bungling with beaux and jobs, go and talk it over anyway. A little first aid couldn't hurt. Your family doctor (unless he's impossibly stuffy) or county medical society can give you a list of medically accredited psychiatrists.

If You're Shy, But Oh My . . .

The other night I watched a thirteen-year-old boy conduct himself in a way that I think could be profitably aped by shy single girls. He lasted out one full hour of conversation among a group of adults without ever getting "on" himself, but apparently without dying of boredom or making anybody nervous either.

His lovely dark eyes snapped from one talker to the other. He never opened his mouth, but he seemed pleased and happy to be there.

A woman alone is not a child, and I don't mean that she should act like one or be treated like one. Sometimes, however, she finds herself among a group of people with whom she has little in common. It happens so easily.

She accepts a date with a man she doesn't know well, and he yanks her off to be with "foreigners" to whom she doesn't relate. They're all married or older or younger or play guitars or something.

She finds herself sitting there listening to a conversation in which she absolutely *cannot* participate and wishing she were dead. The boredom of it all is bad enough, but she wouldn't mind *that* so much. It's the impression she must be creating. Do they think she's a toad? A glumpf? An idiot? Worse still, unfriendly?

The hardest thing in the world to do is be tranquil and smiling while a conversation flows along without you. If you can keep listening, however, stay tuned in and keep the miserable look off your face—eventually they get around to you.

If *you* don't feel ridiculous about not participating, *they* certainly don't mind. Most groups could use more listeners. There are usually too many talkers talking on top of each other.

I have one or two other thoughts on shyness. Some people simply do not come on scintillatingly the first time out. Sometimes people even misjudge you and think you are snooty and unfriendly, heaven forbid, when you are only painfully shy.

I can remember having people say I was "stuck up" as a young dating girl and all I really was was too scared to open my mouth. Never mind. Most of the time you have a second and third chance at people. You run into them again at another party and gradually you sink into them. I think finally the sinkers-in have more power and perhaps charm than the early impressers who have shot their entire bag of tricks on the first outing.

As you get older, you usually become less shy, too. You're able to think about men as people, not as ogres about to do you in or princes you're afraid won't respond to your charms. A man is just another person with needs and fears. You can even smile when a truck driver whistles at you and be grateful that he has such good taste.

Shy people usually become good at certain things to cover their shyness. They are the best tennis players, bridge players, cooks, dancers, career girls. It's not a bad bargain to make. If you had been the most popular girl in the world just by standing there or being completely, utterly at ease in the world, you might not even have known what you could become.

251

A Special Kind of Problem

It takes all kinds to make up the population of women alone. We no more all fit into a mold (I'm including myself in the group, because I was single so long and identify with you) than all business executives, nurses or airline pilots are cut from the same cloth.

I lunched with a single woman last week who might be from another planet so far as seeing eye to eye with most women about men is concerned. She is, I believe, a nymphomaniac.

What is a nymphomaniac?

The dictionary says a nymphomaniac is somebody with a "morbid and uncontrolled sexual desire." That description doesn't exactly fit my friend—and only a doctor could accurately say who is and who isn't a nymphomaniac.

After hearing about nymphomaniacs all my life, however, and never knowing for sure whether I'd ever met one, because how could another girl know, I decided last week that, yes indeed, this is what my friend was—despite the fact that she doesn't fit the dictionary description.

Louise is just short of fabulous-looking. She has large brown eyes, red hair, a beautiful bustline, skinny ankles and makes $17,000 a year as a photographer. She has never been fired, out of work or even late for work very often in her life.

She hasn't had a nervous breakdown and has lots of friends. Her problem is that she has to have male admiration by the basketful, and the admiration must take the form of a man desiring her. "Thou shalt not pass without noticing me and wanting me" is Louise's motto.

"There has to be one man in my life in whose consciousness I am just about every waking moment," Louise says. "He must spend a great deal of time pleasing me. That's for openers. In addition, I find most men that I work with, meet socially or on business trips to be objects of 'wantability.' "

A man to be wanted by Louise apparently doesn't have to be a jewel, or wanted by other women. "I'm very uncritical," she says. "I can get absolutely mesmerized by a man other girls consider ordinary. Once a particular man has interested me, however, I concentrate on him exclusively for the evening or however long it takes to win him over."

"And what happens when he is won?" I asked.

"Since the attraction isn't based on friendship necessarily, but only on attention, it usually doesn't last too long. I want new attention from somebody else."

"It doesn't seem to be a problem for you to attract men," I said. "At least you're very successful in your collecting."

"Yes, but it's like alcoholism. If you can take a drink or not take a drink, that's wonderful. If you simply *must* drink, you're a victim without free choice."

"But then there's no peace of mind for you ever, is there?" I asked. "Or resting on your laurels."

"I'm afraid not," she said. "I'm thinking of marrying somebody who is really devoted to me and will at least supply part of my need. I won't be sitting every night plotting how to meet men."

Rather than taking a husband, I suggested taking a psychotherapist—my first-aid solution for almost any emotional problem. "I'm sure one can help," I told her. She promised to think about it.

Flight from Depression City

Some women alone are depressed pretty regularly for "real" reasons—the illness of a parent, problems with a child, the loss of a lover, the firing from a job and the more obscure, emotionally based reasons that are tied in with these stresses but not altogether brought on by them.

Whatever the cause, I don't think you can be jolted out of depression by the appearance of a jolly friend who whisks you out for an evening. Once you're unwhisked and back home again, Depression is waiting for you with your robe and slippers and a highball in its hand. "Hello dear, I made myself at home," Depression says. "Sure, I'm still here. Did you think I had any place *better* to go?"

I think you can't successfully run away from depression either. Whether you run to the movies, the bar or the tip end of Portugal, depression will tag at your heels. "For the love of Pete, slow down!" it will say. "I can keep up this ridiculous pace if you want to but wouldn't it make more sense to conserve our energy?" Pretty soon you find yourself slowing down.

Frankly, I don't think you can fight depression. I think you have to go straight through it—chug, chug, chug like a choo-choo train. What do you do then to keep from jumping off a roof? These are Mother Brown's simple home remedies.

You don't try to talk yourself out of a depression by counting your blessings. The kind of depression I'm talking about doesn't respond to such reason. You do, however, count wholeheartedly on your subconscious to count your blessings *for* you while you work, sleep and go about your business. Pretty soon you feel better. (All chronically depressed people know that sooner or later they feel better again automatically even though the trying conditions stay about the same.)

You *work* at your regular chores and extra ones if you can stand it. If you are only mildly depressed, the extra workload may lift your spirits and bring you out of it. If you are too seriously depressed to charge with that much enthusiasm, you treat depression as you would a common cold. You know you don't feel as well as usual but you get as much work done as you can. What you don't do is crump and go to bed—not for long, anyway.

You try to keep sublimely healthy between bouts—unless your emotional state is dragging your tissues down with it. You most assuredly *can* eat good high-protein meals day after day; scrupulously and continuously avoid junk. You can get enough sleep most of the time. When depression strikes, this sound little body of yours will help you strike back. While the depression is around, you continue to eat good foods, of course, even if only a fraction of the amount you usually crave.

If you don't feel like sleeping during this siege, okay, don't sleep. One afternoon you will be unable to hold your head up any longer and even if you have to leave work on the excuse of cramps or nausea I think you should sneak away to have the long restorative sleep your body now needs and is willing to accept. I'm against sleeping pills because again the depression is only there waiting

254

when you wake up. (The same is true of drinking.)

Should you see an analyst? Of course you should, if you can possibly afford it (or a minister, friend or anyone who will listen with genuine concern). An analyst can't cure chronic depression but he can help you understand and lessen its frequency. The people who are anti-analyst give me possibly a bigger pain than anybody I know. Are they going to sit there and say some people don't start out with more strikes against them than others? These people need more help.

Depression by me isn't anything to get excited about. It's just something to get *through*.

What to Do About Your "Craziness"

Many women wonder just how neurotic they are. Are they very much crazier than other people? I have come to the conclusion that almost everybody has plenty of neuroses. The only difference between the person you like to be around and the one about whom you say, "Oh, dear, she's too neurotic," is control. The "normal" person has his neuroses under better control (*i.e.*, he gets his work done, and having worked on his fears through the years, possibly with an analyst, they crop out less frequently).

Are you interested in my own special craziness which never abated during all my years of being alone and still hasn't now that I'm married? It's such a dull, ordinary, run-of-the-mill neurosis I hesitate to mention it and only do so because it's *mine* and I need it to make a point.

I think I am not pretty. I mean I *know* I am not pretty.

On Big N days I think I am not even passable. On those days or nights, I really suffer.

It's no good telling a neurotic (which in my own mind I have established as *nearly* everybody) not to worry about his own neurosis because he can't help it. He will be happy not to worry about *other* people's problems, but his own special pet fear is something else again. When this not-pretty gloom comes over me, I go into a private shell that would make a turtle seem outgoing. The thing that long self-training and psychoanalysis have taught me is not to show it.

I didn't get cured. I just got brave.

255

To continue with me, because I'm so fascinating, some time ago I had to make an appearance (as I've told you before) in the New York Supreme Court in connection with my book *Sex and the Single Girl*. With all the strangers around and with all the talk about sex, I thought I ought to be a symbol.

Well, at age forty-three, how can you possibly be a sex symbol, especially if you have a thirty-three-inch bust measurement and were never pretty to start with? I tried, of course. I wore my beautiful wig, but hadn't had a chance to check it out the night before. It looked like a wig, if you know what I mean. It was done in an up-flip, and the flip part was shooting straight out at a ninety-degree angle instead of whisking up prettily.

Being nervous, my mouth was set and tense—the "smile lines" deeper than usual. I had on a new dress that didn't pan out. (I wish these accursed formless, shapeless, sexless, little-nothing wool dresses would drop dead and small waists and hips could show again.)

Anyway, the wig, the dress, the strained face, the need to be gorgeous and not making it all combined to let my Big N get a foothold that day. It was gruesome. I became the frightened, wan, colorless little girl I must have been when all those ideas of "unprettiness" started.

Still, I don't think anyone was aware of how I felt.

Whatever your Achilles' (or Josephine's) heel is—you're unmarried, fat, tall, short, thin, shy or whatever—if you're doing everything possible to correct conditions, you can get by fine.

If you crump occasionally, well, crump! I want you to know that you are *not* alone.

"Eat Beautiful" and Feel the Difference

A famous health expert once wrote a book called *You Are What You Eat*. I don't know whether you *are* what you eat, but you certainly look like and feel like what you eat. As a woman alone, you have a chance to eat healthful, glamour-girl food most of the time. There's nobody around to demand those calorie-laden, figure-misshaping meals. If you *yourself* demand them, forget it! And children have to eat what you fix them so they shouldn't be able to ruin your healthful-eating plan either. Besides, what's good for you is good for them.

Here are four glamour-girl recipes gleaned from my friend Mildred Schroeder, who is an attractive and svelte newspaper reporter. Two of them require an electric blender, which is rather expensive—usually between $20 and $30. You know, of course, that I would never ask you to spend money wantonly or foolishly; however, when you feel you can afford it the blender is a lifetime investment, along with your steam iron. I believe it belongs in the kitchen of every woman alone because of the quick, healthful, delicious things you can mix up in a blender. (Sometimes it's much easier to *drink* a meal than cook and *eat* one.)

MILDRED'S DIET SALAD

Two or three kinds of greens (though one will do), crisped in the icebox
One small can of tuna
flaked into the salad
Oil and vinegar
Salt and pepper

Handful of Grapenuts (the Grapenuts give the salad a satisfying, dessertlike quality and make it a one-dish dinner or lunch)

NONBREAKFAST BREAKFAST

(full of voom and vigor)

1 raw carrot   1 stick of celery
1 small can of tuna
(you may eat the oil, too)

SEXY MILK SHAKE

(because it's full of protein)

Mix in the electric blender:
About half a cup of powdered skim milk
About a fourth cup of water
2 ice cubes
Spoonful of instant coffee (or you can flavor with fresh fruit)
Honey or Sucaryl for sweetening

257

HANGOVER CURE

Mix in the electric blender:
One avocado (without the seed, silly)
One cup of cottage cheese
Tomato juice with spices added

The avocado soothes your stomach, the cottage cheese is for protein and health. The tomato juice binds them together and tastes good.

The Gourmet in You

It came to me in a crystal-clear flash of insight the other night what a woman alone can do to become beloved and popular. She can learn to cook like Escoffier!

I realize this isn't a blazing new idea. As a matter of fact, it's about as old as goat-herding and the worship of primeval hemlocks. I'm not talking about just being a *good* cook, however. I'm talking about being a very *fancy* cook.

During the holidays I went to the dinner party of a very fancy cook. There were eight courses of the highest French cuisine—Les Filets de Boeuf en Croute, Endives Braisées Flamandes and that sort of thing.

Dinner took three hours. Nothing but champagne was served, and the twenty guests acted as though they'd all died and gone to heaven. They moaned in ecstasy. They rolled over on the floor. Some of them kissed the hostess's hem and refused to go home. Since no dinner could ever possibly be quite so heavenly and ambrosial again, what was the use of going on?

It occurred to me that if a woman alone could cook like that, she would have people—men in particular—dogging her footsteps, hoping, praying, yearning, hinting, dueling for invitations to dinner every day. It isn't a possibility to be taken lightly.

I asked the hostess, Yvonne Becker, what the chances were for a woman to become that kind of cook. Yvonne did the entire dinner herself—marketing, preparation, serving and cleaning up.

"Any woman could do it if she cared very much about

food," Yvonne, who happens to have attended the Cordon Bleu Cooking School in Paris for three years, said. "It would have to be a pretty strong drive. You see, I don't do anything else. I don't paint. I don't sew. I don't write. I don't gamble. I cook!"

"We don't have cooking schools like Cordon Bleu in most of our cities," I said.

"No," Yvonne admitted, "but you can still cook exquisitely if you care. You need time, patience and, as I say, a real passion for cooking. A beginner could learn the basics first. You can't start right out with Les Petits Chassons a l'Indienne or Crêpes. *The McCall's Cook Book* is an excellent basic book. So is *The Joy of Cooking*. You could probably learn basics quite thoroughly in a year. Then you would work with the *Gourmet Cook Book* or something more complicated."

Yvonne favors French cookery for "really showing off." With Chinese dishes, which are delicious, she says, "It doesn't really matter which comes first. You could serve the fortune cookies in the middle. French cuisine has harmony and beauty and ritual to it. It is probably the most complicated but also the most delicious."

In encouraging single girls to cook beautifully, Yvonne says, "After a cocktail party you are all alone with the dirty glasses and full ashtrays and perhaps one drunken guest, and you feel so let down. After a gourmet party, there is no loneliness or post-party blues. You feel warm and happy and rewarded because you have given your guests so much warmth and pleasure."

She also points out that cooking is feminine. Men adore you to do it and are never jealous if you turn out to be the best cook in the world. If you entertain without a host, any man at the party loves to carry things for you and help serve.

You might consider this cooking thing before you pop off for your next ballet lesson or frontal attack on the principles of contract bridge.

The Mole on the End of Your Nose

An enchantress I know has a big red mole on the end of her nose to which she is absolutely devoted. She wears chic clothes, keeps her nails manicured, her hair coiffed, her heels shod, her face made up and she can charm leaves out of a book, but the mole stays.

"Why don't you get rid of that thing?" friends plead. "You're such a pretty girl." "I just kind of like it," Marie Teresa tells them. "That mole is *mine*. Besides, Carter (her beau) doesn't mind it. I asked him and he said no." Carter, her beau, wouldn't tell a woman he didn't like something personal about her if she were growing a long red beard. He's just that kind of man, but that doesn't mean he's really in love with Marie Teresa's mole.

A young friend of mine is taking an apartment with a girl friend. The girl friend is from a wealthy family, speaks four languages, buys most of her clothes in Paris, and when she opens her mouth, sounds like a tough cab driver. That's because she's from a section of the country that has marvelous people but not beautiful voices. Her pals entreat: "Lola, why in heaven's name don't you take diction lessons and do something about that voice?" "But that's just the way I *sound*," Lola says. "My whole family sounds that way. (True. They all grew up in the same city.) Why should I try to have a voice that's unnatural?"

Joan's teeth are darkish, spaced too far apart and crooked. Joan grew up in a European country whose people aren't so fussy about giving babies plenty of milk to supply calcium; therefore, lots of adult girls from that region have terrible teeth. "But why should I have them capped?" Joan says. "As far as I know, no man has ever failed to ask me out because of my teeth." As far as she *knows*, that could be true.

Some of you have probably quit reading to take pen in hand to say "Good for Marie Teresa, good for Lola, good for Joan; they are showing guts and individuality." Maybe so. And maybe they are following an old American custom of being a little bit lazy, a little bit complacent, a little bit scared, leaving something imperfect about themselves so they won't be *too* beautiful and get too many rave reviews.

The list could be endless of things girls don't do to themselves that could help win friends and influence beaux. I had messy hair for years. It's casual and sexy, I said. It's unkempt and messy, people who really loved me said. I finally saw the light—or *really* saw the hair—

and did something. I'm glad. Another friend of mine has finally stopped declaring, "I think men really prefer chubby girls" and has husked off the thirty pounds that have been spoiling her looks. It's bringing her a new life.

Conformist as it sounds, cowardly as it may be, unnatural as it may seem to you, I think it's criminal to put off doing something about the mole, the teeth, the voice, the hair, the weight or whatever it is that keeps you from being a smashingly good-looking girl and getting the rewards you ought to have. Do you *hear* me?

Are You a Scaredy-Cat?

Many of us raised-in-the-Depression kids have a built-in horror of changing jobs very often. Way back when banks were failing and apples were hawked on street corners, we gleaned the idea that smart people get on a payroll, stick with one company through thick and thin and grow old gracefully together (company and employee).

Companies, of course, love this attitude and encourage it with such things as profit-sharing and twenty-five-year wristwatches with a teeny-tiny diamond in them for the faithful.

In my opinion, sticking around is good for the company but not always good for the sticker. It isn't categorically true that you must change jobs right and left to develop your full potential. Some girls rise from the mail room to become vice-presidents, working in one and only one firm all their lives.

Still, other girls who are capable of and deserve much more—often women alone—stick around through the years to become little more than faithful "family retainers." Sometimes it's the company's fault. They just don't see the girl in any other light than she shed ten years ago when she joined the firm as a shy secretary.

Often it's the girl's own fault, however. Out of fear and inertia, the company is so safe and comfortable—the girls are so nice and congenial—she fails to keep herself watered and throw out new shoots.

Don't you miss out on profit-sharing and pension plans if you're a butterfly? Possibly, but how much do they amount to? A friend of mine, age sixty-five, just retired from a major advertising agency after being employed by them and their parent company almost forty years.

For twenty of those years they had profit-sharing but Betsy's job classification didn't put her in the salary range to qualify. The company has, however, always given a pension to retiring workers, age sixty-five. Do you know what Betsy's pension is? A cool sixty dollars a month. It's something but it isn't much, so upon "retiring" last week, Betsy went right across the street and went to work for another company. Maybe if she'd done that at age forty-five, her retirement pension might have been more impressive. (Incidentally, I held jobs in twenty-one different companies, starting at age 19, before I became an author, columnist and editor.)

To see whether you might be ready for a change of company, I suggest you ask yourself these questions:

1. Can I do my present job practically blindfolded?

2. Have I made any stimulating new friends at work this year?

3. Do I ever meet men I can go out with?

4. Does my company really respect me or do they rather patronize me like a faithful collie dog? (A girl can be only thirty-two and still make this statement.)

5. Do I feel compelled to dress up, make-up and look chic every day or can I get away with run-down heels, sweaters and skirts?

6. Am I scared to death at the thought of a new job?

If the answer to the first five questions is "no" and the last question is "yes" I think you may be just about ready to go list yourself with a good employment agency.

TEN	**SOME WORDS TO THE WISE**
	or,
	Advice on Just About Everything

Whatever didn't seem to fit anywhere else in this book we've put in the last chapter, most of it having to do with —what else!—relations between men and women. The third article, "Should She or Shouldn't She," drew a ton of mail when it first appeared, 99 percent of it "frothing at the mouth" over the idea that an unmarried girl might cool-headedly and with malice (or pleasure) aforethought make a decision to have an affair . . . horrors. It's too late to take sides. The young lady went ahead with her plans. I won't tell you how it worked out. She's still involved, and it's too soon to say.

How to Lose a Man on the First Date

Some pages back we gave some rules for dating procedure. My friend Kriss Karlsson suggests that while we're at it, we ought to list these twenty-three rules for *losing* a man on your first date.

When your date arrives, don't be ready. If you've been ready for hours, return to the bedroom for at least a half hour of primping so that he doesn't think you're overeager to go out.

If he lets you choose the restaurant, pick the most expensive one in town.

Give him careful driving instructions, including when to stop for red lights or try to sneak through yellow ones.

At the restaurant, talk to the maître d' yourself and try to line up a good table.

When ordering dinner, select the most expensive items on the menu.

Order a vintage wine.

When dinner is served, complain about at least two of the dishes.

Talk with your mouth full.

Talk loudly.

Always comb your hair at the dinner table. While you're at it, do a painstaking make-up re-do.

Entertain your date by telling him your life's history from the day you were born to the present moment. Don't

265

leave anything out. If you forget minor details, go back and fill in—"Oh, I forgot—before that I was with the girl's band at Mineola High School and then I transferred to Watts Polytechnic."

If your date doesn't use correct English, don't be backward. Tell him the right word. Finish sentences for him if he hesitates.

Talk about former boyfriends. Tell him about all the money they spent on you, where they took you and how attractive they were.

If things get dull, pull out an old letter from someone in the family and clue him in on all the family troubles.

While he is talking, let your eyes wander around the room. Wave at somebody if you can.

While he's talking, interrupt constantly.

Smoke while you are eating.

Be sure to drink him under the table.

Don't be afraid to argue. Religion, race issues, politics, woman's place and sex are good meaty subjects. Try not to let him make a point. Top him on every subject.

If he suggests leaving and you are having a great time at the piano bar, insist on staying for one more drink.

When he takes you to the door, be sure to ask when you're going to see him again. If he hesitates, try to pin him down to a date.

If he doesn't offer to kiss you goodnight, kid him about being bashful or better still, grab him by the ears and kiss him.

Be sure to call him first thing in the morning. Get him out of bed. If you're up, he should be up, too. If you don't hear from him after that, call him every night for a week.

How to Say Goodbye and Make It Stick

A woman alone doesn't *always* have the problem of finding a man. Sometimes she has the problem of telling one she doesn't want to see him anymore. And maybe there's nothing particularly wrong with the man. He just isn't her cup of tea although he apparently thinks she is *his*.

How do you tactfully tell someone you don't want to see him again and not to ring you up any more for dates?

If you're deeply involved with a man, you just tell him

266

the truth. The romance isn't working out and you must let each other go. If it is a more casual friendship, there are several systems. One is to say you're going to be frightfully busy with your work or your skiing, or your sewing or your family or some guests from out of town for the next couple of months and you don't see how you can fit him in. That doesn't sound very plausible, however. A girl always has time for the man she really wants to see.

You can tell the man he's a bore, but that's pretty cruel. You can be obscure. "John, I just don't feel we're relating." He'll want to know what you mean by relating and you're still faced with trying to explain why the friendship can't continue.

You can profess conflict of interests. He's an arch-conservative. You're liberal. He's for Swinburne. You're for Streisand. When did different views ever keep people apart? Real lovers spend fascinating hours explaining their heroes to each other.

I think the best way to dismiss someone you don't want to see any longer is to tell him there's somebody else in your life whether there is or not. This explanation is convincing, unequivocal and in the long run less painful because it doesn't impugn this particular man's charm. Everybody knows there is such a thing as a cliff-hanging romance. If a girl has found it with another man, it doesn't mean the man left behind is a boob. The girl is just temporarily out of her mind, that's all.

This is your dialogue when the soon-to-be-discarded friend calls up.

"John, I really must talk to you about something. I seem to have got involved with someone and I think perhaps you and I shouldn't see each other for a while. I guess I'm going to do what is called 'going steady.' I know this may seem a little inappropriate for a woman my age—going steady—but I think I have to spend some time with this man to see if it's going to work out. Frankly, I'm not sure he's the right one at all. (Make your new love sound a little seedy and you save this man's ego.) Anyway, I feel I must try it."

If John sooner or later sees you out with two different men two nights in a row, this doesn't necessarily negate your story. Maybe man number one is your love and man number two is his father or brother. The important thing is to make the initial break so that your friend stops bugging you for dates. Within a few weeks he'll probably find a new girl to bug and it doesn't matter whether you keep up the pretense of having a new *amour* in your life or not.

Should She or Shouldn't She?

"I have been going with (I'll call him Bill) for almost a year now," stated the young lady. "He is a nice person —gentle, kind and also very romantic. He takes me to the best restaurants, buys me flowers and courts me devotedly. I'm in love with him and he wants to marry me, but here's the problem:

"About five years ago, Bill was divorced. He tells me his wife was a virgin when they married and later they discovered they were simply *not* compatible. He said she was a wonderful girl but that (if you'll pardon my frankness) they didn't have sexual relations because it was unsatisfactory and frustrating to both of them. They went to a doctor and also a marriage counselor and even these people advised a divorce.

"Bill says that before we get married we should know if we are compatible. I've never married before, and I'm still a virgin. I just don't know what to do. Suppose we do sleep together—the thought isn't repugnant—but then discover we aren't well mated. No other man would want me, would he?

"How do you feel about it? I can see his point, but I also feel that I have a lot to lose, too. Or do I? I'm thirty-five, if that makes any difference in your answer."

"Jane," I said, "I like to think I have the answers to some problems or at least good advice, but in your case I feel like dropping the problem right back in your lap and running for the nearest train.

"To advise somebody to take the step you are contemplating would be taking too much responsibility. Your own religious and moral standards are important, too, and must be weighed against any 'practical' advice you get from the outside.

"In my opinion, you would not be 'ruined' if you take the step. And, of course, other men would still want you, but your man's rationale is what bothers me. If people are loving and kind, they can usually work something out in the way of a physical relationship even if it never quite reaches black magic or Fourth of July fireworks.

"You rarely hear of a doctor and marriage counselor advising marriage dissolution for sexual incompatibility alone. Your friend is either not quite telling the truth, or actually he has a physical problem that worries him and he wants to check ahead of time.

"I don't think it unwholesome or wolfish that your friend *wants* to have a relationship with you and *now*. You are not an ingenue, and you are probably extremely attractive to him. I just find his reasons a little phony."

Should Jane do what the man wants? Or shouldn't she? Should a girl be chaste for marriage no matter how old she is? Read on.

Well, Should She or Shouldn't She?

This is what people said about Jane's dilemma:

"Mrs. Brown, tell her *no!* Don't ever give yourself to a man before marriage. Even if he married you, there'll always be a little something missing that ought to be there."

"Helen, if this pipsqueak really loved this girl he wouldn't ask such a thing of her. Don't let a man hunt on your reservation without a license is what I say—a marriage license, that is."

"Should she or shouldn't she? You bet she should. This girl sounds like the woman I married two years ago. We waited and my wife turned out to be cold, unresponsive and determined never to have anything to do with me. If she'd been a little more honest or willing to experiment before marriage, we could have saved ourselves the heartache and pain of the divorce we're now going through."

"Regarding that thirty-five-year-old woman. She should not give in to that man. He is just a modern-day treacherous stinker. They should both go to a doctor and let the doctor decide this question. One or the other of them may be out of proportion and a doctor could advise them about this."

"Mrs. Brown, I'm not against Jane experimenting, but it wouldn't work. She'd be tense and under the strain of knowing this was a test. She'd probably flunk out no matter how hard she tried."

"Helen, tell that girl I, too, once knew a man named

Bill who asked me to do the same thing. I said no, not until we're married. I really loved him, but we broke up and I married another man. I have now been unhappily married for twenty-five years. If I had it to do over, I'd do what Bill wanted instead of having the sister-brother relationship I now have."

"Helen, how could they tell from one try? It might work just fine then and fizzle out later. Tell them to go ahead and get married and take their chances."

"Stop this woman before it's too late! I read recently that one out of every seven brides in England is pregnant before she gets married. If people like Jane go around doing what their boyfriends propose, the rate could get to be one out of three in this country."

"This man is strictly a wolf in sheep's clothing. He wants to sample the fruit before he buys it. After it's bruised, he may throw it away. I am a wolf, and I know what I'm talking about."

"Helen, I am very much in love with my husband and he with me after three years of marriage and one year of an affair. I think experience before marriage— experience with caution and meaning—is both necessary and advisable."

"Mrs. Brown, if Bill had problems in his last marriage, I don't blame Jane for wanting to know if she's going to have the same kind of trouble. I say she should do what he wants, but be very careful."

"Don't be silly. This is about the biggest nut story I have ever heard. If Jane and Bill were supposed to get together, they would have by now. Making an appointment to conduct an experiment is ridiculous. Tell her to wake up and go find a man with whom she has more 'natural' desire."

"Mrs. Brown, I find your comments about Jane not being ruined if she does what he wants completely nauseating. Tell her absolutely no. No woman can ever face herself again knowing she has sacrificed purity to satisfy the lusts of the flesh."

Sorry, Jane, there doesn't seem to be *one* correct answer.

Let's Face Facts—We Outnumber Them

I'm convinced that friends of a woman alone sometimes have no more idea than a salamander how few and far between the marriageable men are in a girl's life. Not *all* people are so gauche as to corner you after Sunday School or at a garden party and say, "Gretchen, why *isn't* a nice girl like you married?" but their little ears are always perked up and they are sniffing the air to learn that Yes, you've finally come to your senses and done what every good, smart, normal girl always does—got yourself a husband and gone straight. They act as though any girl who doesn't marry is just plain stupid or perverse.

Whom are you going to marry? Sometimes I think a girl *herself* forgets there is a very real and serious man-shortage. She fears there really *is* something wrong with her that she doesn't know *one* man, let alone three or four, she could carry off and mate. Somewhere in another town, must *be* those eligible bachelors she's entitled to.

There are more single women than men at this writing —a whole lot more. I personally have fourteen unmarried girl friends between the ages of twenty-two and forty here in New York where I live, and I wouldn't have the foggiest idea where to go to get a date for any *one* of them for dinner much less to march down the aisle with. By contrast a "bachelor" I know was able to date about thirty different girls while waiting for his divorce to become final. All this time his divorcing wife was trying to get him back. He eventually picked one of the thirty girls and got engaged. Four weeks before the ceremony still *another* girl managed to sneak in and get him away from the first girl. They were married last week. Cary Grant type? Good heavens, no. A reasonably attractive man, five-feet-two-inches tall with a fabulous job and—single.

A few men, very few, complain of a girl shortage. They are usually pathologically shy or much older men. A few girls, very few, have more beaux than they know what to do with (I personally don't know any such girls). Some girls don't really like men or are afraid of marriage and run, run, run from the entire sex and from the institution. Naturally with them there's *always* a man shortage, which is just the way they want it. To my knowledge, however, these exceptions noted, there is a genuine shortage of bachelors in the lives of most "normal" women over the age of twenty-five. (It gets worse after thirty-five and worse still after fifty.) Now I'm not telling you this to depress you, only to say let's face how things *are*. Under the circumstances, to have a happier life, I think you should:

1. Give up your dreams of glory of having ten or twelve young men after you as Scott Fitzgerald's heroines did. (Your great, great pioneer-woman grandmother had a lot more choice of men than you do, *also*.) Realize there are perhaps five girls for every eligible man and you have to be clever to get one of them. (It's kind of like landing a job in the Depression. Then there were plenty of husbands to be had but no jobs. Now there are loads of lovely jobs but few men. As you had to shape up and compete for the jobs then, you have to shape up and compete for the men now.)

2. Don't consider that you are *without* men in your life. You're surrounded by them—your boss, the men at work, your brothers, your father, your minister, your insurance agent, husbands of your friends (Oh, come on, they won't bite. They can at least be friends in your life.), your broker, your lawyer, gas station attendants, grocery store clerks. Just because they aren't yours to marry doesn't mean they can't be buddies.

3. Remember it only takes *one* man to marry and chances are, sooner or later, you can get that *one* if you keep caring and charming and work as hard to get him as girls did to get jobs in the Depression.

4. One marriage in three ends in divorce so that men are being liberated all the time. Whether it's good for the moral fiber of society or not, it does give you new leads.

Happy New Year All Alone

It's not a minute too soon to face it. What *are* you going to do next New Year's Eve if you get stuck without a date?

The Christmas festivities are behind you, and I assume you got through them somehow even if you didn't have a man.

New Year's Eve by yourself is something else again. The old year is konking out and whether it was a good year or a miserable one, you're still a year older with your hi-fi equipment not yet paid for. The new year is crashing in and that calls for your being a finer, nicer, better-informed, more attractive *you* than you were last year. You

272

aren't sure whether you're going to be up to *that*.

There's also that wretched business, and now we are getting down to cases, of every single girl being expected to have something glamorous and exciting to do that night. (They're selling all those sequined gowns to *somebody*.) The truth is that by some incredible set of circumstances beyond your control, you not only may not have a date for New Year's Eve, you may even wind up without even a girl friend to spend the time with. Worse, you can't even talk about the situation openly because it's too humiliating.

I wouldn't tell this to just anyone, but it happens that not once, but numerous times, I, too, was stuck whack, smack absolutely flat in the middle of my apartment alone on New Year's Eve and you know what a lovely girl *I* am. The last time it happened before I got married, I finally abandoned all hope of rescue around 5 P.M., got to a department store just before closing time, bought a pattern and six yards of pink outing flannel and made pajamas all evening. Can you imagine? I don't even wear pajamas.

I think New Year's Eve could very nicely be struck from the list of national celebrations; however, there are ways of coping alone. One way not to cope, in my opinion, is to round up all the other girls you know who don't have anything to do either and make the best of it together. That just seems too pitiful to me. I think it's better to make pajamas, read Baudelaire out loud, take the stove apart and clean it or do something else constructive this particular evening. While you're at it, you can drink a bottle of domestic champagne, think about next year and map out some plans. (Remember that Ghandi, Nehru, Victor Hugo, de Valera, Stalin, Jomo Kenyatta and Mussolini *all* did some of their best thinking in jail.) After you've made a few unostentatious but sincere resolutions, I suggest you finish the champagne and take a hot bath, being careful not to slide down into the tub so far that your head is under water. Go to bed around 10:30 long before the bells are ringing and the chimes are chiming. You'll feel much better the next day than those nuts who were out in all that racket.

As for what to tell people you did on New Year's Eve, you have a number of choices:

Big party—Pick one that's been infinitesimally described

273

in the society pages and say you went to it. You can pick up what everybody wore, table decor, door prizes and sound very much there.

Multiple parties—You went to *several* parties. People will hesitate to ask for details for fear the descriptions of five parties might take all day.

Big twosome—An old beau came in from out of town and you spent an intimate evening together (obviously too absorbed in each other to want anybody else around or to want to talk about it either).

Sports event—You and some friends took the train right after work to the nearest ski trail. If anybody figures you only got in about two hours skiing in order to get back to work on time, say two hours of good skiing are better than none.

The truth—"I hadn't a single solitary thing to do and went to bed at 10:30." You'll find a number of other people did exactly the same thing.

The Rich, Full Social Life—What's That?

Aside from the emotional fulfillment marriage is supposed to bring, many an unmarried woman feels her social calendar would fill up like magic if she just had a mate.

It doesn't necessarily work out that way, you know. An excellent article in a recent periodical is called "Why Young Couples Feel Trapped"—subtitled "Husbands and wives across the country talk about their minor pleasures and major dissatisfactions of social life after marriage."

It's an eye-opener! The magazine held seminars of married couples in six medium-sized cities, and from these writer Sam Blum concluded that "many newly married couples have very little social life at all. They neither entertain nor go out with other couples." He was touched by the fact that many of the couples participating in the seminars seemed reluctant to go home, this possibly being the most rewarding social evening they had had in weeks.

Young couples apparently have trouble getting their social life off the ground because:

1. A wife keeps putting off and putting off having people in until everything in the house is just right and she can be proud. Time marches on.

2. Money is a problem. The couple is making so many

payments on mortgage, television set and car there isn't much money left for the rich, full social life.

3. Finding somebody to be rich and full and social *with* is rougher than you'd think. Many of the friends each had in "singlehood" have also married, moved to different neighborhoods or cities. A husband who depends on associates from his office to join him and his wife in the evening may find them all living in town whereas he commutes to the suburbs.

4. There are few community centers where people may just go and talk and be sociable. The centers are usually meeting places for service organizations and special interest groups. We have no equivalent of the French café or the English pub where the entire neighborhood is welcome to enter and speak its mind.

5. Parents who can't hire a baby sitter very often simply stay home with young children rather than take them along to somebody's house to which the kids aren't specifically invited.

Many young couples, says Mr. Blum, "can only look back with nostalgia on the kind of recreation and sociability patterns they once knew—certain people (gave) the impression that the true social excitement in their lives ended with marriage and that they were still trying to recapture it."

Many a woman alone reading this could probably say, "They think *they* have problems—they should be *me!*" A chock-full-of-fun-and-satisfaction social life probably isn't that simple for anybody, married *or* single, and lots of the people you envy and think are having it *aren't*. You just hear about the high spots. Some women are just better at making lively things happen to them than other women but really very often they are *single*. While lunching with a divorcee the other day, I watched her get herself invited to a country estate for the weekend by the couple at the next table, lined up to see *Hamlet* two nights later with a second couple who had a bachelor arriving from Dallas and invited to lunch the next day. I know several single women like her. Put them down alone in a potato patch and twenty minutes later they've rounded up at least five people to have a party with.

It's up to you. You have to make the phone calls and say, "I'm going to be in your neighborhood next Friday, can I drop by and bring you that gazpacho recipe I promised you?" Or, "Why don't you come over for cocktails Thursday?

Aunt Meg is going to be here and she wants to meet you." The single or married people who have it best *make* it happen.

Surrounded by Loved Ones, but Oh So Lonely

As I've said, not all women alone are without husbands. Recently I heard from one who was married at seventeen but is still alone most of the time except for her children. Her husband is in the service but stationed near home. There is no on-base housing, however, so the service personnel are all scattered around and not centralized.

Here is what this young "wife alone" says. "We have a one-bedroom apartment in a very unfriendly area. Most of the couples work and have no children. My oldest child is twenty months, too young to keep in tow without chasing after him. He doesn't just follow verbal commands. My youngest is three months old and must be carried. Just getting out the door is an ordeal. We have very little money so baby sitters are out of the question. My husband has an extra job and is active in the base judo club. Therefore, with his regular duty nights, he is not home much. I am not trained to work, but I'm not stupid either. I had a scholarship before I married, but I gave it up to become a wife. I read quite a few books, but they just can't replace people. I'm seeing too much of myself, so you see, I really *am* a woman alone. Do you have any ideas about how I could become less so?"

It isn't easy for me to advise this girl because I've never been in remotely the same situation. (Unmarried and childless, you can always scat around to a new job or new community and stir up some action. With three permanent people in your life, it isn't so simple.)

I would hazard these suggestions:

1. Without carping, I would try to explain to my husband the fix I'm in—that I just have no adult companionship. Is it possible you could see each other anymore often if he really tried? Have you become a bore or a nag, so that he doesn't *want* to come home?

Perhaps your husband was raised by a mother who assured him marriage and babies were all a woman could

276

possibly want and he doesn't understand that you are actually frustrated.

2. Looking toward the future when the children will be in school and you can work, I would try to decide what my most consuming interest, aside from my family is. Usually everyone has a predilection toward *something*— flowers, law, medicine, politics, money, beauty, physical fitness, costume design. I would then read and study everything I could get my hands on about the subject or send myself to college at home. It couldn't hurt a thing to be steeped when the time comes to get a job.

3. The few times I was out I would poke around to see if there's one other young mother in the same boat. Then trade off an afternoon or two of caring for each other's children. Keep poking. Ask your husband to ask the fellows on the base who have children about reciprocal sitting with their wives.

4. When the children are a bit older, poke around some more and see if there isn't a job you can do several afternoons a week without training—cashier, receptionist, salesgirl. Even if your wages all go for baby-sitting, it might be a good exchange.

5. Remember you are only twenty. There'll be lots of years ahead when your husband is out of the service and life can be more normal.

Getting a Lonely Young Mother Out of the Gloom

A number of people took to heart the problems of that young mother who is married to a serviceman but is a "woman alone" most of the time because she lives off the base, her budget is low and her husband is involved with base (the military kind) activities which keep him away from home. Several young mothers in approximately the same situation as this girl have these suggestions. (And some of their ideas can also be utilized by young widows and divorcees with children.)

1. Don't feel sorry for yourself and don't wait until the babies are older before you do something. Act now. Make up your mind that a portion of your life belongs to *you* in addition to the portions that belong to your husband and children. Force yourself to get out every day if

277

only for a walk around the area with the children in a stroller or buggy. Take a different route each time. When you see small children along the way, stop and talk to them. Their mothers may be just as disconsolate as you are and friendships can form.

2. Smile and speak to your neighbors every day. Even if they're childless and go off to work, most people will be friendly if you are and you can visit with them on weekends.

3. Have a "coffee" some morning. Just write out the invitations and put them in a few of your neighbors' mailboxes. You'll be surprised at the response. If your neighbors work, ask them over in the evening for dessert and coffee.

4. Go to church regularly and take the babies. Most churches have a nursery, and church is a wonderful place to meet other young people. Offer to teach Sunday school. If you have no transportation to the church, somebody will probably come pick you up.

5. Get a collapsible stroller and take the children on the bus. You can visit a park and bring a picnic lunch.

6. Stretch your food money to purchase at least one home magazine each month. Get a different one each time until you see which has the most practical and inspiring ideas. Buy a beauty magazine, too, and try out all their suggestions.

7. Join the Y.W.C.A. or Y.M.C.A. They often have a fine program for young mothers and will care for the babies while you are in class. Any adult education class will get you together with people your own age and enrich your life. If you're married, firmly but lovingly suggest to your husband that he take over the children one evening a week no matter how busy he is with his own projects. If you're divorced or widowed, try to trade baby sitting with another young mother.

8. When the housework is bugging you, stop! Make yourself a cup of tea, go sit by the window and think for a while. After that ten- or fifteen-minute break, you'll feel better.

9. If you need extra money, see if they need part-time help at the commissary or post-exchange (or drugstore or restaurant). Even if your wages go for baby sitters, this will at least get you out of the house and give you a new interest.

10. Remember that other people need you as much as you need them. Figure out ways you can help them.

The Weekend That Was

We all know that women who are technically free to have dates are *supposed* to have some pretty rollicking times on national holidays. You're supposed to sail away in a romantic little sloop with a chemical engineer and make chemistry or at least dance till dawn under the stars with a star insurance salesman.

What single girls really *do* on holiday weekends is something else again. Some of them have romantic times. Often the romance just doesn't happen to fall when the holiday does, and that's the way the mop flops! I interviewed twelve unmarried girls in a large publishing company, and this is how their Labor Day weekend shaped up:

Sandy: I went camping with my family. Mother and Daddy were delighted to have me because I usually turn up my nose at family outings. We slept in tents. The temperature was a bracing 29 degrees. It took me all morning to thaw out. My tent fell down one night, too. I also caught a bass.

Elizabeth: I took all the pink-striped sheets I'd bought at the August white sales and made bedroom curtains out of them. They look smashing! I also put up twelve hems and made face towels out of some old bath towels that were getting ravelly. Boy, was I virtuous!

Margo: My girl friend and I went to the races. We bet one dollar apiece on each race and made enough to pay for lunch and getting in. It was *very* successful. I recommend race tracks.

Claire: I spent the weekend drinking and looking for men. You go down to the docks where the restaurants are located and there are about fifty men to one woman. What *else* would you do on a weekend?

Ruth: I went on an eating binge—waffles with melted butter for breakfast, blueberry pancakes for lunch, chocolate soufflé and salami pizza for dinner. At least it was kind of creative because I cooked all this stuff myself.

Ursula: Seven girls and I have this beach house and naturally I went there. We dug clams and actually found some but couldn't get them opened. A lovely old clam digger showed up from nowhere and opened them for us. He ate most of them.

Pat: I refinished a mahogany chest antique white. It was like me and the monster locked in a death grip—I kept thinking of Hemingway's *Old Man and the Sea* bringing in that marlin. There's quite a lot *to* refinishing furniture.

Mitzi: The city was deserted and I had the art galleries, museums and aquarium to myself. I'm pretty good about doing what's worthwhile when there's time to *do* it instead of sitting on my fanny.

Rae: I got engaged. He's been saying no-no-no and I've been saying yes-yes-yes and finally he said yes-yes-yes.

Lureen: I hiked, and then I hiked some more. I didn't have another bloody thing to do and decided this was the weekend to get at the hips and biceps. They're coming along nicely.

Mickey: I gave a cocktail party but it was kind of a flop. The married people only talked to each other in little bunches and the single people didn't have any fun. Next time I'm going to invite some characters to liven things up.

Regina: I had a date with a different man all four nights and two afternoons. I think holiday weekends are very depressing if you don't have dates.

And how was *your* holiday?

How Do You Keep from Getting Murdered?

That brutal murder of two career girls in New York City made all women who live alone uneasy, I'm sure.

One frightening aspect of the crime was that the girls seemed to have done everything right. They were nice girls. Three of them lived together in a good neighborhood. One of their families lived only a few blocks away. They held respectable jobs. Where did they go wrong?

I asked Deputy Commissioner Walter Arm of the New York City Police Department, and he said, "We haven't been able to figure out anything they did wrong, except it looks like maybe they left their door unlocked. Anyway, there was no forced entry."

"Is there so much more crime in New York City that girls should stay away from here?" I asked.

"No," he said, "of the twenty-five major cities, New York ranks eighteenth in murders committed, seventeenth in rape, tenth in aggravated assaults." (Though that still adds up to a lot of crime.)

"Well, maybe girls alone should stay away from all big cities entirely," I suggested, hoping he'd say this wasn't so.

"No," the commissioner stated. "The FBI has found that crime is on the increase more in suburban areas than in major cities. There's more crime because there are more criminals. That's about all we know. You just can't tell when a woman will attract some sort of psycopath, and it will have nothing to do with where she lives."

Asked his advice about defense tactics, Commissioner Arm said a girl's lungs are her best protection.

"If somebody is following you on the street and gaining," he said, "scream. That usually frightens this kind of fellow away."

He also sent me a little booklet telling women alone how to protect themselves. These are some of the points:

Notify the police promptly of any suspicious person loitering in the vicinity of your home or on routes that you ordinarily take. When traveling alone at night, walk where it's well lighted. Don't take short cuts.

If awakened at night by an intruder, don't try to apprehend him. He might be armed. Do not panic. Lie still, observe carefully and at the first chance call the police.

Never open the door automatically after a knock. Insist that callers identify themselves. Install a window peephole.

At night, double-lock your door and chain lock it, too. Equip your door with a lock that has a "dead bolt" as well as a spring lock.

Install locks on windows so that they will be secure when open as well as closed.

In case of burglary, don't enter residence if door has been forced. Don't touch anything. Notify police.

If threatened by a robber, do as you are told. Observe as much as possible and notify police.

Don't place keys under mats, in mail boxes or other receptacles outside the door.

If you lose your door key, have locks changed immediately. Make certain your door is locked at all times. Some burglars make a career of finding open doors.

Employ servants only on bona fide recommendation and after thorough investigation.

When you go away, do it quietly. Be sure paper and milk deliveries are stopped in your absence. Don't leave notes.

Don't flash sums of money in public places.

When shopping, don't leave your purse lying on a counter. In the theater keep your bag on your lap, not beside you on the seat.

Last-Minute Christmas Gifts of Love

When Christmas rolls around, you may well find yourself, at the last minute, plowing through stores looking for the perfect Christmas gift. Well, here are some little gifts you tuck into somebody's stocking—and they don't take a single minute of shopping time. They also don't cost a cent. They are gifts of love—backed up by some of your time.

Don't underestimate their worth. To be technical about it, everyone's time is worth a certain amount and you are giving a promissory note of some value. Just hand-letter in gold ink on red paper or some such combination these "promises to pay," and you have a wonderful present for somebody who has everything, somebody who doesn't have anything or for anybody you genuinely care about.

1. Twenty hours of free baby sitting any time during 196—. (Two days' notice required.)

2. Three weekends of cat sitting or dog watching. This is a present that can't even be bought by people who adore their pets. They can purchase kennel care, but someone to come and stay in their house while they weekend in Mexico is a gift without price.

3. Written offer to take goldfish, parakeets (or dogs and cats) into your house for the vacation period. Word it officially. "This certificate entitles the recipient to bring his parrot (or whatever) to my house for three weekends in 196—. Written instructions must accompany pet."

4. Six backrubs—as close to real Swedish massage as you can dish out. This is expensive fare in salons but there's

282

hardly anybody it doesn't appeal to—especially tired
mothers and worn secretaries.

5. Twenty hours of hair-brushing. (This is one I have
been giving to my mother for many years now.)

6. Three afternoons of labor (or however long the job
takes) to map out, cut and sew up draperies and curtains.

7. Alterations of three hems and three waistlines during the year. (Women who don't sew are thrilled with
this kind of help.)

8. Four mornings of scrubbing or any kind of actual
household help an overworked mother needs.

9. Offer to be part of the clean-up crew after the next
party. This could be for a bachelor who claims it took him
three days to dig out of the last one.

10. Sock-mending. Jacket elbow-patching. (I know one
girl who made Bermuda shorts for a fellow out of a pair
of his old Levi's. She just whopped off the legs and hand-
hemmed them, but he never got over it—thought she was
a real wizard.) Most men have things like this to be done
and don't know who to ask.

11. Volunteer service to type a speech or rehearse lines
with somebody who's studying acting.

Tailor the gift to fit the recipient, of course. And do
the gift certificate up "gorgeously" so it will look official
and the recipient won't hesitate to collect.

And Bring Your Young Man ... Oh Sure!

What do you do when a thoughtless but well-meaning
hostess invites you to a party and says, "And be sure
to bring your beau"—and you don't have one!

As I see it you have three choices. 1. Scrounge up just
anybody even if it's your little brother. 2. Say your gout
is worse and you can't leave the house. 3. Level with the
hostess and go to the party alone.

Now none of these solutions can be ruled *out* all the
time or *in* all the time. It depends on the party.

If it's the kind you must bring a man to—couples for
dinner, fashionable cocktail bash, charity ball—and
there's no little brother or any other male to round up
unless you go out to the airport with a butterfly net,
then it may be better just quietly to skip the party. Dye

your hair that night. There'll be another party along.

As for leveling with the hostess on the chance she can scare up a man for you, that's all right if she's a hip and friendly person. You may not know the hostess well enough to do that, however . . . and no girl likes to be thought of as a charity case. Again, skip the party.

It's all right to attend many parties alone or with another girl. By all means do. Again you must use your instinct to pre-analyze the party.

As for bringing a man who isn't quite up to snuff socially, go right ahead! That's what everybody else does sometimes. I've seen some very attractive unattached heiresses who ought to be able to round up a prince arrive at parties with specimens you'd swear they had plucked from night court. Nobody pays that much attention.

When you *do* have a gorgeous man in your life, may I suggest you *give* a party or round up a friend to do so. Show him off and impress them during your fat times so they don't have a permanent impression of you as Little Orphan Annie.

How to Argue and Be a Lady

How mad is too mad to get when arguing a controversial subject at a party? Too mad is when you wake up the next morning and realize that you didn't have a good time, that you and one of the guests were almost at each other's throats. You know you probably gave the host and hostess some terrible moments and that you'd give your new orange T shirt if the discussion hadn't taken place.

As a woman alone you probably carry an extra burden of responsibility on your frail shoulders to be charming and not too controversial as a guest. For one thing you don't have a husband to defend you (my husband is always on *their* side of course!) or drag you out of the fray when things get too bloody. The hostess can't say to her husband next day, "Well, she's a bit of a hot-head, but he's so nice we really can't cross them off the list." There's just little you, running the risk of ostracism by getting too angry.

I don't think you should stay away from discussions

at parties—that can be the best part—but as a single woman I do think you have to keep your shirt on. Let's see if we can put down some ground rules.

1. Before you categorically attack dog worshipers, Fair Play for Cuba, spoiled children, NATO, ladies' clubs, the Beatles, modern furniture or yoga, think what the object or philosophy under attack may mean to the person you're discussing it with. It could be a whole way of life for him and not just an abstract idea, in which case you must pussyfoot. A public figure you are gossiping about or criticizing may be this person's idol, in which case you might as well be attacking his own mother. In other words, you must be aware of whether you can have an all-out intellectual discussion (ha! fat chance) or whether you are dabbling with somebody's psyche.

2. Even with your *own* friends, there are things you absolutely must not talk about by tacit agreement. A friend of mine believes all members of a particular ethnic group are dangerous and keeps a loaded gun in his house against attack. If he and I ever discussed this bias again (once was enough), I'm sure I'd be unable to resist trying to find the gun and shoot *him*.

3. If one particular member of your discussion group is a professional troublemaker, drunk or spoiling for an argument, lie low. Don't *you* be the one to trigger him into a mouth-frothing rage, thus doing yourself in with the hostess.

4. When somebody is saying ridiculous things you know to be untrue because you were *there* or know the attacked person, quietly state the truth but don't whip yourself into a lather. Some people are just great blabbermouths and don't want facts. By the same token, if it's the kind of argument in which everybody is yelling so loud you can't get on, stay off. Even if you're well informed, those "discussions" are no fun anyway.

5. Daub your conversation with a great many "I certainly can see your point about *that*, but on the other hand," and other gracious statements. Let your protagonist finish his sentences. Compliments and courtesy from you mean your arguments will be more forceful and effective.

6. I think you can discuss politics but almost never religion. At least those are my ground rules for the world's two most controversial subjects.

Joseph, the Fiend, Took Her Flying Machine

A successful young career girl says, "I recently purchased a car and wonder if you would give all us girls who own cars your opinion on how to handle a situation like the one I found myself in the other day.

"My date's car was being repaired and he asked if I would mind using mine. I didn't but let him drive. After our date, I dropped him off at his apartment and drove on to my house alone—about twenty minutes away.

"The next day he asked me to a football game. I picked him up at his apartment and drove about 150 miles round trip. On the way home I noticed my gas tank was just about empty. He thought it didn't look quite empty and said if I waited, there was a station near his apartment where I could get gas two cents a gallon cheaper.

"As I wasn't sure just how much gas was left in the tank, I pulled into the next gas station and told him I was going to get ten gallons. He said, 'Put in two dollars worth, I'll pay for it!' This, however, didn't cover all the gas we had used both days. How would you handle this? Also, should he have come home with me and then gone on in a cab?"

I think no matter how well-to-do a girl is (she doesn't say), there really is no excuse for a man not having filled the tank of a girl's car after a long trip. If he is strapped for cash, he can use his credit card. My correspondent was right in not having said anything at the time. If she cares to see this young man again, however, I think a friendly little chat is in order. "Joe, you probably have your side of the story, but I'd like to tell you how the football game-gasoline situation struck me the other day." I think it's possible and necessary sometimes to be honest with beaux about matters of this kind.

In my opinion it's all right to use your car on dates. If it's just a sometimes thing, there's no need for a man to pay for gas.

If a friend is visiting from out of town and has no car, having a car of her own makes a girl a more desirable date. If any distance driving is done on a date, however, "tanking up" is always a young man's financial responsibility. At least those are Mother Brown's rules.

As for loaning your car to a man without you in it, that's all right if you know your borrower extremely well and won't be in for any rude shocks like a call from the border patrol telling of an abandoned Chevvy in Juarez.

As for dropping a man off at his place and driving on home alone, that's bad. It's so bad I don't even think a friendly chat is in order. A man who doesn't realize that he should "see a girl home" doesn't deserve the chance to do so.

They're Needing You More But You're Needing Them Less

Do you remember that when the Big Bad Wolf couldn't get into the houses of the three little pigs any other way, he tried to blow them down? He huffed and he puffed and carried on outrageously. For the life of me I can't remember whether he got the houses down or not, but I have decided, like the Big Bad Wolf, to resort to still another ruse to get you to do what I want. What I want you to do is get up the will power and do—power to learn to cook sensationally, take the weight off, scramble ahead in your job, learn a foreign language or do whatever thing you haven't got to which will make you a more terrific woman alone.

If it would do any good, I'd try to blow your house down, but the ruse I am going to resort to instead is a promise. I promise if you do some of those things just mentioned or others like them, people will be needing you more and you will be needing them less. That's a brand new promise from me to you.

Why on earth would it be good not to need people? Well, it wouldn't be good not to need *anybody,* but it is indeed a pleasant thing to be asked to more parties than you can attend, to be sought for jobs by several companies when you can work only for one, to be requested to chat with a friend of a friend because the friend thinks you can do him some good, to be asked for your recipes, asked to make a speech.

Let me go on. It's a good feeling to be asked to contribute to charity because people figure you can afford to, asked to work on committees because people know you're capable of getting the work done, asked your opinion about hanging a drapery or taking a picture because you're known to be expert.

Believe me, it's a lot more fun to be in the position of being asked and have to turn people down because you're too busy and overextended than it is to be the one asking all the time. Will you concede that?

I think a woman of fifty can be asked to do more things—*i.e.*, be more needed—than a woman of twenty-five if the fifty-year-old continues to be active, searching, interested, curious, restless and to better her past record.

Have you watched a woman who has been vegetating for a few years go back to work again or become involved in a civic project or start raising three grandchildren when both parents were killed in a plane crash? Gradually or suddenly this woman takes on a new aura. People want to be around her more because she's actually too busy to spare the time.

I suggest that every woman who lives alone, unless she is physically ill, ought to be hopelessly, pitiably, irretrievably overextended with not enough time to shop or read or talk leisurely on the telephone or play bridge or browse in the library. She ought to have at least once and a half too much to do!

To get overextended you can sign up for too many night school courses, take on too many extra assignments in your job, have people over to dinner too often in a month, try to remember too many friends' birthdays with a personal note, try to put up too many jars of jelly for the orphanage. Pretty soon you'll be in the enviable position of saying "no" to a great many people. People who need you *more* but you need *less*.

Were *the opinions outrageous? No, of course they weren't. Goodbye, dears, and ah men! until we meet again.*